Lloyds of London

FARMS AND FORTUNES

AN AUTOBIOGRAPHY

By Michael Godwin

Bright Pen

A Bright Pen Book

Text Copyright © Michael Godwin 2011

Cover artwork by James Oses ©

British Library Cataloguing Publication Data.
A catalogue record for this book is available from the British Library

ISBN 978-07552-1340-5

Authors OnLine Ltd
19 The Cinques
Gamlingay, Sandy
Bedfordshire SG19 3NU
England

This book is also available in e-book format, details of which are available at www.authorsonline.co.uk

I dedicate this book to my grandchildren, Evie and Jack.

Contents

CHAPTER 1   EARLY DAYS 1

CHAPTER 2   LIFE CHANGING EVENT 18

CHAPTER 3   THE BEGINNINGS OF THE COLD WAR .. 24

CHAPTER 4   END OF VINEYARDS FARM 37

CHAPTER 5   LOVE AND NUCLEAR PERIL 48

CHAPTER 6   AN EXTRAORDINARY WINTER 58

CHAPTER 7   A LUCKY BREAK 68

CHAPTER 8   A FARM OF OUR OWN 75

CHAPTER 9   A SON AND HEIR 81

CHAPTER 10   AN IRISH ADVENTURE 97

CHAPTER 11   A NASTY LETTER AND

ANOTHER FARM 112

CHAPTER 12   A BIG BANG AND BACK TO

IRELAND 121

CHAPTER 13   CONSOLIDATION, FIRE AND FEAR 126

CHAPTER 14   A LOOK AT EUROPEAN

AGRICULTURE 141

CHAPTER 15   MILITARY JETS 149

CHAPTER 16   A FATEFUL INVITATION 163

CHAPTER 17 MAKING PROGRESS 181

CHAPTER 18 AMERICAN ADVENTURES 192

CHAPTER 19 MOMENTOUS EVENTS 204

CHAPTER 20 ANOTHER FARM 211

CHAPTER 21 IMPENDING DOOM 223

CHAPTER 22 FIGHTING FOR SURVIVAL 231

CHAPTER 23 A DREADFUL TIME AND A RAY

OF HOPE 242

CHAPTER 24 SALVATION AND A HOLIDAY 257

CHAPTER 25 DESPAIR, AND A SECOND CHANCE 269

CHAPTER 26 AND FINALLY 279

CHAPTER 1

EARLY DAYS

The winter of 1939 began in earnest early in December with blizzards sweeping across the south of England. Jack and Sarah Godwin were struggling to feed the cattle, pigs, geese and hens on their rented farm near Bath. The cows provided the main source of income, but had to be milked by hand twice every day. Sarah would normally be expected to help with this, but was heavily pregnant, expecting their third child at any time. The eldest boy, Raymond, was eight, the second boy, Brian, was six, and Ern, the live-in farm worker, made up the household.

Conditions in the house were pretty primitive even by the standards of the time. There was no running water or electricity, no bathroom or proper kitchen; the main source of heat was the big wood-fired range in the living room. Cooking was done on the range or the small paraffin rings and oven, which sat on two of the rings. Lighting was paraffin lamp and candles in the house and paraffin hurricane lamps out on the farm. Great Britain at this time was three months into a war with Germany, which was to escalate and eventually engulf the whole world for years to come. The scene was set for my arrival into this most beautiful and cruel world, in the early hours of the 15th December, 1939. The following very early recollections of my life are based on my memories of my parents' conversations and what I was told.

The morning of Thursday 14th December dawned very bright,

but terribly cold, after a week of high winds, blizzards and an ice storm on the Tuesday morning. The storm had left a coating of ice over everything including the trees and the drifted snow. The weight of ice on the trees was too much for some and they would crash to the ground with an enormous cacophony of noise, accentuated by the silence of the night.

The improved conditions enabled Jack and Ern to catch up with the farm work, the most urgent being to replenish the stock of hay in the cowshed from the hayrick in Lodge Ground. Ern was able to make an improvised sledge from some old corrugated iron, which was quite easy to pull over the frozen snow; the only problem was controlling the speed when coming back down the hill with a load of hay.

The in-calf heifers and young stock were wintered on the hill in a field called Bushy Norwood, very close to the present University of Bath. Hay was provided quite close in the adjacent field, but it had to be cut out with a hay knife and carried to the cattle in the form of huge flaps carried on the head. The cattle were surviving the conditions very well because, as its name suggests, Bushy Norwood had lots of trees and bushes for the animals to shelter amongst. During the worst of the weather, Jack and Ern would make their way up the hill through the snow together but today the going was easy for Ern on his own, over the frozen snow, in the sunshine.

Having helped with the morning milking, Jack joined Sarah and the boys for a real country breakfast of home-cured bacon and eggs. Next the pigs had to be fed; also the geese, ducks and hens; eggs had to be collected and cleaned, then into the cow shed to carry buckets of water to all the cows from a brick trough outside the cow shed. This trough was supplied from a stream, by a pipe. This stream was eventually to give me so much pleasure in my childhood.

It was now time to prepare the rations for the cows to last about seven days. This entailed the use of a chaff cutter and a root pulper, both driven by flat canvas belts, via a shaft and pulleys fixed to the wall, and driven by the open crankshaft petrol engine downstairs. Quantities of hay and oat straw were cut to chaff and piled in one corner of the barn. Then mangolds, swedes or turnips were pulped. All this was then spread on the barn floor in layers, together with the contents of various sacks, which were stacked around; the whole lot was then turned several times with a shovel until it was really mixed. It was then ready to be shovelled into large round baskets to be carried to the cows. As soon as all this was done it was time for Jack and Ern to do the afternoon milking. It soon began to grow dark and Jack filled the log basket and coal scuttle and went into the kitchen where Sarah had already filled and lit the oil lamp. He only had to take one look at her and he knew that tonight was going to be the night.

Sarah said, "You had better fetch Marjorie, Jack". She was referring to Marjory Cooper, the midwife, who was also a friend of the family and lived near Combe Down. Without further discussion, Jack lit a hurricane lamp and went to the stable at the back of the house, put the harness on Toby, led him out to the yard and hitched up the trap. Jack filled and lit the paraffin lamp for the trap and thrust it into its holder, picked up a shovel and, leaving Ern with Sarah and the boys, he set off through the brook and into Barn Ground.

The farm track and country roads were blocked with drifted snow, which had been blown away from open ground. Up over Barn Ground and up through Poor Ground he went, keeping well away from the wood and hedgerows to avoid the deepest snow. Toby was skilled in helping to pick a way through and seemed to appreciate the urgency of the mission. On they rode into the top field where the icy wind swept across the hilltop, stinging Jack's face and making Toby turn his head away.

The main road was not far now; they were heading for a gate near Keeper's Cottage. It was difficult to find but thankfully it was open, and the snow no more than four feet deep in the gateway. Toby lunged forward into the drift and stopped. Jack allowed him to rest a while then, with a few encouraging words, Toby made a gigantic effort and they were through and on to the road. It was much easier going from here on, but very slippery for Toby on the hard-packed snow, so progress was only at a gentle walking pace. Marjory was not a bit surprised to see Jack, but was obviously worried about the journey and fetched some blankets to wrap around herself.

The return journey was much easier as once they left the main road, it was all down hill and by nine o'clock they were back in the kitchen warming themselves by the fire. Sarah had by now taken to her bed, and Ern had put the boys to bed and busied himself making up the fires, assembling saucepans and kettles of boiling water, and filling and lighting the paraffin heater for the bedroom. Jack spent a few minutes with Sarah, and then went to the stable to feed and groom Toby, and make sure he was OK. Jack looked at Toby and felt very proud of him. All must have gone reasonably according to plan, for I was born in the early hours of the morning.

Jack, my father, was a lean, wiry figure of medium height with a ruddy complexion. I have the impression of a very fit, strong man in his younger days. His health was damaged during his time in the army when he used to look after horses and mules.

My Father, far left, shoeing mules

4

Vineyards Farm. 1940s

At that time he was an accomplished blacksmith and I have seen photographs of him shoeing mules. Jack was born and brought up in a farm worker's cottage in St. Catherine's, near Bath, and worked on various farms and estates before and after his army service. When his right elbow was severely damaged in the army, the surgeon told him that he would lose the movement in the joint and asked how he would like it fixed. Jack told him he would one day own some cows and to fix his arm so he could milk them; consequently his elbow was fixed from that day on at ninety degrees.

Eventually Jack met my mother, who was much younger than he was, and they rented a small farm at Downhead near Frome. They farmed there for about five years, had the two boys, and then moved to Vineyard's Farm, Claverton, near Bath. This farm was much larger than the previous one, but due to its run-down state, steep land, and the poor condition of the house, the rent was very low. If my recollections are correct, I had heard that the place was free of rent for two years. Agriculture was in a serious depression at this time in the early nineteen thirties and this was a way of finding someone to live there.

More than anything, Jack was in every respect a countryman, very hard working, and turned nature to his advantage to feed his family. He took pleasure in rough shooting and catching rabbits with ferrets, and enjoyed the occasional cigarette, a pint in the local and a pipe in the evenings. We were to live very much off the countryside, eating wild rabbit, pigeons and the occasional rook pie when they were in season. My father would find pigeons' nests and watch for the young to be hatched; he then used a technique he had developed to wire them to the nest. The parent bird would continue to feed these fat and overweight youngsters until Dad judged them ready for the pie. His own birds and animals were looked after very well but he had no qualms about killing any one of them for dinner. The large kitchen garden provided fresh vegetables in season, and the first picking of peas accompanied by new potatoes and the best duck Jack could find, made a super treat after our long winter diet.

My first childhood memories seem to relate to some rather dramatic events in April 1942. A widespread outbreak of Foot and Mouth Disease occurred in North Somerset and quickly arrived at our farm. This must be one of the most distressing things a farmer has to endure. All cloven hoofed animals had to be slaughtered by government decree with market value compensation. I remember lots of strange men at the farm, and when my mother took me into the yard, I was very frightened when a man in a white coat shouted at her "Take that child indoors! He should not be out here watching this," so she hustled me away. Anyhow, despite this admonishment, I can remember a dragline excavator negotiating the farm track with great difficulty, and later, seeing a huge pit behind the cowshed, with dead cows lying in the bottom.

The pigs must have been suitable for meat because I remember them as carcasses hanging from hooks in the back of a big lorry. The young stock on the hill at Bushey Norwood were allowed to survive, so long as no one from the farm went near them. I think Jack must have arranged for someone else to oversee them. This was most fortunate as these young cattle formed the nucleus of the new herd when the time came to re-stock. No one was allowed to visit us and I used to go with my father up to the end of the farm track to collect deliveries such as post, groceries and milk. These were deposited in a large wooden box. It seemed strange to get milk from bottles.

The second dramatic event that April, of which I only have fleeting memories, was our involvement in the war. The conflict had gone badly for Britain up to now but at least the outcome was no longer in doubt, as both the Soviet Union and the United States of America were embroiled on our side. On the two weekend nights of the 25th to the 27th April, the Luftwaffe bombed Bath in a revenge attack in retaliation for the bombing of Luebeck and Rostock by the RAF. On Saturday evening the sirens sounded, as they had many times before, but on this occasion the target was not Bristol - Bath was the target of the enemy's spite and malice. A savage attack started before midnight. Then there was a short lull for a few hours. This was followed by a second attack which lasted until daybreak on Sunday.

That day many people decided to leave the city and spend the night in the countryside. Lots of people came to our farm, and my mother, who was heavily pregnant again, did her best to accommodate some of them. People also slept in the barns and even in our old Ford car. Not very far from Bushy Norwood, there is a rocky area known as Hampton Rocks with lots of huge caves in the limestone. These caves were used that night as sleeping quarters by hundreds of people using straw as bedding from my father's straw rick. It was very fortunate that these people had left the city, because the bombers came back that Sunday night for a second and heavier attack. The sky glowed red from the fires and, between bouts of sleep, the house shook from the explosions and the sound of German planes roaring overhead. In the morning I came downstairs and was shocked and frightened to see the kitchen ceiling had fallen down, with lathe and plaster all over the place.

Sometimes Mother would take us to Bath to have our hair cut, and she would have her own done at the same time. After a shopping trip to Bath, we would take a bus to a place in Twerton, where the hairdresser was a friend of the family and we always stayed for tea. Dad sometimes came for us in the car after he had finished milking. I remember pestering my mother to take me along the bombed streets, to see the wrecked houses. It must have fascinated me to see inside a remaining part of a house; to see staircases, fireplaces, even upstairs, and pictures still hanging on the walls at odd angles. Only the solid brick and concrete shelters in the streets remained intact; the homes were little more than piles of rubble, and remained that way for a long time.

As was very common during the war on family farms, the boys helped with much of the work. Ern had long since gone to do his bit for King and Country. I am told that Ray was hauling cow manure from the farm to a field called Bowshot, a field next to Bushy Norwood. He was using Dad's lovely old carthorse called Colonel. On the first trip the horse refused to go through the gate into the field. Eventually Ray persuaded him, but he was not a happy horse. On the second trip the horse again refused and Ray tried to coax him in but to no avail. Suddenly the horse collapsed between the shafts of the cart and was obviously dead. Ray was stricken with grief and blamed himself to his dying day. He wandered around in despair inside the gate and then spotted a hole in the ground. He peered down inside and saw the fins of a bomb, so he raced back home to tell his Dad. Maybe Colonel knew that bomb was there as he was out in the paddock during the attack. All I remember about this incident is my Dad being very angry because the bomb disposal people did so much damage to his crop of wheat when they removed this unexploded device. I expect the last thing on their minds was my Dad's crop.

May saw the birth of my sister Susan; so important was this event that I remember absolutely nothing about it. I do, however, remember my new velvet suit with lots of buttons which Mother had bought me for the christening.

The farm was a wonderful place to spend one's early childhood, with so much to do and learn about. I loved the hens, geese and ducks which were free to roam about all over the place. The sows were also free to wander about and I had to keep a safe distance from them, as I did the cockerels and gander. One day, misjudging the speed of the latter, my coat was caught by the gander and he gave me a good thrashing with his wings, until my cries alerted my father and I was promptly rescued.

The sows wandered around in various stages of their reproductive cycle so occasionally they required the attention of a boar. This meant loading the appropriate sows into the trailer behind the car and taking them to a little farm at Batheaston where they kept a suitable boar. They were left there for a few days then we picked them up and brought them home. This mysterious business was explained to me by saying the sows needed a holiday.

On one such trip to collect a sow, we were nearly there when we crashed into the back of a bus that had stopped quite suddenly to turn right. I was thrown against the windscreen but thankfully no serious harm was done. The car must have suffered much worse for we had to get a bus to Bath, followed by another bus to Claverton Down. We had walked most of the way home from the bus, before climbing a fence to take a short cut down across the field. A while later at home Dad realised that he had lost his chequebook which he subsequently found where we had earlier climbed the fence.

There were about six sows and sometimes they could be very funny. They wandered around the farmyard and the fields and would seek out nice things to eat, such as acorns under the oak trees. When they discovered the cider apples they would eat too many, and we sometimes watched them coming home down the hill in a drunken stupor, falling over and then struggling to their feet again, only to fall over once more. It really was very funny.

Many of my most vivid memories of this time were concerned with military activity. The Home Guard used to come through the farm quite frequently as part of their on-going exercises. I used to watch with fascination the practice launching of barrage balloons on Claverton Down, which I could see from our house. There were often lots of aeroplanes to watch, the most exciting of which were the squadrons of bombers towing huge gliders. I know now of course, that these were on exercise in preparation for the long awaited invasion of France by allied forces, and for the ill-fated attack at Arnheim. There was also the occasional appearance of enemy aircraft, and the noise of local anti-aircraft batteries.

A friend of the family - a Frome businessman called Arthur Edwards - once took me with him on a trip to Bristol where I saw masses of barrage balloons strung out across the city. Occasionally my mother would take Sue and me to Bath for shopping, which entailed a long walk to catch a bus at Claverton Down. Walking along the avenue took us past a camp for prisoners of war where we saw lots of men behind tall wire fences. As we passed they would whistle and call out to my mother who would take no notice and just hurry on past. All this was a bit frightening and mystifying at the time. Many of the prisoners were given useful employment on farms during the war. I remember several coming to our farm in an army lorry when the threshing drum was working on Dad's wheat ricks.

It was always very exciting when the threshing drum came to thresh our ricks. During peacetime the cereal crops were grown to feed the livestock - oats, barley, and something called dredge corn. This consisted of wheat, barley, oats, peas and beans all grown together, cut with a binder and stacked in a rick to mature. When it was eventually threshed and ground into a meal, it provided a cheap source of protein for the animals. During wartime my father was compelled to grow as much wheat as possible; food rationing had been in place for some time and the nation had come close to starvation.

Although bread was never rationed during the war, it was rationed soon after and remained so for several years. The rations were regulated by everyone being issued with a ration book containing tear off tickets like stamps, and produce in the shop carried a price plus the number of coupons required. The week's ration was very meagre but farmers and miners were given extra coupons to compensate for the heavy manual labour. We were much better off in the countryside than city folk were as we could increase our meat ration with wild rabbits and birds; we also grew our potatoes, fruit and vegetables.

The kitchen garden was so important in those days and my father would spend a lot of his evenings working there. Very often the men working on the farm would be brought in to help for a few hours if there was a break in the farm work. Early and main crop potatoes and many types of root vegetables were grown and stored for the winter. We also grew all sorts of greens, from spring cabbage to winter greens like curly kale and sprouting broccoli, early and late sown peas, and broad and runner beans. Salad crops were grown throughout the growing season. Horseradish and herbs of all kinds were available and even watercress from the stream. Ample dressings of farmyard manure maintained the fertility of the soil. Scattered around the farm were apple trees with lots of cooking apples; these were wrapped in newspaper and stored in the attic. Several varieties of damsons and plums were made into jam or stored in hundreds of Kilner jars. Walnuts and hazel nuts were all collected and stored. Oranges and bananas were no more than a treat at Christmas.

The baker called at the farm two or three times a week. The butcher called once a week when Mother bought the beef and sausages. Bacon, ham, chicken and duck were produced on the farm and, as I mentioned before, anything that could be snared or shot served to increase our variety. Fish was rarely available unless Father brought some home from his trip to the market

A little man on a bicycle came to the house every two weeks to collect an order for groceries. These were delivered a few days later from Bath. Milk, cream and butter were provided by the cows. My sister and I spent many hours of drudgery churning the butter which Mother used to sell, together with eggs, to a few stout-hearted customers who walked to the farm. It was a rare event for Mother to go to the shops in Bath; this still amazes me when you consider that there was no fridge or freezer or even electricity. I always remember our diet as being very salty - salt being used to preserve food such as bacon and butter.

Although I don't remember the steam engines, I do remember

the threshing machine, which seemed huge, being towed into position between or adjacent to the rick by a large tractor. The machine was then set level with jacks and blocks so that its four iron wheels were clear of the ground. The tractor was then positioned accurately, some distance away, where it could provide power from a pulley on one side, through a long, flat canvas belt to the threshing machine. The whole area was then fenced in with netting wire to stop rats from escaping. This was a legal requirement and the local policeman would sometimes appear on his bicycle to inspect the fence.

First, the thatch was stripped from the roof of the rick, then the threshing began. Two men worked on the rick with pitchforks, throwing the sheaves of corn onto the top deck of the machine, where another man would pass them to a skilled member of the crew who would cut the strings and feed the sheaves gently into the drum. Two men worked at the other end, on the ground, removing sacks of grain and attaching empty sacks to the spouts, the sacks of grain being stacked nearby to await collection.

The straw came out of the machine in bundles tied with string, at the opposite end to the grain, and was made into a rick by two or three men with pitch forks. This straw would be used as bedding for the animals, and the rick would be thatched to keep out the wet. Another man, armed with an enormous fork with lots of prongs, was responsible for clearing the chaff and piling it up away from the machine. With the large fork he could move substantial quantities of this very light material. Towards the end of the day a lorry would arrive to collect the wheat, or, if the crop was for the animals, the sacks were hauled back to the farm by horse and cart and stacked in the barn. It could then be rolled or ground to make rations for the animals.

After considerable progress had been made, reducing the height of the rick, the rats began to attempt their escape. When I was a little older this was great fun, as it probably meant having a day off from school and being joined by other children from the village armed with sticks to kill the rats. The number of rats increased as the rick reduced to ground level; sometimes there were hundreds if the rick had been there all winter. All the men working with the threshing machine had the bottoms of their trouser legs tied with string, to prevent the rats running up inside.

Looking back on those happy times, I am horrified that children were running around those machines with lots of moving parts and exposed belt drives. Today's Health and Safety Executive would be appalled at the conditions, but even so, I do not recall hearing of any accidents. The belt drives were all of the flat canvas type and needed to be kept moist to maintain their grip; if the weather was hot, a man went around them at intervals with a watering can. All this involved a huge amount of manual labour, and a day's threshing would produce only about ten tons of grain. Threshing was carried out all the year round, with the tractor and threshing machine, and maybe four key men, moving around the countryside from farm to farm.

Farm work in those days was very labour intensive and a huge amount of work was carried out by hand. Before my brothers were old enough to carry out much of this work, my father employed two full time men and the productivity was very low by today's standards. About twenty milking cows and followers were kept, being fed mostly on feed produced on the farm in the form of grass, hay, mangolds, turnips, swedes, kale, oats and barley.

Six or seven breeding sows and a couple of hundred laying hens made up the income producing part of the farm; a few ducks and geese were kept but these were primarily for family use. The hens were housed in moveable chicken houses out in the paddocks. A lot of work was involved cleaning them out and providing fresh straw, collecting the eggs and making sure that all the hens had returned to the chicken house before dark and, of course, shutting them in for the night. 'Mr Fox' was always on the lookout for an insecure hen house.

A huge effort was made to avoid waste of any kind. One such effort involved the inevitable shedding of good grain in the fields at harvest time. The hens and their mobile homes were loaded on to trailers and transported to the stubble fields. Here they scratched around, eating the shed grain and laying their eggs in the fowl houses. It was very important to shut them in at night and this was often my job. It always seemed to me to be an awful long walk up the hill and, lost in my own thoughts, I would be on the way home when I suddenly couldn't remember shutting them all in. There was only one thing to do - go back up and check; needless to say they were always shut in.

The crops that were grown on the farm, such as root crops and kale, were planted in lines across the fields and these had to be hoed by hand. Firstly, when the plants were very small the crops were hoed between the lines to control the weeds - this was called flat hoeing. Secondly, as the plants increased in size, they had to be thinned out using the same hoe; this was called singling, so that single plants remained at about six inch intervals. Thirdly, by the time all this was done, the weeds were again beginning to take over, so another bout of flat hoeing was required.

Several acres were grown in this way and if they could not cope with the amount of work, or if the weeds began to overtake and threaten the crop, then extra help could be called in. Gangs of workers would roam the countryside looking for just this type of work. These men would carry out the work at a certain price per acre, called piecework. Much of the hedging and ditching was carried out by these workers. I remember my father measuring and marking the work to be done with a chain and paid the men so much per chain. A chain is 22 yards long, the length of a cricket pitch, 10 chains equal 1 furlong and 8 furlongs make 1 mile.

My school days began when I was four years old. Mother took me two afternoons each week. The school was then very much overcrowded by the continued presence of the evacuees from London. The children seemed very grown-up and difficult for me to understand, which I found very daunting. Enemy air action was, by now, very limited and spasmodic so the occasional appearance of a plane carrying the black crosses and swastika caused great excitement. I suppose there was still a danger of an attack because our gas masks had to be with us at all times. There was also a new threat from flying bombs (doodlebugs) and I remember discussing with my older brothers, a diagram and description of these weapons in the newspaper. By the time I began to attend school full-time, the war had ended and the school population had reverted to normal. The evacuees had returned to their homes and I could at least understand what the other children were saying.

It must have been within a year or two of the end of the war, when I overheard my dad having a rather heated argument with a family friend, Frank Fisher. Frank, I was to learn years later, had leanings towards the Communist Party, and had some sympathy for the Russian system. Dad was outside the kitchen door with one foot up on the garden wall, smoking a cigarette, when I heard him make a very emphatic statement, and I quote, "We shall be at war with Stalin within five years". The significance of this statement was to become clear to me as I grew up.

Over the next few years I was to gradually understand what this was all about. Britain had declared war on Germany in 1939 in order to stand by an agreement with Poland that we would go to her aid if she were attacked. In the event we could do little to help that unfortunate country, but our wartime Prime Minister, Winston Churchill, hoped that Poland would be free again after the war. The Russians, who had also been attacked by Germany, and had beaten them back in a long and terrible war, decided to extend their western frontier into central Europe, engulfing several eastern European countries and imposing communist rule.

Just before the end of the war, at the Yalta conference, President Roosevelt of the USA, who alone had the power to stand up to the Russians, was very ill and did not support Churchill in his endeavours to see the East Europeans free and self-governing. This situation was very understandable, as a confrontation with Stalin at that time may well have meant war between east and west. We were now to embark on 45 years of 'Cold War', of which more later. Germany was now divided into four zones of occupation, the Russian zone in the east, and the American, British and French zones in the west and south.

After the war Britain was in a critical state, with thousands of homeless people and not enough to eat. America was not very helpful at this time, expecting repayment of wartime loans and only sending food if it was paid for. It was only when Britain told the Americans that our troops were to be withdrawn from Turkey and Greece, where they were resisting the communists, as the cost was too great, that they realised that the whole of Western Europe was at risk. The Italians and French were very close to going communist when Churchill made a famous speech to the Americans at Fulton, Missouri, in which he warned that an 'Iron Curtain' would be drawn across Europe, from Stettin on the Baltic to Trieste on the Adriatic.

Until this time the Americans just wanted to go home and let Europe fend for itself. With this wake up call they realised that something must be done and General Marshall introduced the famous 'Marshall Plan'. This plan involved sending food and massive aid programs to rebuild European industrial capacity. On the farms, a huge range of tractors and agricultural machines were arriving from America, including combine harvesters. All this aid began to take effect soon after the very severe winter of 1947 when people could not even get enough coal to keep warm.

The village school was about a mile from the farm. I always thought it was a long way to walk and Sue and I were delighted to get a lift on the milk lorry on occasions. The milk was collected every morning by the milk lorry loaded with churns, the driver exchanging clean empty ones for full ones. These churns contained either ten or twelve gallons of milk. Walking was something I must have been good at, as when I was three the milk lorry driver found me wandering on Claverton Down and delivered me back to the farm. The result of the ensuing enquiry was that Mother thought I was outside with Dad, and Dad thought I was inside with Mother. School was fun in those early days but I did not learn very much. Mother, in desperation, taught me to read when I was eight.

During this period my mother had some help with the housework. Mrs Duckett used to come from the village most mornings, bringing her daughter, Mary, with her if she was not at school. Mary was a little older than me, but I remember she was a good playmate. Mrs. Duckett's husband, Ern, worked for Dad on the farm and they lived in a tied cottage in the village.

Holidays were unheard of until I was about seven. Dad announced that we were going to a small hotel at Bowlease Cove near Weymouth. Dad, Mum, my sister Susan and I, set off amid great excitement one Saturday morning, leaving the boys to help with the farm work. The little bunny that always went to bed with me was, after much agonising, left at home. It was my first holiday and I felt far too grown-up to take him. At the hotel I had a small room of my own and missed my bunny very much on the first night or two.

Sue and I played on the sand and in the sea and had a lovely time. Arthur Edwards came down for a day and brought some inner tubes for us to play with; these were great fun in the sea. Arthur and Dad went off to Bournemouth in the evening. Other evenings were spent taking lovely walks along the sea front; it was so unusual and enjoyable to have Dad with us so much. Mum and Dad seemed so very, very happy. The week soon passed and we were back in the old Ford for the journey home.

CHAPTER 2

LIFE CHANGING EVENT

July 28th 1948, disaster struck our family with the sudden death of my father. He had been going to hospital on a regular basis for some years to have blood transfusions - something to do with injuries and infection received during his service in the First World War. The worst moment for me was a few days later, while helping load and spread manure on Claverton Down with Ray and Brian, Dad's car suddenly pulled up where we were working. A total stranger was driving, having been given the job of returning the car from the hospital. It was then that the awfulness of the situation sunk home, life was never to be the same again.

Dad's funeral passed unnoticed by me. I have always regretted that I was not permitted to attend and I was probably sent away to stay with friends or relatives: I just don't remember. From the family's point of view the question of security in our rented home and farm was most traumatic. As Dad was the tenant we expected to receive a notice to quit at any time, so we just sat tight and hoped it would not come. After three months my mother could legally claim the tenancy, which is what happened. Mother ran the farm for about ten years, or at least made sure the bills and rent were paid, while Ray was in charge of the work routine.

Ray, who had recently left school at fourteen, was assisted on the farm by Brian, who now had little time for school, and Mother lived in dread of the School Attendance Officer. I remember him as some sort of ogre. Also working at the farm by this time was John Vaughan, a few years older than Ray, and a powerfully built young man who reminded me of screen tough guy Robert Mitchum. Three young men or boys working together, and my mother trying to keep some sort of order, was a recipe for disaster I remember lots of rows and fighting over the years, with blood flowing on many occasions - mostly Brian's.

My Uncle Rowland, mother's brother from Marshfield, took Ray to Chippenham market a couple of times to show him the best way to sell his stock and introduce him to the intrigues of the auction system. Ray proved a quick learner and soon saw opportunities to make a few pounds around the auction ring. This was to be the beginning of a life-long career wheeling and dealing in cattle, pigs and horses.

This caused an awful lot of friction at home as Brian was left to do most of the work while Ray, using the family money, did deals of his own at the markets. Of course he didn't win all the time and if he ended the day with animals that he could not sell, he brought them back to the farm, and many times there was no room for them, so makeshift accommodation had to be provided. One night there were twelve pigs in the coal-shed and of course these were not 'Ray's pigs'- they were bought for 'the farm'.

Long-standing friend of the family, Arthur Edwards, had been appointed executor to Dad's will and was a constant source of advice and support to my mother in her struggle to keep the farm and family together. As the boys became more confident with experience, they were keen to modernise the farm by introducing new technology and increasing output. Mother could not accept the necessity of this policy and spent many sleepless nights worrying about the expense and generally being negative. Considerable investment was required from time to time; a new Fordson Major tractor being one of them. This was to supplement the old Fordson which had been on the farm for years.

The new tractor was needed to plough the old pastures, (most of which were very steep) and re-seed with new leys. These leys, after correcting lime and phosphate levels, responded to applications of nitrogen fertiliser and dramatically increased the amount of grass produced. This, in turn, called for more efficient methods of conservation as haymaking could no longer be relied upon to conserve enough grass for the increasing number of cows. Field-clamp silage was introduced, these clamps being covered with a six-inch thick layer of lime to seal them.

The price received for milk was much higher in the winter months, so the output was concentrated for winter production. Trying to persuade the landlady to invest money in more buildings was an ongoing problem, and when she was eventually persuaded the rent was, of course, increased. Mother could not see any sense in this and constantly worried and argued.

The government at this time was fully committed to agriculture and the 1947 Agriculture Act confirmed this commitment. A system of guaranteed prices was introduced together with an annual price review. All this was designed to give farmers the confidence to invest and increase production, to reduce our dependence on imports.

While all this expansion and improvement was progressing out on the farm, the much-needed improvement to our living conditions were very sparse. Originally, the only water tap was in the dairy, adjoining the house. The landlady agreed to connect the water supply to the cowshed and install automatic drinking bowls. The opportunity was taken to include a sink and draining board in the kitchen, together with a coldwater tap as part of the scheme.

Calor Gas lighting was installed, but only downstairs, providing very poor light but was probably rather more convenient. Because of the poor light from the gas, the old oil lamp was to see a few more years of use in the living room. A big improvement came with the replacement of the old range in the living room with a Rayburn. The often-discussed bathroom was never to be. There was a bath in the washroom but this involved lighting the copper to heat the water. As the washroom was no more than an outhouse it was not much used in the winter. A tin bath by the fire or Rayburn with a rota system on a Saturday night had to suffice.

School Photograph 1948
Me, second from left and my sister, Sue, fourth from left

After Dad's death, Ray, who increasingly took on the role of a father figure in my eyes, began to take an interest in my education. This interest, I believe, was partly inspired by his and Brian's almost total lack of a reasonable education by the time they had left school. I continued to attend the village school for about a year with my younger sister, the number of pupils falling all the time. There were only eleven of us by the time I left. Ray decided that I should go to Combe Down Secondary School, where I would have gone in any case when I was eleven. The local education authority provided a taxi service for secondary children from Claverton and I eventually found a seat in that. The village school was closed soon afterwards so my sister and I could claim a legitimate place in the taxi.

All went well for a while until the Education Authority decided, in their wisdom, that Combe Down School was within walking distance of Claverton. It probably did come within their criteria for walking distance, but it took no account of the dreadful conditions, especially during the dark winter evenings. The walk included some particularly nasty woods and a very muddy lane called Lime Kiln Lane. Despite parental protests the taxis were withdrawn at the end of the Christmas holiday. Consultations took place among the parents and the consensus was that the children would not attend school until the transport was restored.

There were probably about eight of us involved who thought it was wonderful. I found myself fully occupied enjoying life on the farm. As well as playing in the woods and stream, I did a lot of tractor driving, carrying out some of the simpler operations such as rolling, chain harrowing, disc harrowing and sweeping hay to the elevator. One of my brothers would start the tractor and take me to the field and set me up with the job to be done, and leave me to it. A bottle of cold tea and some jam sandwiches would keep me going until evening, when I would switch off the tractor and walk home. If I made a mistake and stalled the engine, being too small to start it, I would have to walk home and find someone; sometimes I got a poor reception.

It was nine months before the school transport was restored. In that time there was considerable interest by the local press, referring to us as the 'Claverton Strikers'. Although we all had a good time, it did nothing for our education, which was now plumbing new depths. Soon after this I was faced with my Eleven Plus exam paper. I was totally incapable of understanding the questions, even if I could just about read them. Having been unable to put pen to paper I left that exam room in a state of shock, which proved to be a turning point in my educational fortunes.

One of our great joys was playing in the stream or brook as we called it in those days. Dams were constructed using large slabs of turf torn from the side of the brook. These were laid across the bed of the brook and weighed down by a layer of heavy stones. Another layer of turf and more heavy stones were laid as the level of the water rose. There was a limit to the height that these dams could be built as the pressure from the water was enormous. We soon became very experienced at knowing when to stop after several wash outs and rebuilds. The flow of water in the summer was very low and our dams were built across a narrow part just downstream of a wide area of stream bed. The water then spread out into a large lake, perhaps three or four metres across.

A really successful dam would result in a trip to the workshop to make some ships from odd bits of wood to sail on the water. If we left a dam intact and went and did something else, the geese and ducks quickly took over; they so enjoyed thrashing about in the deeper water that they must have thought Christmas had come. Of course, a great part of the fun was watching the rushing torrent of water overwhelming the course of the brook when we eventually became bored and caused it to collapse.

As we got older and got to know other boys and girls in the area, some used to come to Vineyards Farm to play during the school holidays or the long summer evenings. Together with my sister Sue, we went through a phase of rolling old tyres around and taking them to the top of a field and watching them roll down, jumping into the air when hitting a bump.

This seemed to be great fun at the time until one day we rolled our tyres to the top of the front paddock where there were several mobile poultry houses. Releasing our tyres, they sped off down the hill but, to my horror, I saw that my tyre was heading straight for one of these poultry houses. Then, to my utter despair, I realised that a sow with her litter of piglets was lying in front of the poultry house. Just when I thought some pigs would be killed, my tyre hit a small bump, jumped over the pigs and smashed right through the poultry house, bursting from the far side in a shower of splinters.

With great relief we retired to the workshop to fetch some wood, tools and nails, and repaired the poultry house as well as we could. After that we went a little further from the farm where we continued to enjoy watching our tyres leaping into the air as they hurtled into the valley.

CHAPTER 3

THE BEGINNINGS OF
THE COLD WAR

The original capital of Germany was captured by the Russians during the war, but in accordance with the Yalta agreement, was also divided into four zones, the same as the rest of Germany. East Berlin was the Russian communist zone and the western part of the city contained the British, French and American zones. As the city of Berlin was isolated in communist East Germany, beyond the 'iron curtain', three corridors were arranged to maintain road and rail communications with the West.

In 1948, the Russians tried to force the western nations to vacate Berlin by closing the three corridors. The fear of a third world war now loomed large, with the frightening thought of nuclear weapons being used. The western allies decided against an armoured attack to reconnect Berlin to the West, but to try to supply the cities 2.3 million people by air. It was to become the largest airlift in history, and was gradually built up from a few tons per day, to a maximum of thirteen thousand tons on the best day. The blockade lasted almost a year, and as a counter blockade of East Germany began to hurt the Russians, they backed down and reopened the land communications.

During the blockade of Berlin, the western nations had been engaged in talks to create an alliance of nations to resist Russian aggression. An agreement was signed in April 1949, by America, Canada and ten western European countries and was called the North Atlantic Treaty Organization, or NATO. From that time, an attack against any of these countries was to be treated as an attack on them all. This agreement confirmed the United States of America as leader of the western world, and committed them to the defence of Britain and Western Europe.

It was during the early 1950s, in June - because we were haymaking near the school at Claverton - when a large number of huge American bombers flew slowly over at quite a low level. As one plane disappeared over the south-eastern horizon, another was overhead, and another was just appearing over the north-western-horizon. They continued roaring over for some time; there must have been twenty or more. These were B36 strategic bombers of the United States Air force, or USAF, the largest planes in the world. They had six enormous piston engines of 3500 hp each, with propellers at the back, plus twin jet engines near each wing tip. After a trip to the cinema, and watching 'Movietone' or 'Pathe News', I learned that these bombers were flying right around the world, as a demonstration to the Russians, or anyone else, that they could deliver an atomic bomb anywhere in the world. I was destined to meet one of the pilots many years later.

Convair B36 Peacemaker 1953

25

These bombers were slow and vulnerable to attack by enemy fighters and were only in service for a few years. The Americans went to extraordinary lengths to provide fighter protection, including a trapezium device fitted in the bomb bay of a number of the planes so that they could carry a North American Thunderstreak jet fighter. These fighters would be launched if they were under attack, and recovered for the journey home. More experiments included towing a fighter from each wing tip, ending in the destruction of all three planes. Another experiment involved carrying three specially designed mini fighters in the bomb bay, also unsuccessful.

America then developed a medium range jet bomber, with six engines, the Boeing B47 Stratojet, which was based in many countries surrounding Russia. This was called 'Operation Many Baskets', and provided a nuclear deterrent to the Russians, should they consider invading Western Europe. We were now in the midst of the cold war and were able to watch these bombers being refuelled by Boeing tanker planes, glinting in the sun at high altitude.

It was considered at this time that a threat of nuclear destruction was the only way to deter the Russians. There was no way that the western countries could fight a conventional war in the east as the Russians had thousands of tanks stationed in Eastern Europe, together with huge standing armies.

As the cold war intensified, and the East/West confrontation deepened, the West was determined to resist communist expansion wherever it appeared - a situation that continued until 1989. In order to help resist the Russians in Germany, the western powers set up a democratic government in Western Germany to control the three Western Zones of occupation, and to re-arm the new West German nation. The Russians were, of course, very much opposed to this policy and saw it as a threat. I believe that this perceived threat on the part of the Soviet Union was understandable to a certain extent, as the Russians had suffered terribly during the German invasion of 1941.

Early in the 1950s, Boeing introduced a new strategic bomber with eight jet engines, and with a very long range, called the B52 Stratofortress. Five hundred of these bombers were in service by 1959, and many were to remain in service until well into the next century. As the stocks of nuclear weapons held by both sides continued to grow, it was realized that there was no defence against a surprise attack, so a new policy was evolved. This was a policy of Mutually Assured Destruction, or MAD, for short. The USAF Strategic Air Command, or SAC operated the B52 and B47 bombers in a constant state of readiness, to attack the Soviet Union in the event of a surprise attack.

A large number of these Stratofortress bombers were airborne and armed with nuclear weapons at all times, and it was hoped that the threat of instant retaliation would be sufficient to deter the Russians from mounting such an attack. Thankfully the policy worked, but all the while there was a constant risk that nuclear war would break out, caused by accident or a mistake by one side or the other. I believe we were very fortunate to have survived this intense period of the 'cold war'.

Britain and the USA were involved in another war in 1950, which was to last three years, and have an impact on our local community, this time in the Far East. The North Korean communists, with the backing of the Soviet Union, invaded South Korea. At a meeting of the United Nations Security Council, a vote was carried to resist the communist attack; this vote was carried because the Soviets were boycotting the UN at the time, so were unable to use their veto. American, British and forces from other countries, under the flag of the United Nations, quickly moved into South Korea, only to be thrown back south in disarray by the ferocious and relentless attack by the communist forces.

The UN held on to an area around Pussan, on the south coast, and built up their forces and eventually began to fight their way north. This saw very heavy fighting and not much progress. The UN forces then made an amphibious landing on the coast at Inchon near Seoul, the capital of South Korea, way behind enemy lines, wrong footing the communists and forcing them back into North Korea.

The UN then decided to follow up by invading the North, destroying the communist forces and hopefully uniting the country. All went well until they were near the Yalu River. This river formed part of the border with communist China and Chinese forces joined the war, and pushed the UN forces back into South Korea. The Chinese forces attacked in enormous numbers and only US and British air power had any hope of holding them. The British regiment, the Gloucesters, made an heroic stand against superior numbers at the battle of the Im Jin River, and held the communist forces long enough for the neighbouring American troops to retreat to safety. There was intense discussion in the US government as to what to do; there were even proposals to bomb mainland China with nuclear weapons. The situation stabilized into some sort of stalemate, eventually leading to an armistice that divided the country along the 38th parallel. North and South Korea were to remain in an official state of war during the life of my story.

When the UN forces began fighting in Korea, they were using aircraft left over from the world war. They were shocked and totally outclassed by a new Russian fighter, the Mig 15; it had swept wings, and a copy of a Rolls Royce jet engine. A couple of years before, the British Government had exhibited the engine at a Moscow trade fair, where the Russians secretly copied it. Not until the Americans rushed the North American F86 Sabre into service did the UN have anything to compete.

In Britain at that time, all young men had to do two years National Service, unless they were in a reserved occupation. Several of Ray's friends were doing their National Service at the time of the Korean War, and after basic training were posted to fight in Korea as part of the UN force. Some were captured by the communists and were subjected to incredible hardships and psychological re-education programmes called 'brainwashing'. I remember when they eventually returned home, they were almost unrecognisable. My brothers were lucky that farming was a reserved occupation.

During this period of my life, there were no more family holidays, but I did have a couple of weeks each summer at

Marshfield. Uncle Rowland and his brother, John, were farming the farm where they were all brought up, including my mother with her sisters, Hilda and Edith. Hilda, my favourite aunt, was a single lady who, I believe, had fallen in love with a young man who lost his life in France during the First World War. She never ever looked at another man and spent her life living with Rowland and his wife Laura.

I always gained the impression that Laura was lazy and Hilda did most of the housework as well as helping her brothers on the farm. When Dad was alive we used to spend Christmas Day at Marshfield, arriving in time for Christmas lunch prepared by Hilda. Dad and the boys went home in the afternoon to feed the animals and milk the cows. When they returned in the evening we enjoyed another lovely meal, then played games and cards before returning home very late. A few more memorable Christmases were spent at Marshfield after Dad's death but eventually, as the boys wanted to pursue their own interests, Mother, Sue and I began to spend Christmas at home. Despite huge efforts to instil some Christmas spirit they were far from memorable.

We were reliant on either Ray or Brian for transport, which in itself caused a lot of friction. Mother expected the boys to offer to take us shopping or visiting, and the boys expected her to ask, but she was too proud to do this, and the situation went from bad to worse, with the boys convinced that Mother enjoyed being a martyr. Ray was very good and would take us for an occasional day at the seaside. We would arrive in Weymouth in time for lunch in a restaurant on the front, where Sue and I would order fish and chips, a real treat for us in those days. The afternoon was spent on the sandy beach before driving home. During one of these outings Ray took me on board the huge Battleship Vanguard as it was in the harbour and open to the public. This was the last battleship to be built in Britain and never fired its guns in anger. It was, I believe, a big mistake on my mother's part not to learn to drive the car; she did have a go, but once behind the wheel she was terrified and seemed to freeze. I realise now that she should have persevered and insisted on professional tuition.

My Sundays were dominated by my mother's insistence on our attendance at our village church. Sue and I had to go to the morning and evening services every Sunday, and Sunday school every fourth Sunday. I was in the choir for years and my big moment came when I sang solo at the Carol Service. When my voice broke I was promoted to pumping the organ. This involved some concentration on the proceedings, and several times, immersed in my own thoughts, I heard the organist trying to attract my attention. This tended to make him very cross. My friend in the village, Jim Anstey, would sometimes throw small stones at the window to attract my attention and the noise could be heard throughout the church.

A gentleman from Bath used to come to the farm on Saturday afternoons to give me music lessons on the piano. I did quite well in the early stages and passed several exams, attending at the Guild Hall to collect my certificates presented by the Mayor. Another friend, Ray Dyer, who lived in a flat near Claverton Manor, was a frequent evening visitor and loved playing the piano. Hours of practice were necessary for me to play my exercises and set pieces to anything like a reasonable standard. Ray, who could not even read music, played my pieces beautifully within a very short time. We then discovered that he could play tunes after listening to them on the radio. This so discouraged me that I decided I was not sufficiently musical and gave up my lessons.

Quite soon after my Eleven Plus fiasco I began to take on a much more serious attitude to my education. Also a lot of consideration and discussion took place about what I wanted to be. Due to my having to do lots of work on the farm after school and at weekends, cleaning out pigsties and cow stalls etc. farming, as a career, looked less and less attractive. Arthur was of considerable influence in this; he was involved in building projects around Frome and had his own drawing office. He used to take me to his office to look at plans, and later we would go to the various building sites to talk to the men. I considered this a much more civilised way of earning a living, and as I was always drawing things, I made it my ambition to become an architect.

I now had tremendous motivation. After two years of intensive schoolwork I passed an exam to attend Bath Technical School. Five boys passed this exam out of thirty-three, but only two of us passed the final interview. It was now 1953 and I was on my way.

At about the same time as I was starting at my new school, Brian had been courting a girl from the Domestic Science Hostel at Claverton Manor, and she was now pregnant. The first I knew of this was when Brian and Christine arrived home one evening with a newborn baby boy, Robert. Such was the state of communication in our family. They moved into a room in the attic and preparations were put in hand to buy a caravan to be sited in the garden. I remember feeling sorry for Chris; she seemed so sad and was often left in tears by my brother's sharp tongue and quick temper. My mother was very unkind to her and blamed her for bringing this perceived disgrace upon our family. The caravan was to be their home for just over a year, after which they moved to a smallholding at Limpley Stoke on the eve of the birth of their second child, a girl, Marion.

Brian had bought a smallholding at Limpley Stoke where he milked his own cows and came to the farm part-time. This just left Sue, my mother and myself at the farm as Ray was out most of the time. Ray was by now courting Myra, a farmer's daughter from Crewkern, whom he had met at the Manor. Sunday mornings saw an opportunity for local lads to meet the Domestic Science students from the Manor, as most of them attended the village church. Ray had planned his work so that he was on the road with the tractor at the time the girls were walking back to the Manor. Eventually Myra began a teaching career at Dorchester and Ray corresponded by telephone and letter. The latter caused us a lot of amusement with Ray spending hours trying to write a letter only to have it returned by Myra corrected and almost rewritten in red ink.

Mother was very unhappy, being so isolated and not having a car. On reflection, it might have been much better for all of us if Mother had remarried. Sue continued to take the taxi to Combe Down School, and I walked to the bus or rode my bike to Bath.

My new school had a very different regime, with a master for each subject, and the necessity of moving from classroom to classroom according to our timetable. The immense amount of homework that was handed out by each master was quite a shock. Everything was geared to obtaining the maximum number of General School Certificates in three years' time. The standard of work required was much higher than that at my old school, and I felt out of my depth in some subjects, maths in particular.

During this period of my education, Ray was seriously injured in a car accident. As Brian had his own cows to milk, I had to get up at five, and with the help of Ray Dyers' father, Allen, did the morning milking. Thankfully, an electricity generator and milking machine had been installed some years earlier, but the thirty cows were still milked in the cow shed and parlours were still in the future. I then had to wash and change, have breakfast and cycle to Bath by nine o'clock. Sometimes I fell asleep at my desk, if the lesson was a bit boring, which often had unpleasant consequences.

Time came for GCE exams and it was decided that I should take eight subjects consisting of Mathematics, English language, English literature, General Science, History, Geography, Technical Drawing and Art. The maths master complained for some weeks prior to the exam that I was going to be his first failure for five years. However, surprise, surprise, I passed in all subjects, scraping through maths on the pass mark. The sixth form in those days was very small, consisting of the very brightest of boys, and in any case I had by now had my fill of school.

1956 saw Britain involved in yet another war, this time in the Middle East. A dictator called Colonel Nasser had become ruler of Egypt and tried to unite the Arab nations by taking an anti-western stance and building strong links with Russia. Our Prime Minister, Anthony Eden, was very concerned about the effect of all this on our interests and oil supplies in the region.

The situation came to a head when Nasser decided to nationalise the Suez Canal, a vital link in Britain's communications with the Far East. Britain, France and Israel colluded on a plan of action.

The Israelis launched an invasion of Egypt across the Sinai desert and a few days later the British and French launched their own well-prepared invasion to regain control of the Canal and safeguard it for international shipping. The action was a great success and all objectives were achieved in a few days.

This action was denounced throughout the world. The Americans were furious because they had not been consulted and insisted that we withdraw our forces and supported a United Nations resolution to that effect. The Russians, who were already involved in a war in Hungary, threatened to bury us. Israeli, British and French forces withdrew, but the Suez Canal was blocked by sunken ships for many months.

This unpopular action caused political turmoil for the government and a huge loss of international prestige, leading to a realisation that we were no longer a world power and a gradual shedding of our commitments east of Suez.

During the few weeks before the invasion, I used to go down to the main road and watch the tanks go past on their transporters. This went on for many days and it seemed like hundreds of them all in their desert colours. They were on their way to Southampton to be shipped to Malta in preparation for the ill-fated invasion.

While I was still at school, a succession of various second-hand cars were used by the boys for the farm, and their own private use. It was always in a dreadful state whenever Mother found someone to drive it and take us out. Eventually she bought a Ford Prefect to be shared with Mrs Owen from Claverton Down. The car was kept in a garage near Claverton Manor, so it was away from the farm, from the mud and the boys. Mrs Owen used it for shopping and local trips and we used it at weekends if we found a driver. Arthur Moody, a single young man from Combe Down, took us on many trips and visits during those few years. I believe he was a bit lonely and enjoyed the company and somewhere to go; we enjoyed his company too. Whenever he came to the farm he would hurry off down to the stream to pick watercress.

Mrs Owen had been a friend to Mother for a long time and was also Sue's godmother. Her husband, Jack, was chief engineer to Bath City Council. When I left school she suggested, if I still wanted to be an architect, that I should see her husband who may be able to advise me on a course of action. I did see him in his office, and also pursued other career avenues. Mr Owen explained that there were two options to consider: Firstly, I could attend the Royal West of England Academy of Architecture at Bristol, full time for a minimum of seven years. He thought I was probably too young for this and recommended the second option. This was, to be articled to a local architect and attend the academy part-time, one day a week. He made an appointment for me to see F W Beresford Smith, as he knew he was looking for a new pupil. I followed this up, was articled to the architect and enrolled part-time at the academy.

The drawing office at FW Beresford Smith was just one large room next to Mr Smith's office, which was about the same size. Mr Smith's office was well furnished with a large polished table and chairs in the middle, some smaller tables and bookcases, and a number of architects' presentation watercolours on the walls. The tables contained a couple of beautiful models of previous important projects. It was an ideal room for meeting clients and business people, and of course it was where Mr Smith had conducted my interview a few weeks before.

The drawing office was, by contrast, a bit drab and I felt that a coat of paint would have improved the working environment. The room contained an old arc lamp printing machine, a huge plan chest and four double elephant drawing boards. The boards rested on tables and a pile of books at the back adjusted the slope. Two professional draughtsmen made use of the boards near the windows; the other two were for me and another pupil. Both of the professional draughtsmen were middle-aged and had passed the RIBA intermediate examinations. They took a week's leave most years and trotted off to London to retake their finals. Another articled pupil, who had been there about six months, used the third board. It was good to discover that Clive, like myself, was also enrolled at the RWA and we were to start on the following Monday.

Working in the drawing office was enjoyable, not only working at the drawing board, but also visiting the sites. Holding the end of the tape or helping the staff when surveying was most interesting. I seemed to fit in well with the two draughtsmen and soon became friendly with Clive. The RWA was a different cup of tea, and consisted of an old building with lots of stone stairs and corridors and a very serious atmosphere. Most of the students were older than I was; one was thirty-three which seemed very old.

The routine consisted of three lectures during the morning, then time to eat my packed lunch. The first period after lunch was 'Criticism' followed by an hour outlining and explaining the new project for the week, then finally deciding the subject of the weekend sketch The 'Criticism' was horrendous! Work from the previous week was displayed on the wall of a corridor, stamped with either a 'P-', 'P', or 'P+' for a pass, or 'E' for excellent. If the work failed to attain the necessary standard it was stamped 'RESUBMIT'. We were each given a few minutes in which to criticise everyone else's work. It was a nightmare and I dreaded Mondays.

If the work was stamped 'RESUBMIT', it meant that it had to be resubmitted the following week as well as the new week's work. If, as happened several times in my case, it still did not pass and the new work failed as well, I found myself with two weeks' work, together with the new week's work plus a small weekend sketch. At home space was limited and without electricity, lighting was inadequate for technical drawing and watercolour painting, and as the amount of work increased my standard fell. Every student was assessed at the end of the first year and both Clive and I had to repeat the first year; this was disheartening! Hoping the first year would be easier the second time around, we set about it with renewed determination. Alas, this did not last very long and I was soon overwhelmed with work again.

Both Clive and I decided to pack it in, but there was the problem of the Articles which were for three years; however after two years, Mr Smith agreed reluctantly, that to continue would be a waste of everyone's time and released us. I went back to farm work. I don't know what happened to Clive. Maybe if I had completed a couple more years at school and passed some 'A' levels, and then attended the RWA full time, being older and more mature, it may have turned out differently.

CHAPTER 4

END OF VINEYARDS FARM

While I was concerned with architecture, dramatic events were occurring back at the farm. These events were set in motion by the death of our landlady, Miss Skrine, who lived across the river at Warleigh Manor. The estate consisted of five farms and many cottages, including our farm and Mrs. Watson's cottage at the top of the farm lane. The estate was to be sold, and all the tenants were offered an opportunity to buy their properties by negotiation. If a price could not be agreed then the properties would be offered on the open market.

As all the tenants had security of tenure, there was no great need to buy, except the tremendous opportunity to purchase at a price level generally considered to be about half. By this time Mother had had enough and saw this as an opportunity to get out and into her dream bungalow. With the help of Arthur Edwards, she decided to buy the farm including the cottage at the top of the lane, which was already condemned as unfit for human habitation. Mrs. Watson was then given her cottage, it being considered a liability, and the farm was divided into various lots, each being offered for sale with vacant possession. Most lots sold reasonably well except the farmhouse and buildings, together with fifty-six acres of steep pastureland. This lot returned only three thousand pounds. A field adjacent to the village was withdrawn from the auction having not reached its reserve. This field of about six acres

Vineyards Farm, 1957

was eventually transferred to my sister Susan. Brian continued to farm it and paid rent to Sue.

A sale of all the live and dead stock was arranged through Cooper and Tanner, who had auctioned the property. A temporary auction ring was constructed in the yard for selling the livestock. The tractors and trailers, implements, tools, stores, scrap and what could only be described as 'rubbish' all had a price and was laid out in lines in the paddock. On the allotted day parking proved to be an enormous problem as there was no room in the yard and the available fields were too steep for cars. There were crowds of people; most of them had left their cars on the road and walked to the sale. It was a very busy day for all of us, thankfully, but even so I remember feeling a bit sad seeing people milling about our things. This was especially so when household items, such as our old cast iron mangle went under the hammer - things that I had been familiar with since my earliest memories.

After a few days all the animals were gone and all the lots in the paddock had been collected. For Sue, Mother and myself the farm suddenly became a dead place, very quiet and lonely. We were scheduled to move out soon and Mother was busy looking for a house, which must have been very difficult, living where we did with no transport. Mother arranged for us to stay on at the farm for another six months. However when this time expired we had still not found a suitable house. She then took up an offer from some farming friends at Hinton Charterhouse, George Dix and his wife, to live with them until we found a place. We lived at Stroud Farm with the Dix's for about six months, enjoying all the trappings of modern living - kitchen and bathroom with hot and cold water, flushing toilets, electric lights and even a television.

After the sale of the farm, Ray went to work for Fred Joyce, from Rode, a well-known cattle dealer and market character. Fred wanted to ease up a bit and needed someone to drive him around in his Jaguar, drive his lorry, and generally act as his agent. This was ideal for Ray and was to be the start of his bull hiring business, when he eventually bought Fred out, and ran the business from his rented cottage on Claverton Down. Brian continued to farm his smallholding at Limpley Stoke, adding to his income by building a small agricultural contracting business. Sue left school at fifteen and started a job in an estate agents in Bath. She and I cycled to Bath if the weather was reasonable and continued to do so when we moved to Hinton Charterhouse. When we moved, Mother bought her share of the car from Mrs. Owen as I had by now passed my driving test. Mother and Sue were now dependent on me for driving them around, and the car was available for my weekly trips to Bristol, and for Sue and I to get to work in bad weather.

During this period I began to realise that there was more to life than work and became interested in girls, visiting pubs, and coffee bars. As I only received ten shillings a week from the architect's office, (£9 at 2009 values), I was always short of cash to finance my newly discovered lifestyle so I spent any free time doing odd jobs. Picking up litter after a cricket match at the Bath recreation ground was a good example. My relationship with my mother reached an all time low during this time as she was very disappointed at the collapse of my architectural career.

The summer of 1958 saw me totally free of my studies, with the responsibility of earning a living. This coincided with Colin Dix investing in a second-hand combine harvester to carry out contract combining in the area. There had been, for some time, a gradual increase in the acreage of cereals, as the number of small dairy herds continued to decline. Although a few years older than me, Colin was great fun to go out with; he knew where to go and what to do. He could afford good cars and despite being married was not averse to our having a drink with a couple of girls in the pub. I remember being very impressed when he told me that he spent £6 a week on beer, cigarettes, and eating out. This was like a fortune to me as farm worker's wages were about £8, plus 5 shillings an hour overtime.

The combine was a Massey Harris 726 bagger, which meant that a second man was required to deal with the sacks. I worked for Colin that summer on a casual basis, as I was not required during wet weather, and there was a lot of wet weather that year. The work involved helping to service and refuel the machine, cutting binder twine to the required length and stocking the combine with empty sacks supplied by the farmer. I then spent the day attaching empty sacks to the grain chutes and removing the full ones. These were then tied with the twine and lifted off the platform on to a sloping chute, which would hold three or four sacks. Pulling a rope would then release them, to fall on the ground behind the machine. These sacks were to be collected by the farmer's tractor and trailer.

As I have said, Colin could afford good cars, and about this time bought a second-hand Ford Zodiac, with two-tone colour, overdrive and white walled tyres. Colin loved to drive it fast and put it through its paces through the corners; the local girls loved it. I enjoyed driving the car when given the opportunity but was very careful and cautious.

Colin was always ready to drive anything to the limit. One Saturday afternoon I had just finished washing the Prefect, when along came Colin, keen to give it a go. As soon as he was behind the wheel we were out of the yard and hurtling down the lane towards the busy main road. He quickly discovered that the brakes were ineffective due to my washing. I was in a state of shock, but Colin grabbed the hand brake and locked the steering fully to the right. With this the car immediately turned ninety degrees to the right, accompanied by screeching tyres, went up on two wheels and came to a halt on the edge of the main road and dropped back on four wheels. As far as I can recall, we abandoned the rest of the test drive and returned home for a cup of tea.

Having some spending money at last, I bought an old Royal Enfield 125 to give myself a little more independence. I was still able to borrow Mother's car to go to dances or take out a girlfriend. The dances were very popular among young people, and Freshford Village Hall was a great venue. Drinking and driving was no problem as there were no breathalyser tests and the only chance of being charged with drunken driving was if you had an accident. Many times I saw people too drunk to walk across the car park who considered themselves to be OK once they were behind the wheel. There was very little traffic on the roads in those days and we were generally driving on country lanes. After a while I changed my motorbike for a better one, a Royal Enfield 350. This motorbike was a disappointment so I soon changed it for a Matchless 500, which was pretty good and enabled me to keep up with a few friends on weekend outings.

Although I had a license to drive a car, it did not include my motorcycle, so I had to take my test on the Matchless in Bath. After completing the practical part the examiner invited me to a roadside bench to answer some questions. The first question was, "Was I keen to commit suicide?" I was taken aback and thought I must have failed; but he went on to say that my only fault was not looking behind enough. He then showed me photographs of horrendous accidents where motorcyclists were run over by lorries because they had been unaware of their presence.

Jim Ansty was a great friend who was keen on motorbikes. At one time he had a shaft-drive Sunbeam, which was a big cruising machine, but not over quick. We were out and about most weekends, and the evenings too in the summer. Looking back on those days we must have been crazy as we never even had a crash helmet, but at that time no one did unless they were keen on racing.

My working life consisted of odd jobs for cash - sometimes driving a tractor for Colin Dix, milking cows and tractor driving for my brother Brian, or long-distance lorry driving for my brother Ray. Some of these trips were very long... to bull sales as far away as Perth, when climbing over Shap Fell in Cumbria was only half way. The age of the motorway and the HGV licence had not yet arrived and heaters, de-misters and power assisted steering were unheard of. It really was hard work but also quite exciting.

At this time the idea of working on an arable farm began to appeal to me. The experience with Colin's combine and the small amount of cultivation work I had done seemed to suggest that it would be much better than messing about with cows. I had already applied to a couple of farms when Brian told me that Bert Bowles at Winsley needed a tractor driver. I knew the farm as I had been there baling straw with Brian during that summer and had admired the tanker combine and bulk handling of the grain, something I had only seen on films. Some years before I had come across the name 'Bowles' when a young man had been tragically killed by an overturning tractor on Winsley hill. This young man was Bert's younger brother, John.

After contacting Bert and arranging to see him one evening, I found myself in his warm, large kitchen enjoying a cup of tea. I had met Bert a few times out on the farm so he was not a complete stranger to me and I found him easy to talk to. We chatted about tractor driving and ploughing and he assured me that the fact that I had not done much ploughing was no problem; he was prepared to teach me. Bert suggested that I start as soon as possible and asked if I could start after the weekend.

After living with the Dix's for about six months, Mother found her bungalow. It was near the garage on the main road at Monkton Combe, called 'Overvale' and overlooked the Limpley Stoke valley at the back. The property had a wooden garage, which required a bit of manoeuvouring to get the car in and out of, and a lovely garden, which was to become Mother's pride and joy. I often wonder why she didn't get a job or at least a part-time job as she was only in her mid-fifties; I think she would have been a much happier person. My greatest regret from this time is not having persuaded her to learn to drive but I suppose I was too wrapped up in my own life. Mother, Sue and I moved into Overvale early in December and I was quick to discover the delights of my new local, 'The Viaduct Inn', which was within walking distance.

On my eighteenth birthday I set out for my new job at Church Farm, Winsley, where I met the only other employee, George Godwin, (no relation as far as I know). George had worked for the Bowles family for many years and was now nearing retirement. His job was to look after the sheep, attend to the grain drier at harvest time and to do all the odd jobs necessary to keep the farm clean and tidy. For this George was provided with a little grey Ferguson tractor, which was also used for drilling and harrowing at planting time. My job was to drive the Fordson Major Diesel if and when there was work for it, help service and maintain the tractors and machinery and to help George with his many and varied jobs.

There was also the combine harvester, a Massey Harris 780 Special, which I was expected to learn about and operate during the next harvest. There were two farms, managed and run as one unit by Bert, my new boss. He lived about a mile up the lane at Parsonage Farm and his mother and two sisters lived at Church Farm. Bert arrived at Church Farm soon after I did and, after a general chat, suggested that I hitch on the plough and meet him in a particular field in about an hour. I had, at my interview, explained that although I was a competent tractor driver and had done some ploughing, I knew very little about the technicalities.

On meeting Bert in the field he explained that as the land was over-lying rock, it was necessary to have a special top link incorporating a hydraulic pressure valve. This automatically depressed the clutch should the plough hit an obstruction, but even so ploughing was to be carried out fairly slowly. First he showed me how to mark out the headland, then, using marking sticks, instructed me how to strike out. Using the sticks again we marked out another strike out which I then completed under his supervision. I explained that I was happy to continue with the general work but would like some advice when it came to the finish off, so he arranged to come back to the field after lunch.

I very soon realised that my clothes were insufficient to keep out the cold so I drove the tractor back to the farm at lunchtime to eat my sandwiches in the shed. George had gone home to lunch and when he came back he saw I was frozen and immediately went back home to fetch a World War I army greatcoat. He said I could have it as it was far too heavy to work in and he had not worn it for years. George then went on to suggest that I should buy a second pair of wellington boots for the winter and make sure they were two sizes larger. If these were then lined with fine hay, to be changed every few days, my feet would never be cold again.

Returning to the field I found that Bert was waiting. He complemented me on the general work and then proceeded to show me how to finish off. From then on I was on my own and with lots of practice became a very competent ploughman. The December weather was dry and cold and I wondered what I had let myself in for, but once I had my new boots with the hay lining, I was never really cold again.

An old Combe Down school friend, Alan Christopher, used to enjoy pigeon shooting and we did quite a lot of this at Bert's farm; we were both pretty good shots. In the evenings we sometimes went to the United Services Club on Claverton Down where we could drink, play snooker and chat up the girls. Jim had moved and was living near Chippenham so we didn't see much of him. The three of us planned a summer holiday. Mother agreed to lend us her car, not the old Prefect but a second hand Ford Zephyr she had recently bought. We were delighted to have this car as we considered it a real 'bird puller' with its large front bench seat and column change; also there was room for six people.

Gradually a plan came together to spend a week in early July touring north Wales, as we were all keen to see some mountains. The holiday was great fun, staying at cheap bed and breakfast places and eating loads of beans on toast. One wet afternoon, in a cinema, we met some girls and took them dancing in the evening I think we all fell in love that night and promised them that we would return for a weekend after harvest. We then drove home through the night as our week was up.

With the prospect of more money in my pocket in the run-up to harvest, I traded the Matchless for a second hand Norton Dominator 500 twin. This was a really good bike to ride and was in much better condition than any of the others I had owned and I was happy to go on longer trips. This was a really enjoyable time as I was in a job that gave me huge satisfaction and apart from harvest there was plenty of free time. It was also still possible to continue helping my brothers on occasions so generally it was a very interesting life.

At work during that first few months, I made the most of wet days and slack periods, learning about the combine to ensure I was competent to handle the coming harvest. The weather for the harvest was exceptionally good and the crops were standing well which made the job much easier than had been the case with Colin's combine the previous year. A conflict of interest arose out of the fact that my two brothers purchased a large part of the straw to bale and haul away - some for Brian and some to trade on. The straw was sold by the acre, so the shorter I cut the crops the more straw my brothers got for their money, but cutting it short was not good combining practice as it overloaded the separating capacity of the machine, and consequently slowed it down. I managed to resolve this to no one's satisfaction by compromising on cutting height. Bert did most of the grain hauling with the little Ferguson and a three-ton grain trailer; it was a great advance to be rid of the sacks. Bert's sister, Mattie, used to drive the Ferguson at weekends or on her days off from her work at County Hall in Trowbridge.

My life continued in very similar vein for another year with

Me driving Massey Harris 780, harvesting wheat 1960

my interest in arable farming growing from day to day and I thought about how I might improve my prospects if I made it my career. I began to look at positions as a Farm Manager and it soon became apparent that I lacked a suitable agricultural education. I regretted my wasted years in architecture, but no doubt it was all useful experience, especially the introduction to city life and a very different lifestyle.

The second harvest at Church Farm was even more interesting. I was much more confident operating the machine and I had some company on occasions. Chas (that's all I knew him as) was a jovial character of about fifty who spent his two weeks holiday with relations in the village. When he appeared in the field he would hobble across to meet the combine, so I would stop briefly for him to struggle aboard where he then sat on the toolbox behind my seat, sometimes for hours. All this was a struggle for him as he had a wooden leg, but it did not stop him from doing what he wanted to do. Chas referred to it as his peg leg and apparently he had a metal one with a knee joint at home, which he wore for 'best' and referred to this one as his artificial leg.

Alan Christopher came on the combine some evenings for

a chat, and Mattie was often driving the tractor. After dark we sometimes went to the pub to wash the dust down. This was always enjoyable after a hard, long day in the sun and I began to take more interest in Mattie. We started going on secret trips to various pubs; having rushed home to bath and change, I would race to Winsley on my Norton and meet her near the shop. Sometimes I had to wait a while and as I watched her walking towards me I thought how lovely she looked and she made me feel like no other girl had made me feel before.

One warm summer evening I finished a bit earlier than usual and met her in the yard. She told me she had relatives visiting in about an hour so she couldn't come out with me. So I suggested that if she walked up to the shed in the top field, I would ride my bike along Stoke road, park it inside the gate and walk up to the shed from there. Mattie was lying on a pile of loose straw looking really sexy and inviting. Before she could get up I had dived on to the straw beside her and began cuddling and kissing. Before long I had removed all her clothes, never before had I held a girl so closely in my arms. As I began to remove some of my own clothing, she suddenly pushed me aside, jumped up and started putting her clothes back on, explaining that she must get back and that we had gone quite far enough in any case. She said she wanted to see me again so we kissed goodbye and she went back across the field. I waited a while in the shed thinking that perhaps I was falling in love, then I walked down to my bike, riding home in a tangle of emotions.

CHAPTER 5

LOVE AND NUCLEAR PERIL

Work continued through 1960 and Bert bought a brand new Fordson Power Major. I enjoyed operating this tractor, using it for ploughing and heavy cultivations, but sometimes I was required to use the little grey Ferguson for lighter jobs such as drilling and spraying.

Spraying was only carried out to control broad leaf weeds in the cereal crops, as in those days there were no fungicides available. The farm was well served by water troughs supplied from the water main. The water system had been installed several years earlier when the farm was a dairy farm carrying lots of livestock. It was my job to visit the various fields to be sprayed and clean each trough in turn with a bucket and scrubbing brush, therefore ensuring a clean water supply when I arrived to spray the field. The sprayer was mounted on the back of the Fergie and consisted of a power driven pump, forty gallon tank and a twelve foot wide spray boom. The sprayer was backed up to a trough and filled using a bucket, each fill covering about 4 acres.

This year saw me engaged to Mattie, an occasion we celebrated with a party one Saturday night at Claverton Down Village Hall. We often went to the pictures in Bath and on Saturday nights went to dances at venues such as the Weston Hotel and the Old Mill at Bathampton. All the while plans were being made to marry in June the following year. Bert arranged for one of his houses on the edge of the village to be available in May, so we could do some decorating and generally get the house ready for our return from honeymoon.

At about this time Mattie informed me that her father had left her a farm, In fact he had left each of his four children a farm Bert's farm was Parsonage Farm where he lived. John, who was killed by the overturning tractor, would have had Church Farm where Mattie, her disabled sister Mary and her mother lived. Mary's farm was at Grittleton and let to a farmer and Mattie's was at Rowd near Devizes, also let to a farmer.

We visited the farm one afternoon in the summer and met the tenant who kindly showed us around. The land consisted of about 100 acres of wet heavy clay and was all permanent pasture supporting a small dairy herd and followers with a small range of traditional buildings. We did not go inside the farmhouse but from outside it was not very appealing. The approach to the farm was along a very long, rough, pot-holed track with very wide grass verges where gypsies parked their caravans and grazed their horses. It was of course apparent that there was very little for us to do apart from continuing to collect the rent and probably spend most of it maintaining the property, as the tenant had security under the law.

Mattie and I were married on the 3rd of June 1961, followed by a reception for about sixty at Winsley Village Hall. Our good friends Joan and Gordon helped us escape from the reception when the time came, and drove us to our hotel in Bournmouth where they joined us for dinner. Next morning we transferred to Bournmouth airport for our flight to Jersey - all very exciting as we had never flown before. The aeroplane was a Douglas DC3 - in Britain, called a Dakota; one of many thousands produced during and after the Second World War. Dakotas had been used extensively as military transports, carrying parachute troops and towing gliders.

The flight exceeded all our expectations as we flew at only 2000 to 3000 feet and the view was fantastic. After landing at Jersey airport we transferred by taxi to our hotel at Bonne Nuit

Married to Mattie 1961

Bay, where we were expected. On checking in, the manager asked where the baby was as he had received a telegram asking for a cot to be provided in our room. After scouring the island for a cot, he was, understandably, very cross to learn that it must be a joke by one of our friends; we never found out who it was.

It was a super holiday. We hired a little Renault Dauphine and toured the island, seeing all the sights, making new friends and enjoying lots of strawberries and cream. Mattie got pretty badly sunburnt, so I had to keep my distance for a few days but apart from that we had a very pleasant week.

Settling into married life went fairly smoothly, with me continuing my work at Bert's and Mattie working as a shop assistant at Fear Hills in Trowbridge. Mattie soon became pregnant and we began preparing for a family when in November Mattie had a miscarriage. This was a dreadful shock for us and Mattie took some time to recover, but we were led to believe that this sometimes happens and was nothing to worry about. It would probably be all right next time. Next time, however, was not all right and a second miscarriage devastated us. This was a bitter disappointment and again we were advised that it was nothing to worry about and it would prove third time lucky

Soon after this, in October 1962, the cold war came very close to turning into a hot war during a period that became known as the 'Cuban Missile Crisis'. The island of Cuba in the Carribbean had had a Communist revolution and was now ruled by a dictator called Fidel Castro. Russia was very keen to support this Communist state in the heart of the American hemisphere and trade between Cuba and Russia grew rapidly. Cuba supplied sugar and other agricultural products to Russia in exchange for defence equipment and technical advisors.

This caused tension to build up between Cuba and the United States of America. This was raised to breaking point when the USA discovered that the Russians were installing medium range ballistic missiles on the island. At this time ballistic missiles were gradually replacing manned bombers as a means of delivering nuclear weapons to their desired targets and it was apparent that a huge area of the USA and several major US cities would be within range of these weapons. We stayed up until the early hours of the morning to hear President Kennedy tell us what the Americans were going to do about this volatile situation.

The President told us that after a long and difficult debate, it had been decided that to attack the missile sites was too dangerous as some may be ready for firing, and to mount an invasion of the island would bring the US into war with the Soviet Union. The decided course of action was for the US navy to blockade Cuba and stop, board and search, and if necessary turn back or sink any ships carrying war material. He also told us that there were several Russian ships crossing the Atlantic towards Cuba and some were carrying what looked like missiles on their decks.

The next few days were the most traumatic I have ever lived through. We were involved in the crisis because of our membership of the North Atlantic Treaty Organisation or NATO as it was known, and also by our government's support for the stand the Americans were making. On Thursday, 25th October, an oil tanker, the *Bucharest,* was stopped by the US navy; the captain assured the Americans that it was carrying only oil and it was allowed to continue towards Cuba.

At this time of year we were in the midst of autumn cultivations and I was spending long hours on the tractor which in those days was not equipped with a radio. We used to listen avidly to the BBC news programs morning and evening, but I was cut off from the world by day. For several days we would get up in the morning and wonder if we would survive the day, and go to bed at night wondering if we would see the morning. The next day the US navy stopped a Soviet ship and three US naval officers went on board while the world held its breath. They were satisfied that the ship was carrying industrial goods and it was allowed to continue. During the following days several more ships were stopped and boarded - not only Soviet but other nationalities as well; each time the world's heart missed a beat. Then on Saturday an American U2 spy plane was shot down over Cuba and the world stood still. All the while the Soviet ships carrying the missiles continued their steady and determined course towards the US naval blockade.

Unknown to us during these tense days was the amount of dialogue taking place between East and West at the United Nations in New York. We now know that while the full nuclear arsenals of both East and West were on red alert, a secret deal was being hammered out. This was a plan to give the Russians an excuse to back down. They agreed to remove all their nuclear missiles from Cuba if the Americans removed all their nuclear missiles from Turkey. The American missiles had been installed in Turkey as part of 'Operation Many Baskets' many years before. On Sunday the 28th of October, we learned that the Soviet missile ships had turned around and were on course back to Russia.

Time to say a few words about Bert's farm at Winsley where I had now worked for nearly three years and learnt an awful lot about arable farming.

Bert had taken over the farm from his father and continued milking cows until an outbreak of Johne's Disease, which is carried in the soil. Bert was advised that he should not keep cattle on the land for at least seven years and was persuaded to convert to arable farming in about 1956.

The majority of the soil was known as 'Cotswold brash' which was a variable depth of soil over limestone shale or solid rock, easy to work, with a tendency to dry out in a drought. Damage to implements, in particular the plough, was considerable although tyre wear was low. Ploughing was consequently a slow job and the Fordson Power Major that I was driving at this time was pulling a four furrow Ransomes plough set at twelve-inch wide furrows. This tractor was also fitted with the automatic stop devise that I mentioned on my first day. In the event of the plough striking an immoveable object, this top link compressed and depressed the clutch stopping the tractor instantaneously; even at the low operating speeds of two to four miles an hour this sudden stop could be quite violent.

Stone walls divided the fields, making good use of local materials. They were good boundaries for pigs and cattle but not much use for sheep, whose only aim in life, apart from dying for no good reason, was to escape into the next field. I was once ploughing, with a good view of the sheep and several fields, when I saw them jumping up onto the wall and down into the next field; then before long they were again escaping into another field which happened to adjoin the field where they were supposed to be. It was not long before they were escaping again, but this time into the field where they were supposed to be. Not content with this, they soon escaped again and after a while formed a continuous line of sheep going from field to field in a huge circle of 'follow my leader'. The fields were irregular shapes and quite small ranging from three to seventeen acres.

George was in charge of the sheep, worked on the grain drier at harvest time and kept on top of all the odd jobs around the farm. Wire netting was used to control the sheep and George was constantly erecting and dismantling the wire as the sheep were moved from field to field, using the little Ferguson with its lift box on the back. I used to help with the sheep at lambing and shearing times and also helped with the fencing in the spring when the ewes and young lambs were creep grazed on one-year ryegrass leys. This involved dividing up the field with wire netting fences into roughly one acre paddocks with a creep system being installed between the paddock currently being grazed and an adjacent fresh one for the lambs to creep into, but not the ewes. This system enabled the lambs to have the very best grass in the fresh paddock. After a few days the ewes and lambs were moved into the paddock already grazed by the lambs and the lambs were now able to creep into a fresh one. This was very labour intensive but was amply justified by the rapid growth of the lambs.

Having completed drilling the spring crops, my time was spent spreading nitrogen in the form of Nitro Chalk and spraying the crops with herbicide with the little Ferguson. The fertiliser was supplied in one hundred weight [50kg] paper sacks which were loaded onto a trailer and taken to the field where they were again manhandled onto the spreader. The sacks were cut and emptied, the empty sacks being secured to stop them blowing away until they were burnt at the end of the day. Again a very labour intensive operation for, alas, forklift trucks on farms were still a long way in the future.

It was my impression that Bert was an exceptionally good and efficient farmer, always looking for new ideas and insisting on keeping the farm tidy. Old broken down wooden gates were replaced with new steel ones and fallen dry-stone walls were rebuilt as soon as possible. I was always encouraged to plough as close to the walls as was possible. On rare occasions I recall the plough just gently touching one stone at the base of a wall and a huge section would come tumbling down; once, I remember, it came down on top of the plough. Two new enterprises were introduced around this time, one was concerned with the arable side and the other saw the introduction of more livestock.

Dealing with the arable crop first - it was apparent that there was an increasing demand for home-grown grass seed, so Bert decided to grow a variety of Cocksfoot, which was showing a useful return at that time. The seed was under sown in a spring barley crop in rows 21 inches apart. After the barley harvest it was grazed by the sheep through the winter and early spring, when it was fertilised and allowed to grow up to seed and ripen off, to be ready for harvesting in July. As the seed ripened unevenly it was combined twice - the first time, which was when it was cut, the combine was set very wide so that in effect it just gave the crop a good shaking so that only the ripe seed was collected in the tank and the rest of the crop was returned in lines to the ground to continue ripening.

Next, a draper pick up was fitted to the combine and after a few days the crop was combined again but this time the machine was set tight to give the crop a good threshing to separate all the seed. The seed was then discharged into the grain trailer, which was not so easy, as the seed tended to bridge over the unloading auger in the tank and had to be poked with a long stick. Once in the trailer it was taken to the barn and tipped on the floor where it was shovelled into hessian sacks. A makeshift drying floor had been constructed from gates resting on spaced out straw bales, on to which the sacks were placed close together in a single layer without any gaps between them. Air was blown into the chamber under the gates and so was forced through the seed in the sacks. This airflow was provided by a hired Lister Diesel, axial flow fan, rated at about 40 hp, and run night and day until the seed was dry.

This makeshift drying system was of course only for the grass seed harvest. For the grain harvest Bert had a state of the art Ransomes, oil fired, continuous flow grain drier at Parsonage Farm. There was a specially constructed reception pit into which the grain was tipped from the grain trailer, from there it was elevated up to the top of the drier, where it gravitated slowly down to the bottom. The speed of flow was controlled according to the moisture content of the grain and the temperature of the hot air being blown through from the burner. From here the grain was elevated to a Penny and Porter cleaner that separated the good grain from the seconds, dust and chaff. The good grain could now be elevated and conveyed to six 20 ton steel storage silos built inside the barn or bagged from the cleaner into large hessian sacks, rented from the West of England Sack Company.

George filled and weighed these sacks and stacked them in the barn ready for moving to permanent storage sheds at Church Farm. Hauling these sacks away was done in the mornings before the crops were dry enough for combining to start. The sacks contained two and a quarter hundred weight of wheat (112.5 kilos), two hundred weight of barley (100 kilos), or one and a half hundred weight of oats (75 kilos). Consequently these sacks were difficult to move around and sack trucks were used, plus an electric sack lift which elevated them to shoulder height from where they could be carried to a stack or placed on a flat bed trailer.

Bert and Jean had by this time, three little boys, Stephen, Richard and Geoffrey. A baby girl, Catherine, was born at Parsonage Farm on the very morning that the new sack lift was delivered. I arrived at the farm about mid morning, from Church Farm, to find Bert looking after Geoffrey. Bert was keen for Geoffrey to give me the news, saying, "Tell Mick what arrived this morning". Geoffrey said excitedly "a new sack lift".

After these sacks of grain had been stored for several weeks or months the dreaded time came to load them onto lorries, when we found that mice had created havoc. Instead of a good tidy job the shed ended up with the floor covered in grain and hessian and part sacks too damaged to load. All this had to be cleaned up, re-sacked, and weighed before the next lorry arrived. At least we no longer had to lift these huge sacks onto the lorry as they were now equipped with a simple loader. A tubular framed arm was attached to the back, and with the engine ticking over, and a sack tipped on the end from the sack trucks, a hydraulic ram would swing the arm and sack to arrive at shoulder height of the lorry driver standing on the bed. From this position the sacks could be carried and stacked by the driver without undue effort. The drivers made it look so easy but I could imagine the danger and horror of a new boy catching his first sack.

The second new enterprise to be introduced at this time was breeding pedigree Saddleback pigs. Ten Saddleback sows were purchased and mated with a pedigree boar and the offspring weaned; the males were castrated and fattened for pork or bacon. The females, or gilts, were moved onto the stubbles and lived in movable arks in large pens made with electric fences. When the gilts were big enough to breed they were mated with Large White or Landrace boars. All this was planned and timed so that the gilts could be sold close to farrowing, at what was to become an annual auction at Parsonage Farm. This took place one evening during May and the last bit of land, until then occupied by the pigs, was ploughed and sown with barley.

Getting ready for the sale was a busy time. The first problem was moving the gilts from their pens; although the electric wire was removed, the pigs would not cross the line - sometimes they had to be loaded into a trailer. The pigs then had to be washed and brushed and when they were dry, oil was rubbed into their skins to make them look bright and shiny. Pens had to be constructed from straw bales; gates and hurdles and a sale ring prepared. The auctioneers would send a couple of men to help on the day of the sale. Bert and Jean provided refreshments after the auction and it was usually a very enjoyable evening with farmers coming from all around the locality to bid for the pigs.

CHAPTER 6

AN EXTRAORDINARY WINTER

It was a very short walk across the field to our house from Church Farm, so I used to go home for lunch most days. If there was no tractor work for me, then George and I would be working together and we would stop at around 9.30 am for a thermos of hot tea and a chat in the workshop. We needed a break by then as we started work at 7am and finished at 5pm with an hour off for lunch. During one of our tea breaks, George and I began talking about the weather, a common topic of conversation for people who worked outside. George recalled how past winters had seen heavy snowfalls and drifting snow blocking the lanes and roads several feet deep. This of course was difficult to imagine and we were not to know that we were soon to experience the reality as the worst winter in living memory was about burst upon us.

Mattie and I spent Boxing Day at my mother's house where we enjoyed a Christmas lunch in the company of several members of the family. In the evening it began to snow quite heavily, but nothing unusual, but to be on the safe side we decided to leave early and departed at about 9pm. The snow already covered the roads and our little A40 was unable to climb Winsley hill. Very conveniently Brian's farm was at the bottom of the hill, so we left the car there and walked home, about two miles. If I remember correctly it was a lovely walk as the snow was falling gently, no wind and just the two of us, full of Christmas cheer.

Next morning dawned bright and sunny and about four inches of snow lay clean and beautiful over the landscape. It was to remain like this for several days. On New Year's Eve we were invited to a toboggan party at English Combe, the other side of Bath, to end with a party and mulled wine to see in the New Year. Travelling with Bert and Jean in their Morris Traveller, we found that the roads were virtually free of snow and ice. The party was great fun with lots of people and toboggans but snow began to fall at about 10pm. By the time we had seen in the New Year and sampled the warming mulled wine, the snow was falling fast and the wind was quite strong.

Eventually we climbed into the car. Bert asked me to drive so I took the wheel and we set off. It soon became apparent that the strong wind was blowing the snow into drifts; where ever there was a gateway or gap in the hedge, a drift of snow was forming across the road. Getting the car through these drifts depended on picking up speed where possible to give the car sufficient momentum to propel us through. The snow of course was fresh, soft and fluffy so there was little chance of damaging the car. The journey proved to be quite exciting as the snow was getting deeper all the time. As we continued, I began to suspect that we might not make it; an unpleasant prospect but I kept these thoughts to myself.

As we approached Parsonage Farm, I was thinking that there was nothing this little car could not cope with. It had performed beyond all expectation, when suddenly we came to a huge drift, as high as the roof of the car. We stopped to consider the situation. Seeing the snow blowing horizontally across the lane, and also taking into account what we had already been through, we decided to go for it; the thought of walking in that blizzard was too much. With some difficulty I reversed the car as far as I could, which was not very far, then charged the drift with all the speed I could muster in the circumstances. It was not good enough and we stuck fast in the middle of the drift. Then, to our horror, the doors would not open. Fortunately we were in a Morris Traveller so we all clambered out through the doors at the rear.

Outside the conditions were appalling; the wind was whipping the snow along so fast it was stinging our faces. We had about a quarter of a mile to go to the farmhouse and I wondered if we were going to make it. We did, but by the morning the car was covered by eighteen feet of snow and remained there for six weeks.

Having stayed the rest of the night at Bert's, we woke to find a new white world with huge snowdrifts all over the place - the height of the house in places. After a cooked breakfast of bacon and eggs, Bert and I set off on foot for Church Farm, about one mile away. Thankfully the blizzard had stopped and the world seemed quiet and eerie. On the way we had to keep away from lanes and hedges and head for open spaces where the snow had been blown away. We decided to check out the sheep which were on the new cocksfoot ley. A number of them were busy digging through the snow for some grass, which at this stage was about one foot tall and very stiff, ideal for the sheep under these conditions. It was also evident that a lot of sheep were buried by snow having taken shelter by the dry stone walls.

George was at Church Farm when we eventually arrived, so we found some long sticks and shovels, started the Power Major and headed back to the sheep. The tractor could only travel where the snow was no more than a couple of feet deep so we had to dig through several gateways and eventually made it to the sheep field. We spent a couple of hours locating and rescuing sheep then headed for the pigs. We found the pigs asleep, very warm and cosy in their arks. The rest of the day was spent feeding and getting water to run for the stock. I then collected Mattie and took her back to our house on the tractor where we ate a makeshift meal and collapsed, exhausted, in front of the fire.

The next day we fitted the front loader to the little Ferguson and used it to clear snow from buildings and gateways where we needed access in order to feed the stock. Tractor cabs were not in general use at that time but I still had the old great coat which George had given me during my first few days on the farm, so I kept reasonably warm on the tractor, but when I arrived home that evening the coat was frozen solid at the front and was difficult to remove.

Occasional snowfalls occurred for the next week or so with the sky continually overcast. Most of our time was spent looking after the stock and clearing snow. Water proved to be a difficult problem, as it had to be taken to the stock quite frequently where it was quickly frozen solid. After that first week the weather changed, the sun shone every day for several weeks but the temperature never rose above freezing. By about 2pm each day the power of the sun would loosen the surface of the snow and the wind would blow it along until it settled in a sheltered spot, which was usually in the roads or around the buildings and houses. Consequently snow clearing was a continuous operation even on the main roads. Contractors to the council, with diggers and bulldozers, were working day and night in a fruitless effort to keep the roads open.

The country roads between walls and hedges were blocked for weeks and people used to drive their vehicles through the fields. Our Morris Traveller was recovered in mid February after a supreme effort with shovels and the Ferguson. It started straight away and appeared to have suffered no ill effects from its sojourn in cold storage. The weather generally was quite pleasant once we were used to the cold; the amount of sunshine was amazing. Although the sheep had to be fed hay and a little concentrate, they kept themselves occupied and apparently quite happy, scraping the snow aside and eating the tall, stiff cocksfoot grass underneath. During March, when drilling spring barley, a considerable area of land remained covered in snow, particularly by the dry stone walls.

Mattie became pregnant again during that winter and tragically miscarried in May. She always miscarried at about five months, which was unusual and of course much more devastating for her. This time we decided that further investigation of the cause was necessary. She set about recovery, which was plagued by bouts of depression, which we were told was only to be expected.

While all this was going on we also gave some consideration to what sort of a future we wanted. Mattie was of the opinion that if I continued as a farm worker, then she would like to go back to nursing and complete her training. My ambition at this time was to have my own farm, certainly a possibility now that we owned the farm at Rowde, but the thought of milking cows for the rest of my life held very little attraction for me. It so happened that the tenant at Rowde Croft Farm decided to retire. This was most opportune as we had even discussed the possibility of offering him a sum of money to relinquish the tenancy and leave the farm. Possession of the farm was gained on the 21st of March and we immediately appointed Tilley and Culverwell, the Chippenham Market auctioneers, to sell the farm by auction, in May, with vacant possession.

This gave us about two months to tidy the place and to do anything that might improve its value. Various items, such as hay and straw, manure and minor tenant's improvements were valued by the auctioneers and taken over. We had very little money at this stage so I quickly sold the hay and straw for a good price - the bad winter had increased demand. I then bought some nitrogen fertiliser to spread on the fields. Using Bert's tractor and spreader and Brian's trailer, I spent a long weekend chain harrowing and spreading the nitrogen in the hope that the fields would look nice and green and productive by the time prospective buyers came to look.

These operations gave me a good insight into the condition of the land. It was mostly heavy clay with quite a lot of water logging, and I got the tractor bogged in a couple of times. This entailed walking some distance to find a neighbour with a tractor to pull me out. The farm had another huge disadvantage - the very long track from the road. This had to be kept in a reasonable condition, or the milk lorry would cease to collect the milk.

Bert had a regular supply of cinders from Winsley Hospital boilers, which we collected with the tractor and trailer. It was very good material for making tracks, yards and for hardening gateways.

Several weekends were spent that spring hauling these cinders to Rowde, a long trip with a tractor. Gordon Finch drove a second tractor on a few weekends, which made a huge difference, but a trailer load did not fill many potholes and it was a long job as it all had to be loaded and unloaded with shovels. We will never know if all this work improved the sale of the property or not but it certainly convinced me that our decision to sell was correct.

The sale of the farm was to take place at the Bear Hotel, Devizes, during the second half of May. On the day, Mattie and I had lunch at the 'Bear', then, with our solicitor, met the auctioneer, Mr. Preedy, to discuss tactics. We had a figure of £15,000 in our minds, but were advised that if we set a reserve price of more than £12,000 we would not sell. After much thought and discussion we agreed, as there was still the chance that the bidding could take the sale price above £12,000.

Time came and we went into the room set aside for the sale. I was impressed by the number of people in there and my hopes were raised. I did not appreciate that many people attended auctions just out of interest. After the auctioneers introduction and description of the farm, and there being no questions, bidding began very briskly until it reached £12,000, then the auctioneer told the assembly that the farm was going to be sold. This stimulated a little more bidding and the farm was sold for £12,500 (£187,000 at 2009 values). This was just over £100 an acre. Disappointing, but then I realised that there was probably only one genuine bidder and I was reasonably pleased.

We now set ourselves the task of finding an arable farm, visiting several and attending auctions to get an impression of land values and see how the auction system worked. Our local bank were unhelpful when we talked to them about a loan, probably my own fault. We then had a chat with Mattie's cousin, Peter Archard, who at the time was under manager at Lloyds Bank in Wiveliscombe. Peter was very enthusiastic and arranged a meeting with Mr. Bell, his manager Mr. Bell appeared to be much more of an old gentleman farmer than a bank manager. After a long talk about our history and how we saw our future, Mr. Bell expressed his wish to help, told us to find a farm and come back to him with a business plan.

Eventually, after visiting lots of farms in Wiltshire, Hampshire and Dorset, we found a suitable farm at Whiteparish, the other side of Salisbury on the Romsey road. The farmer was producing wheat, barley and grass seed on 150 acres. By now I had plenty of experience of growing all three and was confident that I could run the farm with only occasional paid labour. Having produced a business plan with Peter's help, I again went to see Mr. Bell at Wiveliscombe armed with the sale particulars. Mr. Bell agreed with my figures and suggested that we go ahead and buy the farm for £200 an acre or a little bit more if we felt that one more bid would secure it.

The auction was held at the White Hart Hotel in Salisbury, where we had lunch then entered the auction room in a mixed state of excitement and trepidation. The room quickly filled and the auctioneer made his introduction, saying this was a rare opportunity to purchase one of the best arable farms in the area. I thought he was never going to shut up.

Then the bidding started, at, I could not believe it, our top price of £30,000 and went rapidly to £45,000 where it was sold. It was all over in about two minutes. This was £300 an acre. After a few weeks, having looked at several more farms and attending two more auctions with high hopes, only to be dashed with no opportunity to bid, it was now clear to us that the average price of good arable land was now over £300 an acre and anything less than 150 acres was not enough to make a living. I was of course disappointed and we talked through our options, one of which was to emigrate to Australia or Canada, but Mattie, having suffered yet another miscarriage, was not up to it, and was becoming depressed at the thought of not having a family.

After discussing Mattie's condition with her gynaecologist, who seemed to be unable to give us any hope, we decided to take up his suggestion to see a specialist. We asked him to find the very best man available, and he said he would like to make some enquiries and would let us know. A few days later he wrote to say that he could recommend a man in Harley Street and advised us to make arrangements to see him.

Our appointment was made for an afternoon, so we took an

early train and visited Australia House for a couple of hours during the morning. There, we talked to people about emigrating, and farming in Australia, asking lots of questions, land prices, capital requirement and where were the best arable areas. They were very helpful and informed us that energetic and enthusiastic young farmers were welcome in Australia. I was impressed by the possibilities and opportunities but considered that it was not the time to discuss it; more important business was at hand.

After having a relaxed lunch, a taxi dropped us at the address in Harley Street where we were quickly introduced to the specialist. He went through Mattie's history, referring to the letter and medical notes forwarded by our doctor. After an examination the specialist told us that Mattie's problems were the result of an ill advised operation, carried out in her early teens, which involved stretching her cervix to ease her problems with difficult periods, and that in his opinion she would never carry a child to term.

However, he continued, there was a new procedure which he would be pleased to carry out if and when she was pregnant. The operation involved inserting a stitch in the cervix, to be removed at the first sign of giving birth. This procedure was known as a 'Shirodka Stitch' and had been performed successfully for several patients. Mattie was so excited about this that it seemed her whole outlook on life had changed.

Mattie became pregnant again in the summer of 1964 and arrangements were made for her to spend a week at the University College Hospital in London for the operation. This time we drove to London in the mistaken belief that the car would be useful; it was a pain, with so much money going on parking. After getting Mattie settled in, I found some cheap lodgings and met a foreman on a building site who let me park the car for a few pounds. It really was a horrible week but thankfully the operation was a success. We motored back to Winsley, and not a moment too soon.

In July that year we took a holiday in the south of France, at Menton on the Mediterranean. This was where Mattie experienced morning sickness, suddenly rushing off from the breakfast table, causing quite a degree of amusement among fellow guests, some of whom quickly became friends. Our flight from Heathrow to Nice was very exciting as our plane was a Comet IV jet airliner. Most airliners of this period were piston engine propeller types and there were only a few jet types, the French Caravelle, the Boeing 707 and the Comet. The earlier Comet I had been the first passenger carrying jet in the world, but the planes were grounded after two tragic mid air disasters, when the planes disintegrated at high altitude caused by metal fatigue, a newly discovered phenomenon.

Arriving at Nice airport, I was struck by the heat and aroma as we left the plane. A taxi took us to the Hotel Royal in Menton which proved to be very up market and quite plush by our standards; it had its own strip of beach called 'The Plage'. Meals were taken at the front of the hotel on a shaded terrace right by the main road. Several times while we were enjoying lunch a man on a bicycle appeared and entertained us with his antics. He was hilarious, performing acrobatics while riding the bicycle in among the traffic, while poking fun at the motorists, some of whom quickly became annoyed, which only added to his efforts to entertain. This fun always lasted until a very cross policeman on a bicycle arrived to chase him away.

The hilarity of our holiday was enhanced by a couple of fellow guests, a well known television comedian, Norman Vaughan, and his wife, who kept us all in fits of laughter most meal times. In a bar late one night we had the pleasure of a chat with Tony Hancock, famous for his radio show, 'Hancock's Half Hour'.

One day we went on a coach trip to the Maritime Alps, which proved to be really interesting. The coach travelled through miles of vineyards which were a little boring, but then we reached the mountains and the scenery became very dramatic, with the roads twisting and turning through deep gorges, passing through rock tunnels and along ledges hewn from vertical rock faces. Eventually we arrived at the pretty Swiss style village of Valberg, high in the mountains, for lunch.

The return journey began by descending into yet another gorge with the drop from the edge of the road to the river marked at

300 metres at one point. Passengers were standing to get a better view, but Mattie stuck to her seat and would not look; this caused some amusement among the other passengers, who were mostly French. However, I must admit that I was quite unnerved by the spectacle, as were a few others, so I had some sympathy for her.

Eventually we left the mountains behind and continued the long journey back to Menton; we were both very tired by the time we arrived at our hotel.

The only other trip we took while on this holiday was a bus ride to Cannes for the day. We enjoyed walking around the town looking at the shops and the gardens along the sea front. The rest of the time we spent soaking up the sun and enjoying the warm Mediterranean Sea. Our two weeks slipped by far too quickly and we returned home renewed and refreshed, determined to raise a family and find a farm.

CHAPTER 7

A LUCKY BREAK

Soon after harvest, during a visit to my mother, I saw an advertisement in a local paper; it described an arable and beef farm at Brixton Deverill. Mattie and Mother laughed when I told them it was 440 acres and they said I was daft to even think about it.

A drive out to Brixton Deverill revealed that the farm had a substantial house and a good range of buildings, but the land was generally very steep. Thinking about it on the way home I realised that there was no way that this farm was going to make £300 an acre. There was also another factor which could have an effect. The country had recently elected a Labour government, confidence in the economy was plummeting, interest rates and inflation were rising, and the new government had just imposed a credit squeeze.

Afraid that the new government policy may effect my loan arrangements with the bank, I phoned Mr. Bell early next morning. Mr. Bell assured me that my loan was unaffected by the credit squeeze as it was already arranged, but added that it would not be available for long, and if I wanted to buy a farm then to get on with it. I also considered what effect the credit squeeze would have on other potential buyers, and thought it could give me an advantage.

This concentrated my mind; how could I do it? Perhaps one

of my brothers would be interested in a farming partnership. The sale particulars arrived so at last I could do some sums. I discussed the proposition with Bert and expected him to dismiss the whole thing as impossible, but no, he just invited Mattie and me to see him that very evening.

We arrived at Bert and Jean's about eight thirty and had coffee and a general chat. Bert then said he wanted to help us buy a farm and that he had a good idea how to do it. Bert went on to explain that when his father had died, his money was put into a trust to be divided, on the death of his mother, equally between Mary, Mattie and Bert. In the meantime this trust money was invested and the interest was paid to his mother. As Bert's mother had other income, her tax liability was quite high and the loss of interest from the trust was no bad thing.

Bert had made inquiries that very afternoon and found that there was about £28,000 (£406,000 at 2009 value) in the trust and that some or all of it could be loaned to us, and we would pay Mrs. Bowles a small amount of interest - one half of one per cent was proposed. This was, of course, fantastic news and I was able to get to work on a business plan for the bank. The first thing was to have a proper look over the place, so I made an appointment through the auctioneers, Cooper and Tanner from Frome, the same auctioneers that conducted the sale at Vineyards Farm a few years before.

Peter Hillier, a friend of mine who had been an auctioneer with Tilley and Culverwell, and now had his own estate agency, came with me to the farm, as did Bert. Mattie, whose pregnancy was progressing just fine, could not come as she had to rest, but told us not to concern ourselves with the condition of the house, she would make a home of it whatever, but could we describe it to her?

On arrival at Whitecliff Farm, we met and introduced ourselves to the owners, Mr. And Mrs. Reeves, who were expecting us. Coffee was soon ready and we enjoyed a pleasant chat, mostly about the farm and its neighbours. Eventually Mr. Reeves said he had things to do and would it be all right if he left us to lock around on our own, then later he would help with any questions if we called at the house. This was ideal and I quickly agreed. An extremely interesting day ensued, walking around the farm and discussing its potential.

We met two of the farm staff, Bill Gunnel and Roger Garrett, who were ploughing on what was known as the far down, using two Super Majors with three furrow ploughs. After chatting with them for some time we headed down a steep slope into an arable field called 'Abyssinia', so named because it was shaped like that country, not because it was a desert!

The land at Whitecliff Farm ranged from 400ft above sea level in the water meadows, to 850 ft on the top of the big down, and consisted of good deep loam over chalk on the lower fields, gradually changing, as we progressed up the hill, to shallow black puffy soil over chalk at the top. About 200 acres were used in an arable system including some three-year leys, to provide hay and silage for the large single suckler beef herd. Some of these cows were out wintered on the big down, and it was agreed that about 100 acres of this old down land could be ploughed and brought into an arable rotation.

Arriving back at the buildings we saw that they consisted of a range of old, traditional farm buildings, positioned to form a square, enclosing a large yard. This yard had, in more recent times, been totally covered in by a steel and asbestos roof, shaped to fit around the old buildings. The most useful of these old buildings was a drive through, wooden framed barn containing an Alvan Blanch grain drier, cleaner, reception pit, and a pneumatic conveying system. At one end there were four circular storage bins of 25 tons capacity each and at the other end, a bulk store of about 80 tons. All this equipment was covered in a thick layer of dust and had obviously never been cleaned.

At the back, away from the main buildings, was a deep litter house with feed store and egg packing room included. Mr Reeves explained to us that the shed contained 1000 hens and 100 cockerels, producing hatching eggs for Sykes at Sutton Veny, a local hatchery. He said it was a very profitable enterprise and produced £1 per bird profit, and also provided a regular income.

It was very common in those days for farmers to own cottages to house their workers, and this farm had four - two occupied by the two men we had met, and the other two let to rent paying tenants. Having seen as much as we could take in for one day, we decided to look at the cottages another day. We were preparing to take our leave when Mr. Reeves invited us for a welcome cup of tea in the farmhouse. After a pleasant conversation with Mr. and Mrs. Reeves, and a quick look over the house, we left with Bert and I in complete agreement that we could describe the house to Mattie by saying that it was an exact copy of her mother's house at Winsley where she was brought up.

The next step was to prepare a business plan with the assistance of Mr. Swan, our local business advisor from the National Agricultural Advisory Service (NAAS), a free service provided by the Ministry of Agriculture, Fisheries and Food (MAFF). This entailed a further visit to the farm, this time with Mr. Swan, to associate him with the practicalities of my plan.

For the first few years the plan was to grow as much spring barley as I could, making maximum use of the machinery, and keeping labour cost to a minimum. Barley was the only crop that I could grow year after year and by ploughing the Big Down, the arable acres would be increased to about 320, sufficient to make good use of a combine harvester. All the grass keep would be sold to other farmers, as I had no money for livestock.

With my new business plan and the promised loan from my mother-in-law, we arranged another meeting with Peter and Mr. Bell at the bank at Wiveliscombe. We spent a fun weekend with Peter and Mattie's cousin Gladys, and had an interesting meeting at the bank on the Monday morning.

My plan showed that we required £28,000 from the bank to add to our own £12,000 plus £28,000 from the family trust. This would enable us to bid up to £60,000 at the auction and still have £8,000 for expenses and machinery.

I was very much afraid that the farm would make much more, maybe as much as £80,000, but my budget showed interest and capital repayment to the bank but none for the family loan, so I was afraid to borrow any more. Mr. Bell said he was confident that the loan would be approved provided that it was a first mortgage and the family loan was a second mortgage. This I agreed to and promised to check with Bert and the trust solicitors.

The auction of Whitecliff Farm was scheduled for late November, and, hoping to move things forward and if possible avoid an auction, I arranged to meet the auctioneer Mr. Quick of Cooper and Tanner at his office in Frome.

We needed little introduction as Mr. Quick had been the auctioneer at the sale, some six years earlier, of Vineyards Farm and the sale of the live and dead stock. I expressed my interest in Whitecliff and explained that I was in a position to make an offer. He told me that the vendors were expecting at least £75,000 and were intent on selling by auction.

The next ten minutes were spent telling Mr. Quick why they would not get anywhere near that figure. (1) The economic crisis, (2) the steep land, making it a young man's farm and few young men would have the money, (3) the altitude of much of the land being some of the highest land in Wiltshire, and (4) the fact that there were only 200 acres of arable land. After that tirade I insisted that my offer of £60,000 be put on record and discussed with the vendors. Mr. Quick agreed to discuss this with Mr. and Mrs. Reeves, but gave me no hope that it would even be considered.

That evening I felt a little downcast but this soon passed. The day of the auction arrived. Bert and I had a sandwich in the bar at the George Hotel in Frome; we then wandered into the auction room, seating ourselves right at the front. There was the usual speech by the auctioneer explaining that this was a rare opportunity to purchase a special piece of Wiltshire countryside, a quarter of a mile of the river Wylye with its own trout fishing and a productive arable and beef farm to boot. He made it sound far too good and I was concerned that I was out of the running.

Eventually the auctioneer asked the assembly to start the bidding and pretended to get an opening bid of £55,000 and quickly ran the bidding to £70,000, constantly looking at me. He then announced that the farm was being withdrawn from sale as it had failed to reach the reserve. It appeared to me that there had been no genuine bids. Bert suggested that we get up and talk to the auctioneer immediately. I explained to Mr. Quick that my offer was still on the table and that there was no way that I could increase it and would they consider it? No, he said, it was way below what the vendors were expecting and in any case there were other people interested.

While all this was going on, I was of course working for Bert, but my mind was constantly thinking about my next move. I was concerned about other interested people, but deep down I did not believe there were any. After a while, I realised that my thoughts had been concentrated on the farm, and I had put the cottages to the back of my mind. The cottages consisted of two semi-detached pairs, one pair at the end of the farm drive, at the side of the main road, and the other pair were about one mile away at Monkton Deverill.

In those days country cottages were not much in demand and consequently not very valuable and rents were low. Unless they were needed for workers, they were not much of an asset and if money had to be spent on them, they were considered as a liability. It suddenly dawned on me that I only needed two, at the most, so I could effectively increase my offer by not including the two cottages at Monkton Deverill. The decision now was either to wait and see if they would accept my offer as it stood, and risk them selling to someone else, or phoning the auctioneer with my new idea. The decision was made for me when I spoke to Mr. Bell at the bank. Having already informed him that we had failed at the auction but it was our view that we were still in the running, he seemed satisfied so long as we did not increase our offer. Speaking to him again, with my new plan, he agreed that it might be enough to tip the balance, but for heaven's sake get on with it, adding that he could not hold the loan much longer.

By now more than a week had passed since the auction, so I phoned Mr. Quick. I asked him if they had any thoughts on selling me the farm and he said they had not even considered it. Explaining that there was a way to improve my offer, he still seemed unimpressed, but I managed to persuade him to put it to the vendors. Then I added that I wanted to buy the farm but could pay no more. Mr. and Mrs. Reeves wanted to sell the farm, and you, the auctioneer, would like to see the farm sold because that's your job. Mr. Quick then explained to me, sounding a little cross, that he did not need advice from me on how to conduct his business; nevertheless he would speak to the vendors and ring me back.

Three anxious days passed before Mr. Quick phoned back, and it was to arrange a meeting with Mr. and Mrs. Reeves at his office. This was what I wanted to hear and I had an extremely good feeling about the meeting as it was arranged for two o clock on the 15th December 1964, my 25th birthday, yippy!

CHAPTER 8

A FARM OF OUR OWN

During the next few days I made another visit to the farm to try to assess how much I would have to pay for in goings, as these could be negotiated away at the meeting, but not after I had bought the farm. These included growing crops, stocks of hay, straw, seeds and fertiliser, plus unexhausted manurial values, and of course any work done towards the next crop, which would include all the ploughing that had been done. Sitting down on a bale of straw and looking around, that day, I really felt that the farm was mine.

With some trepidation, and my chequebook in my pocket, Mattie wished me good luck and I drove to Frome and Cooper and Tanner's office. The girl at the front desk ushered me into a back room where Percy Quick and Stan Reeves were seated on each side of a large desk, obviously having met early to discuss the deal. After the usual pleasantries, Mr. Quick said they were prepared to accept my offer. I then suggested that before we go further could we talk about in going valuations, to which they agreed. The chickens and growing crops I was happy to pay for, as I was for items which I could readily sell such as hay and straw, but could they avoid charging me for those abstract items referred to as unexhausted manurial values and, as a gesture of goodwill, not charge me for the ploughing. This was all quickly agreed and the contract was put on the table, but first they needed my cheque for six thousand pounds, being the ten per cent deposit (£87,000 at 2009 values).

This was the largest cheque I had ever written, and if you bear in mind that in those days six thousand pounds could buy two, three bedroom, semi-detatched houses outright, this was a huge sum. Contracts were signed and Percy Quick went to a cupboard and brought out a tray containing a whisky decanter and three glasses. They both congratulated me and wished me good luck, proposing a toast to my success. A pleasant ten minutes later, our whisky nearly finished, I suddenly realised that I had overlooked something. The completion of the purchase and possession of the farm was scheduled for the 31st March 1965. This was too late for me to plant spring crops and I asked if this could be brought forward a few weeks to the 1st February. They could see no problem with this so long as I came up with the rest of the money. Next morning I informed Mr. Bell who was delighted and said that he would go ahead and deal with the paper work and mortgage.

It was important to decide what to do about the workers, more for their benefit than mine. Stan Reeves gave me the impression that Roger was the expert operator, although a bit difficult to deal with. I decided to talk to Roger and if he wanted the job then it was his. He agreed to give it a go for three months on condition that his father, Percy Garrett, could continue part time until his retirement in six months time. This left me with the unpleasant task of informing Bill Gunnel that he would not be required after the end of January, and as he now lived with his wife and family in one of my cottages, I told him that he was welcome to live there for the foreseeable future. Bill seemed quite happy about this and told me that he had been looking for another job and it was likely that he would work at Sykes, the hatchery at Sutton Veny.

There was now plenty for me to do, developing a detailed plan for running the farm, and buying machinery, seed and fertiliser. The soil in the various fields was sampled and analysed by NAAS. Most samples were low in potash, and a few were also low in phosphate, so I had to use a suitable compound fertiliser in the combine drill. A list of machinery was prepared and I began looking for suitable second hand items. There was, of course, a lot of equipment on the farm but this was due to be sold by auction on the 25th January when a farm sale of the live and dead stock had been arranged.

I decided to purchase as much as I could before the sale, in case the auction prices went too high. A second hand Fordson Super Major was found locally, and a second hand combine harvester was purchased from T.H.White at Devizes. This machine had worked for three seasons; it was a Ransomes 902 with a ten-foot header and a four-cylinder 62hp industrial Ford diesel engine. It was agreed that I would pay £400 now and £800 after harvest. Most of the combine harvesters in the area at this time were Massey Harris, similar to the machine I used to drive at Winsley. The Ransomes machine was, in my opinion, superior, not only having a greater output, it was also a development of a European design, more able to cope with damp crops and conditions.

Brewers of Wilton supplied a new four furrow Ransomes plough and a second hand three furrow. Having used a Cleanacres front mounted spray boom at Winsley, I decided to hire a sixty foot boom to be carried on a fore end loader. Brewers provided a mounted tank and pump and I found a cheap loader to complete the outfit.

At the sale I bought the Super Major that Roger drove for about £700 almost new. Roger was pleased with that. A very old flat bed, four-wheeled trailer was knocked down to me for £2-50, the bargain of the day. Also, I was able to buy a set of Massey Harris disc harrows, a Vicon fertiliser spreader, and a set of triple Cambridge rollers. This was an opportunity to secure some small tools, including a hydraulic jack, spanners, fencing tools, and three small grain augers.

This proved to be a most enjoyable day; neighbouring farmers came to me and introduced themselves, and wished me luck. I had already noticed that if I started bidding for a lot, some bidders would drop out immediately. After the sale Stan invited me into the farmhouse for a cup of tea, and to meet some of his friends, relations and neighbours. Lots of advice was on hand about farming on these steep slopes, and to be very careful with the tractors; all this was accepted with good humour. My early days at Vineyards Farm had given me lots of experience of tractors on steep slopes and I was well aware of the dangers. At that time, not one major tractor manufacturer included a cab, so they were produced by a number of firms, and were commonly made with a very flimsy frame, covered with canvas, and generally not easy to exit in a hurry.

The next day I arrived at the farm around ten, and found Stan, Roger and Bill helping to load cattle and machinery on to buyers' vehicles. Roger had already moved all my purchases from the sale field to various sheds. Wages were discussed with Roger and I agreed to pay him a relatively high rate for the job of eleven pounds, fifteen shillings per week, justified by the fact that I didn't have to provide him with a cottage. It was arranged for him to start work on Monday 1st February, the day I took possession, and I agreed to meet him there at seven a.m.

The next few days were quite hectic, and Stan agreed that we could move in on the Sunday, when Gordon and Joan could lend a hand with the move. Saturday was spent giving Brian's cattle lorry a good scrub, inside and out, which he had lent us to move our few bits of furniture. All went well, despite Mattie having to take lots of rest. We moved in and I reported for work at seven the next morning, with my own farm and my own business. Despite all the risks and uncertainties, I was very upbeat and determined to make a success.

The immediate priority was to complete the ploughing ready for the spring drilling. Ploughed grassland would be drilled with spring wheat and all the other land drilled with spring barley. My plan was to grow continuous spring barley for the first few years, as growing wheat, which was more profitable, needed a break crop, probably grass. With no livestock I had no way of turning grass into money. The area of the big down which I planned to plough was too much to take on this spring - a considerable amount of work, clearing and burning gorse and levelling the ridges and banks was necessary before we could think about ploughing.

Roger, it transpired, was an excellent ploughman and had competed in local matches, winning an impressive collection of prizes. As soon as we had the equipment ready, we were both ploughing in the same field, so a certain amount of competition was involved. I enjoyed the next two weeks; the weather was cold but dry. Roger, who had a cab on his tractor, insisted that I would need one when the weather got bad, and although I was used to sitting in the open, I tended to agree.

The hatching eggs were produced for Sykes who were heavily involved during the first couple of weeks, teaching me about managing a laying flock of hens. Percy Garrett, who I had agreed to employ part time until his retirement, did the feeding, egg collections and the egg cleaning and packing. It was left to me to do the final collection when I came in from the field. The amount of light available to the flock, I learnt, was one of the most important management tools, and was adjusted every week to start the hens laying, then bring them to their peak production and then to maintain a high, but reducing level of production for as long as possible.

Sometime around the second week of February, having made good progress with the ploughing and even drilled some spring wheat, the favourable weather turned decidedly nasty. Roger and I were ploughing in the field called Abyssinia when it began to snow heavily. It was only possible to see half way up the hills on either side of the field. After a while dozens of hares could be seen moving slowly down the slopes seeking more sheltered positions. Before long we decided to go home and realising that we had to find our way across the big down, I asked Roger to lead the way and make sure that I stayed close behind. Not having the luxury of a cab, I found it difficult to see through the blowing snow which was stinging my eyes. We arrived safely back at the farm and found Mattie a little concerned and pleased to see us.

The snow seemed to ease off after dark and we went to bed expecting it to be gone in the morning. However, we were awakened soon after midnight by the sound of men shouting. On looking out of our window, I saw that the snow was again falling heavily, and I could just make out some lights in the direction of the voices After a while I realised that Houghton Brown's men were bringing the sheep off the hills into the shelter of George's Barn, opposite our farm, just across the road. Half an hour or so later, all was quiet again and we went back to sleep.

As I came down the stairs next morning, I was surprised to see, in our hallway, a very beautiful, tall and slender pile of snow. It was a complete mystery where it had come from, and after investigation I found that the snow had been blown through the keyhole in the front door. Outside it was a changed world with deep drifts looking beautifully white and clean. At this stage Mattie became very anxious and explained her concern that if she were unable to reach Bradford on Avon maternity hospital, there would be a serious problem with the Shirodka stitch. Mattie's gynaecologist was all geared up to remove the stitch at the appropriate time. For Mattie's peace of mind, and after listening to the weather forecast, I decided to ask Stan if I could borrow his Land Rover and take Mattie to Winsley to stay with her mother at Church Farm where she would be much closer to the hospital.

Driving the tractor to Crockerton, I picked up the Land Rover and returned to Whitecliff. I set off with Mattie about 10.30am and found numerous main roads totally blocked by drifts. However there were plenty of police and council workers on hand to help and advise on which routes to try. The journey would have been impossible without Stan's Land Rover and we reached Winsley at about half past one. Mattie seemed so relieved and happy that it made it all worthwhile.

CHAPTER 9

A SON AND HEIR

Our first month at the farm was soon past; drilling progressed well once the snow had gone and the land dried out. I was also able to complete other parts of my business plan. The vacant cottage next to Bill Gunnel's was let to a couple from Maiden Bradley, the grass keep on the big down and steep slopes was let to a farmer who also farmed in Australia, and the grass keep in the meadows, alongside of the river was sold to Peter House. Peter and Ann were to become good friends over the next few years.

Travelling every day from Winsley involved a very long day, but well worthwhile as Mattie was much more relaxed being closer to the hospital. On 20th March she felt the first signs of labour so I drove her to the hospital and stayed with her until late afternoon, then went back to the farm to collect the eggs and see Roger about looking after the place next day. Mattie had made me promise to return as soon as possible, which I did, but she thought I had been gone for ages. She told me that the stitch had been removed and labour was progressing, but so slowly. From that moment I stayed at her bedside; she was not enjoying the experience, and I only hope that I was some comfort to her. Eventually after a very long labour, Colin was born in the early hours of 21st March.

All went well with Mattie and the new baby and he was christened Colin, Michael (after me), and John (after his grandfather). The ceremony was held in the church at Brixton

Deverill, in the company of a few friends and relatives, returning to Whitecliff for a little party.

Out on the land, we finished the drilling and began top-dressing with nitro chalk. Next, weeds had to be sprayed with the large Cleanacres boom; this entailed using a certain technique, as there was no way to judge that huge width. With 28ft of plastic clothes line attached to each end of the boom, and one spray width round the edge of the field to complete the headland, a start could be made on the main work. This involved carefully following the lines of wheat or barley formed by the seed drill. On reaching the headland at the far end of the field, the boom was switched off and the tractor was turned to the left or right. With the driver watching the appropriate clothesline and by steering in the correct way, he could fold the line back on itself, which would set the correct width for the return run; then he just had to concentrate on following the lines once more.

This proved to be very easy to do after a little practice. We now had a larger tank and pumped the water from the troughs instead of using a bucket as before, and the larger boom reduced the wheel damage to a minimum. Several farmers came to see the machine in action, as only seeing would convince them that it was possible to use such a wide boom. The chemicals available at that time were limited to broad leaf weed killers, MCPA and CMPP, and so grass weeds such as couch had to be controlled by cultivations.

During May and June there was nothing more to do to the crops of wheat and barley; harvest now depended on the weather. This gave us an opportunity to fence the area of the big down that I had planned to drill with barley next spring. The land sloped from the top and gradually became steeper until it dropped away very steeply to the valley bottom, a fall of some three hundred feet. This made it difficult to decide where to erect the new fence. It was necessary to fence this area, although quite an expense, in order that I could sell the grazing on the steep slopes. MAFF supported the fencing with a farm improvement grant as they did the ploughing of old pasture. They also paid a ploughing grant on leys that had been down for at least three years, such was the importance of home produced food.

Our local NAAS adviser helped with grant applications and advised on cropping. Left to myself I would probably have planned to drill wheat on the big down, but having looked at the results of soil analysis, he advised barley because of low fertility, and recommended a dressing of basic slag to improve phosphate levels, and a high potash fertiliser at drilling time. Roger taught me all I know about erecting barbed wire fences. He was never satisfied if it was not tight and straight - these fences were to last over forty years.

On days when the weather was too bad to work on the hill, our attention turned to the grain stores and the grain drier. Also, removing the manure from the cattle yards and hauling it up to the big down, tipping it in a heap to be spread at a later date. The drier and grain stores had to be ready for use by the middle of July, and Roger told me that it had never been cleaned, as I suspected. All of the machinery, the drier, cleaner, and even the roof structure were covered in a thick layer of dust and debris. With much moaning and groaning on Roger's part, we set about giving it all a good clean. Roger could see no point to this and said, "It will be just as bad next year". I said if that was the case we would just have to clean it again. During this cleaning process we discovered a bad infestation of the dreaded saw tooth grain beetle, one of many pests that can attack stored grain. This meant that all dust and debris had to be removed and burnt and the barn and machinery sprayed with insecticide.

Once the machinery had been relieved of the layer of dust, which was up to six inches thick in places, we could get to work to ensure that it was in a good enough condition to handle a substantially larger harvest than before. The machinery was run and checked, the burner on the drier was lit and tested, and it was decided that sufficient storage was available for my first harvest. This was made possible because I had already sold some to Sainsburys of Trowbridge, for collection in August, to pay for seeds and fertiliser that I had purchased from them in February, on a reciprocal trading agreement. This arrangement was a great help in managing cash flow and keep my bank borrowing within the agreed limit.

In this wooden framed barn was a drive through centre section containing a small reception pit, where the grain, after being tipped from the trailer, was elevated to the drier, with overflow back to the pit. From the drier the grain was again elevated to a small Penny and Porter cleaner, the chaff being discharged into the cattle yard. From the cleaner, the grain flowed down a duct into a pneumatic conveyer, which blew it along a tube, in a tunnel constructed underneath four storage bins of 25 tons capacity each, situated behind the drier.

These bins were emptied via a duct connected to the pneumatic conveyor. The conveyor tube then rose vertically at the end of the barn then continued in the opposite direction, high in the roof, to discharge, either into the bins or into the bulk store at the other end of the barn. There was also a facility to discharge into a square, hopper bottom bin holding about ten tons. This bin was fitted with a long auger used for loading lorries. For out loading, all grain had to be transferred from the bins and the bulk store to this square bin, the big disadvantage being that lorries had to park in the area of the reception pit when it was needed to receive grain from the combine.

Another problem was the 80 ton bulk store, which would obviously hold much more, but the level of grain had to be no higher than a chalk line drawn about five feet from the floor. I was advised that if this line was exceeded, there was a danger that the render and rubble walls could be pushed over, resulting in a total collapse of the barn. It was apparent that improvements would be needed to handle the increasing size of the harvest, but they would have to wait until next year.

During this early period of my business career, I not only had to learn to run our own business, but also the intricacies of the government's agricultural policy. Bert's accountant, Bernard King, agreed to write up my books and deal with PAYE and the Inland Revenue. He advised me to keep all unpaid bills in a separate comparment in my desk and when paid, to mark them paid and dated, and store them in a file for his quarterly visit.

Agriculture, at that time was strongly supported by the government, and the policy was to help farmers produce as much home grown food as possible - a policy formed by the war time and post war shortages and rationing. More recently farmers were encouraged in order to assist with the country's ongoing balance of payments crisis. This helped farmers to feel that they were an important part of the national economy and the community. This support came in the form of guaranteed prices for a range of commodities, the prices being arrived at during negotiations between the government and the National Farmers Union, and announced at the annual price review.

Although the price of grain was guaranteed, it was still important for the farmer to get the highest price possible from the market. When a farmer sold grain to a merchant for a particular month, on completion of the contract the merchant would send the cheque, together with a MAFF form. The merchant completed a section of the form, detailing tons supplied, specification, price and month of delivery. The farmer now filled in and signed his section of the form, and posted it to the local MAFF office, which was in Trowbridge.

At the end of the grain trading year, all the contracts in the country were added up to determine an average price. The farmer then received a cheque covering the difference between the average market price and the guaranteed price. So it was important for the farmer to obtain as much as possible from the market, as the support was the same for every one. The guaranteed price was also increased every month after harvest to encourage farmers to store their grain, rather than market it all at harvest time when the market price was low.

Different systems of support were operated for potatoes, sugar beet, beef, milk and sheep. The government support came in many other ways. Fertiliser use was subsidised together with ploughing grants. A range of farm improvement grants could be claimed, provided that the farmer could afford 60% or 70% of the cost of the improvement. Most important was the free advisory service offered by NAAS which kept us abreast of scientific crop management developments. They also helped us with application forms for subsidies and grants for viable projects.

The most helpful grant in my circumstances was for ploughing the big down, the £12 an acre (£174 at 2009 values), covered the whole operation, from clearing and levelling with a bulldozer to drilling the barley.

The first three months of Colin's life was a bit fraught as he cried rather a lot, and gave us, especially Mattie, very little peace. Everyone, including the professionals, said that he would be better after three months. Sure enough, he settled down and became a very happy baby and so easy to manage. Colin would be quite content in his carrycot when we visited friends or relatives, staying late or even staying over.

Late June saw the weather take a turn for the worst, when heavy thunderstorms swept the country for several days. My crops of wheat and barley were caught at a vulnerable stage and suffered badly from the rain and wind, acres of it were flattened, especially those fields close to the farm. Some of this was my own fault, as I probably underestimated the fertility of these fields and applied too much nitrogen, an expensive way to gain experience.

Harvesting was, as a consequence, quite a struggle, although the performance of the combine in laid crops was impressive, the output was of course reduced and the last thirty acres or so were little more than a salvage operation. My neighbour, Col. Jack Houghton Brown, from Lower Pertwood, came along on his horse one rainy day to commiserate. He offered to send along his three Massey Ferguson 500 combines to finish the job. I declined his kind offer, explaining that if we quickly got the crop into the barn, it would spoil before my drier could catch up. I was also concerned about the cost, as the crop had deteriorated and was not worth much.

However, the weather improved and all was finished in a few days. Prior to the start of harvest, I had purchased two brand new Wheatley grain trailers, with a capacity of 4 tons, having had

Harvesting tangled crop with Ransomes 902, 1965

great difficulty finding good value second hand ones, but I had managed to find one good one. All three of these trailers were easily converted from flat bed use, to grain haulage and also to silage work. At the time, I thought I was being extravagant in having three trailers and only two tractors, but it transpired that because of the very sharp flint stones, there were an awful lot of punctures. Stan's son, Stephen, helped with our harvest that first year, driving a tractor and trailer. Stan had two sons and a daughter and they were all happy to see the farm sold.

The straw was sold to other farmers or burnt, so that Roger and I could start ploughing again in October, getting the land ready for next spring when the whole lot would be drilled with barley.

After several firms looked at the big down, and quoted a huge range of prices, a contractor was appointed to clear, level and leave it ready for ploughing, and to finish it by Christmas. This would give us at least six weeks for ploughing, before drilling began.

Soon after harvest the hens reached the end of their laying cycle and were caught, put into crates of ten, and loaded on to a lorry to go for slaughter. This happened early one morning, before the birds were awake. The next task was to remove and stack outside, all the equipment, including, feeders, drinkers, nesting boxes, dung pits and perches.

I managed to hire a little Ferguson and loader from John Hurd at the watercress farm, to clean out all the manure and litter, load it on to a grain trailer and take it up the hill. Mr Reynolds, a steam cleaning contractor was employed to clean the whole of the inside of the shed and all the equipment stacked outside. He did a superb job and was all done in two days.

Roger and I then spent a few days moving all this equipment back inside and setting it up. A huge lorry load of wood shavings in hessian sacks was then spread all over the earth floor, about twelve inches deep. I really enjoyed this part of the job; the freshly cleaned timber shed, free from dust and grime, the fresh smell of the new shavings, the shiny feeders and drinkers, all gave us the immense satisfaction of a job well done.

Sykes then delivered a new flock of pullets, at point of lay, together with a proportionate number of cockerels. We had to be vigilant for the first twenty-four hours, and often intervene to stop them crowding in corners and smothering themselves. This was a day and a night filled with anxiety, but when they were settled, the enterprise was easy to manage, and showed a useful profit. Sykes were anxious for me to expand to 5000 birds, but my borrowings were too high as it was. I tried to find unused poultry houses in the area that I might rent, but to no avail.

This was a time to assess our financial situation, which was causing increasing concern. Debts for the seed, fertiliser and the combine had been settled by selling barley at harvest time.

Seed and fertiliser had to be purchased for the new season and work needed to be carried out in the grain stores to enable us to handle what I hoped would be a substantially larger harvest in 1966. Interest on the bank loan and the loan from mother in law had to be paid. The bank also required a 10% reduction of the bank loan - £2,800... a substantial sum. Fuel costs and general expenses including living costs, had to be covered until the end of the next harvest. Bernard King helped me produce a budget and cash flow projection to present to the bank, although a genius was not required to see that it would not add up. An appointment with the bank manager needed to be arranged

I tried to explain to Mr. Bell on the telephone, that things had not turned out as planned, and that I should come to Wiveliscombe as soon as it could be arranged but he suggested that he meet us at the farm, and that it would be a good opportunity for him to see the place for himself. I thought this was an excellent idea and invited him to lunch, asked if he liked roast beef, and fixed a date.

On the day, Mr. Bell arrived at eleven and I spent a couple of hours showing him around the farm, the machinery and the grain stores which, despite the poor harvest, were full. All the while I explained the difficulties I had experienced with the weather, trying not to make it sound like an excuse, and outlining my plans for the future. Mr. Bell seemed quite relaxed about the whole thing and was obviously enjoying himself. He said that industry suffered from industrial unrest and strikes, and agriculture suffered from the weather, not a word about finance at this stage.

Mattie had produced a superb lunch of roast beef, roast potatoes, cabbage and carrots, followed by apple pie and custard. Conversation during the meal ranged from general agricultural topics, to the state of the national economy, which was continuing to deteriorate. Mr Bell was confident that the government would continue to support agriculture because of the worsening balance of payment problems, saying they could not afford any other policy.

After lunch we got down to business. He produced a form entitled 'farmers balance sheet' which we filled in with the help of my budget and cash flow. I explained that I could not go on if he insisted on the capital repayment, and all I needed was for the full overdraft facility to be available for another year. He said this could create some problems, because of the government's credit squeeze, but said he thought he could find a way round it. He said he was impressed with our achievements as no business performs well in its first year, with unexpected problems and expenses, and agreed that we had been unlucky with the weather. Expressing his confidence in me, he thanked Mattie for a delicious lunch and took his leave. I felt very pleased with the day's work, but I knew it would be a challenge to get to next harvest without exceeding our overdraft limit.

Unknown to us at that time was the fact that we were about to embark upon two really good years, the harvests of 1966 and 1967 being among the best on record. The only field that did not perform in 1966 was the big down, and I know why. The contractors, with a bulldozer, had completed the clearing and levelling by Christmas; it had taken six weeks. Roger and I finished the ploughing on the rest of the farm, and started on the big down in mid January; it proved to be a slow job. The old matted turf was difficult to turn over, and the slightest thing, such as the plough jolting on hitting a stone, would cause the furrow to turn back to its original position.

We decided to start on the outside of the field, close to our new fence on one side, and Stratton's farm boundary on the other. This ensured that most of the furrows were turned down the slope, so they would not turn back. Because of this slope, and the fact that we needed to turn full width furrows to turn them over properly, our ploughs had to miss a furrow in many places, so my three furrow plough was only taking two furrows for much of the time. This was a big field to plough; we thought it might be more than one hundred acres, and we would only meet occasionally. Roger went up one foggy morning, and I followed later, but I never saw him all day. I knew he was there because each time around the field, his tyre mark, which was different from mine, was in front of me.

The soil consisted of a thin layer of black organic matter containing the turf, overlying the chalk. When these layers were inverted by the plough, the surface appeared as if the soil was all chalk. Before we had progressed very far, our NAAS advisor came and said it was just the same as all the other arable fields on the hilltops when ploughed for the first time; after a few years of cultivation it would look very similar. Reassured, we pressed on.

It was very difficult to make a seedbed as our disc harrows, even with ballast, had difficulty penetrating. Contractors then applied a large dressing of slag, to provide phosphate, making a complete hash of it and spreading it unevenly. We then drilled the barley and a high potash compound fertiliser with the combine drill. A lot of seed could be found on the surface and I remember thinking that I had spent a lot of money, time and effort, producing the only man made desert in the country!

However the rain came and the sun shone and it grew quite well. I was advised to spray with copper sulphate at full leaf cover; standard practice, I discovered, on the top fields of Wiltshire chalk soils, known as black puff. There were a few patches of heavy clay, apparently common in these situations, and these areas were very acidic, the barley being stunted and yellow. A note was made to apply a dressing of lime to these patches for the next crop.

When all the drilling, top dressing and spraying had been completed, time was available to consider increasing the storage capacity and improve grain handling. As there was little money to spend, a great deal of thought was involved. Eventually we decided to lay concrete over part of the covered yard, adjacent to the bulk store in the drier barn, formerly used to house cattle. This would produce storage for at least a further 100 tons, and during the early stages of harvest, could be used for wet grain awaiting the drier, moving it to the reception pit with the front end loader.

Moving the dried grain to this new storage area was to be done by erecting a branch line of pipes from the pneumatic conveyer. The pipes were suspended in the roof trusses and secured with ropes. This new pipe was arranged to supply the square holding bin, which we moved from the reception area, together with its cyclone. This enabled lorries to be loaded in the covered yard, leaving the reception pit area free for tipping trailers. This was a great improvement as I still intended to sell grain during harvest, to ease cash flow.

Our second harvest at Whitecliff was very good and would have exceeded our expectations, had it not been for the big down which, considering the appalling drilling conditions, yielded fairly well at about one ton per acre. Combining the big down that first time proved to be a rather traumatic experience. Where we had erected the fence, it left one very steep piece of land in one particular place. Had we not included this area in the arable field, then we would have missed out on a fairly large area of good land.

Roger was driving the combine, starting at the barn at the top and going round the field the first time in a clockwise direction, adjacent to our new fence. Roger and I had agreed that he would stop and discharge the grain before going down this steep slope. As the grain tank was on top of the machine this would help to maintain its stability. The combine was stopped at this point and an area was cut for me to pull the trailer alongside. The barley was discharged into the trailer but, because of the slope, it must have been piled on the left and lower side unnoticed by me.

I was now anxiously watching the combine going down and across this slope and following slowly with my tractor and trailer, when I just happened to glance behind. To my horror I saw that the trailer was turning over and realised that it would take the tractor with it. Having a flimsy cab with the door on the left or lower side it would prove fatal to stay put, as just through the fence was a very steep slope down into the valley.

Thankfully the cab was open at the back, so I grabbed the roof behind me and threw myself out of the back just as the tractor was beginning to turn over. I must have been in mid air when the hitch gave way and I landed on the trailer drawbar as it hurtled upwards, grazing the inside of my leg, then coming to rest on the stubble. The tractor now had four wheels on the ground again and was continuing slowly down the slope, turning gradually towards the fence and certain destruction.

Pulling myself to my feet, I made a flying leap back into the tractor and regained control. All this happened in seconds but I remember it as if it was all in slow motion. I sat in the tractor, trying to compose myself and thought what a lucky escape I had had, as I followed the combine down to the corner of the field. Roger reached the corner and completed his turn and was now going to the right where he had a good view of the upturned trailer. He was waving an arm and pointing back up the hill, whereupon I pretended that I knew nothing about it and gestured that I did not know what he was on about. Eventually I looked around and gestured my shock; it really was very funny.

We both stopped and walked back up to the trailer where we could see that the barley had been thrown through the fence and was spread out for about twenty yards down the steep rough grazing. Thankfully the trailer had just missed the fence, so the bulls in the field could not escape, but they all gathered around and began eating the barley. It was now urgent that we found some help and plastic fertiliser bags and scraped up as much of the barley as possible before the bulls gorged too much, which can prove fatal. By the time all this was done it was dark and my leg was hurting. I had felt nothing until then, however it wasn't serious and was soon better and it dawned on me how dreadful it could have been. The bulls excreted undigested barley for a few days but suffered no ill effects

After that experience and hoping to make things a little safer, my thoughts turned to the slope at the back of the house. This was divided into six fields with an average size of six acres. Having had considerable difficulty with the machinery turning on these steep slopes, I thought how easy and efficient it would be if these fields were amalgamated and we could operate straight up and down the slope. The problem was that steep banks separated the fields, some twenty feet high in a few places, so a lot of work with a bulldozer would be required. I found that a farm improvement grant was available and obtained prices from several contractors, and decided the scheme was out of the question at present.

At the Smithfield show, I saw the new Roadless Ploughmaster 65, which was a four-wheel drive conversion of the recently introduced Ford 5000. This machine, I decided, was the one I needed to farm my farm to maximum efficiency. On making enquiries, I discovered that a Roadless approved, Bomford and Evershed, bulldozer blade could be fitted, provided that a torque limiter was included in the drive to the front axle.

By investing in this machine, Roger would do the work in the summer when there was nothing of importance to be done to the crops. The fields could also be cropped, as the work would be carried out at the edges only. The scheme would be very cost effective and the grant would pay for the whole project, and possibly a little towards the new tractor. Trading in Roger's tractor, as it was the best value, and being prepared, if necessary to sell extra grain at harvest time, I went ahead with the plan. It was possible to get a very good deal, as the dealers were very keen to get one of these tractors working in the area.

There were few four wheel drive tractors working on farms at that time, and several neighbouring farmers, surprised to see one at my place, could not see how the expense could be justified. However this tractor made a great improvement to farming this particular farm, where only about twenty acres were on the level. Not only did we carry out the amalgamation of the six fields into one reasonably large one, with a single slope from top to bottom, but also did a few other small jobs.

There was also a demand from local farmers for small jobs, from levelling sites to making gaps in hedgerows for gateways. Another added bonus was the contract with the local council for snow clearing on the roads. Deep snow occurred at some time most winters and with nothing to be done on the farm, Roger was away earning good money. To take advantage of the increased power and traction of the Ploughmaster, a new five furrow plough was bought for the autumn, and the three and four furrow ploughs were sold.

The 1967 harvest was even better than the previous year, and the big down yielded much more than expected; the output from the combine was quite staggering in thick crops and good weather. Because we were growing all spring barley, there was constant pressure to get the job done, so early starts and late finishing were the order of the day. Consequently, pressure on the grain drier was relentless, even in fairly good weather. It was my policy to harvest the spring barley, if possible, before it was really ripe, knowing that by the end of the campaign, we would be harvesting overripe crops, when ear losses would be mounting up.

When we started harvest my neighbours would drive into the field, grab some ears of the crop, and rub it in their hands and proclaim that it was not fit. With a laugh, I would say, it will be fit when it's been through the drier. I knew that you did not need to save much grain to pay for the fuel in the drier, and I felt that we could reduce crop losses, if we could combine earlier and faster.

My second-hand Ransomes combine had now completed its third season at Whitecliff and I was concerned about its reliability, down time can be expensive in lost crop. A combine with increased output was desirable, but would overwhelm the grain drier in all but the driest harvest. The grain in store was valued, and Bernard prepared a cash flow projection, which showed that after all expenses and bank charges, but no repayment of capital, there were funds available for reinvestment in machinery. Bernard told me to expect a substantial profit and therefore a large tax liability, something I quickly forgot.

A visit to Wiveliscombe was arranged. I outlined my plans to Mr. Bell and presented him with my cash flow projection. I explained that my plan would not only increase profitability, but also reduce the risk of serious crop losses. All this was much easier than on previous occasions, as now I had a track record of two profitable years and of course more experience. Mr. Bell congratulated me on my achievement and assured me that the original overdraft could be extended for another year. Mr. Bell seemed to be able to get around the problem of the government's credit squeeze. A tot of whiskey was poured and we drank to another bumper harvest in 1968. Alas, this was not to be.

John Wallis Titt & Co in Warminster, who manufactured grain

elevators and conveyors, were asked to design and price a new plant including a new Almet, four tons an hour grain drier, but not a cleaner. Because of the design of this drier, a large proportion of the chaff and dust is removed during the drying process. If this scheme was installed the pneumatic conveyor would be replaced by belt and bucket elevators, and chain and flight conveyors, and would increase drying capacity by 200%.

Combine harvesters were also supplied by JWT but were the modern development of the Massey Harris, now built by Massey Ferguson. Two models were available, the MF400 and the MF500. These machines looked very impressive, and the service and close proximity of JWT had to be considered.

An alternative machine, called a Clayson, could be supplied by A. Brewer and Co. at Wilton near Salisbury - further to go for spares and service, but no worse than Devizes for the Ransomes. Although I had been pleased with my Ransomes, and it had served me well for three years, it seemed to me that compared with the alternatives, the new Ransomes had not kept pace with developments.

As soon as it became clear, that I could afford both the drier and a combine, I finalised the scheme with JWT and gave them the go ahead. This meant selling all the grain in stock as soon as possible, in order that the barns would be empty. Brewers gave me the names of some Clayson users, and Roger and I visited three of them. They all spoke about their machines with high regard, and the words 'rugged' and 'reliable' came through strongly. All these users were previous owners of Ransomes. A deal was soon completed with Brewers for them to supply a Clayson 105, the larger of two models, and take back my old Ransomes. This should increase output from less than four tons an hour to about seven tons.

CHAPTER 10

AN IRISH ADVENTURE

On one Saturday morning that I will never forget, arrangements had been made for a tree stump, about 200 yards up the field at the back of the house, to be blown up with dynamite. Colin, who had suffered from croup on occasions, was unwell and took no interest in the proceedings. This was most unusual, as normally he was interested in everything. Mattie and I discussed the situation and I said that he must be really ill, more than he looked, to miss the fun. We decided to call the doctor who arrived within the hour. The doctor prescribed some medicine which I fetched from Warminster.

During the afternoon, Colin's condition seemed to get worse, and at about three the doctor was called again. After a quick look at Colin, the doctor asked us if we could take him at once to St. Martin's Hospital, adding that there was no time to call an ambulance. Fraught with anxiety we set off immediately on a horrific, high-speed journey, reaching the hospital in about twenty minutes.

At the hospital we were expected and rushed in. Colin was examined by the registrar and immediately put in an oxygen tent, in intensive care. No one actually said that he might die, but gave us little cause for hope either. This was the worst night of our lives, spent at the hospital, close to despair. After what seemed like a lifetime, at five in the morning we were told that Colin had turned the corner and was now out of danger. They explained the condition as a laryngeal spasm, and said it was a close run thing. With huge relief, we drove home to get some rest. We visited Colin a couple of times next day and found him in a children's ward, feeling pretty down. Monday morning, the hospital phoned quite early, to say that we could collect him any time before twelve.

I arrived at the hospital at around eleven; Colin was in the children's ward, in fine shape, as if he had never been ill. He was playing with the numerous toys available, and organising the other children, and seemed really miffed at not being able to stay. This had been a dreadful couple of days, and only parents who had experienced this could possibly know what it is like.

Ray had bought the grass keep on the steep down land for the summers of 1966, 1967, and 1968, and I had agreed to deal with fences and water supply and check the cattle at least once every day. Peter House continued to graze the meadows. The experience gained looking after Ray's cows and calves and keeping some of them in the covered yard for the winter, got me thinking. If I

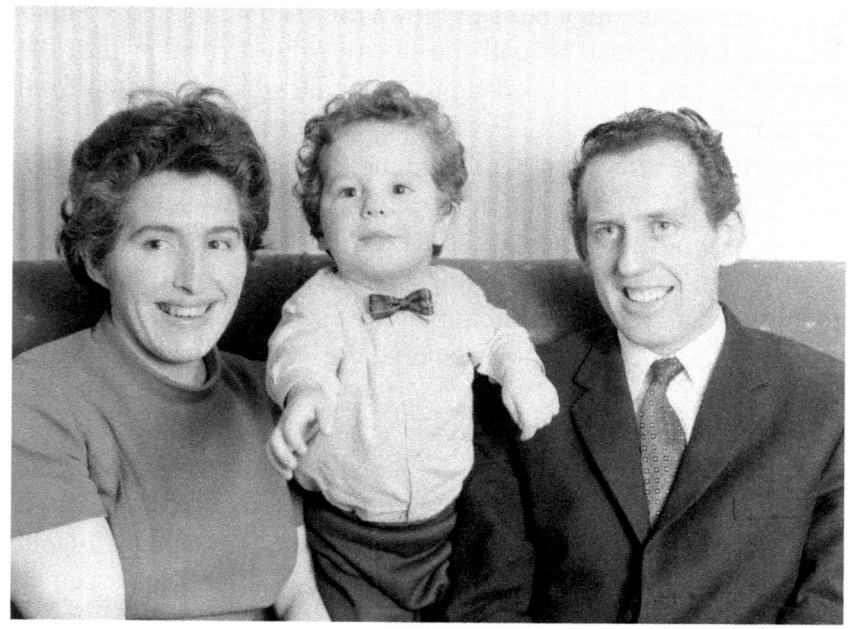

Mattie, Colin and myself

98

could have my own cattle, without reducing my arable land, there might be some way to get back to growing wheat, which would lead to higher yields and higher returns.

My previous experience at Bert's made me take a fresh look at growing grass for seed. Consultations with NAAS and various agricultural merchants led to a decision to grow ryegrass for seed and to start my own beef suckler herd. The ryegrass S24 would have to be under sown in the next crop of barley, to be ready for harvesting in July 1970. This would provide grazing in the spring and autumn, the cows spending the summer on the steep down land.

There was a subsidy on beef cows, so much a head, and a calf subsidy when they were nine months old, if they satisfied the MAFF inspector that they were suitable for beef production. There was no subsidy or guaranteed price for grass seed but it appeared that, because of new technology, we were able to compete on the world market. All these plans for expansion were encouraged by my two profitable years.

The harvest proved to be very difficult, with heavy summer rain flattening some of my very promising crops of barley. The new combine performed well, snatching a few acres when the sun came out. Several farmers came to see the combine picking up the laid crops at quite a reasonable speed but, despite this, losses were high and quality was poor. The new drying system worked well and was able to cope with the output from the combine. My feeling is that had we not made that investment, we would have faced a disaster; as it was we only faced disappointment.

Finishing our harvest in reasonable time, we were able to harvest and dry fifty-two acres for a neighbour, Mr Lister at Manor Farm, Brixton Deverill. At this stage I should point out that one or two extra people were employed each harvest, usually agricultural students. After harvest I sat them on a tractor for hours on end, cultivating the stubbles before they had to return to college. This was our only means of controlling grass weeds such as couch in this continuous arable system.

Cropping plans were now finalised, House field, the one behind the house where six fields had been made into one, was to be planted with spring beans so that we could grow winter wheat for harvest 1970, the rest of the land to be drilled with spring barley, and under sowing the far down with ryegrass for seed in 1970 and wheat in 1971.

Ray had been involved with my plans for starting my own herd and the benefit of his experience was very welcome at this time. Early in September he had a reply to an advertisement from someone called Robert Orr, from County Down in Northern Ireland. Ray had a long conversation with him about the type of cattle available in Ireland, north and south. Ray suggested that we should fly to Ireland and see for ourselves. This appealed to me from the start, as I was keen to have a beef herd that I could be proud of, rather than any old cows from local markets.

Later in the month I drove to Ray's farm near Kidderminster and stayed the night. We set off early next morning to Birmingham airport to fly to Belfast, where we were to meet Robert Orr. On arrival at Belfast, Robert, a weather beaten old cattle dealer, about 55 years old, with a pronounced Scottish/Irish accent, escorted us to his car, a ropey old rusty Ford Anglia, which he referred to as his Irish Ford. Robert drove us downtown to Belfast cattle market, where we met a few of his friends, while we discussed the cattle and the trade.

About noon we embarked in the Irish Ford, on to the M1 towards Eniskillen, where we attended another cattle market. Here, we were introduced to John Molihan and his brother Patrick, cattle dealers and exporters from County Longford, down south in Eire. John, who was very busy, suggested that we meet him at his farm in Longford the next morning. "There," he said, "I can show you lots of heifers and you can show me exactly what you are looking for." We made for the bar, had a cup of tea and a cheese sandwich, before setting off south in the Irish Ford. Ray, sitting in the back, under a coat, already with a bad cold and feeling pretty miserable, soon got fed up with Robert's driving which was atrocious; not only that but he was so slow. Ray persuaded him to let me drive otherwise we would never get there. Robert was quite OK with this and admitted that he did not like driving. We changed over and I drove for the rest of the trip.

Staying the night at a hotel in Mullingar, Westmeath, we motored out to the farm near Egworthstown, County Longford. There we were shown lots of cattle, and picked out the type of heifer I was looking for and discussed prices. The value of the Irish punt had to be checked against the pound. The animals needed to be big enough to take the bull in January. The blue/grey heifers that I saw that day were unique to southern Ireland and were not available in the UK.

Cattle breeders in England and Scotland had explained to us that the true blue/grey cow was produced by crossing a Galloway cow with a pure white Shorthorn bull. This was probably true in the UK as farmers were only permitted to breed with licensed, pedigree bulls. Whereas, in the Republic of Ireland, farmers were able use any animal that they considered suitable for breeding. Consequently, many of their dairy cows were a mish mash of Fresian and Shorthorn with a blue roan colour. When these cows were crossed with a similar type of bull, they produced a superb, relatively small, milky cow, ideal for crossing with one of the larger pedigree beef bulls in England, such as the Hereford, Charolais, Simental or South Devon.

Ray and I were confident that John knew exactly what we wanted and we had a rough idea how much they would cost. John agreed to collect at least 70 for me to see at his farm in three weeks. Although I only wanted about forty, Ray was confident that we could sell any surplus at a profit.

Setting off for Belfast airport, where our plane left for Birmingham at six that evening, I had to push the little car to the limit, and donkeys with their carts on blind bends tested the brakes, which were none too good anyway. Eventually we came over a rise and, at the bottom about half a mile away, I saw the border crossing. Robert, who had been very quiet for a change, suddenly panicked and shouted. "Stop, stop, I will drive." Before I could bring the car to a halt, he had got out and went sprawling, head over heels down the grass verge.

Dashing out to pick him up, I found him already rushing to the driver's side of the car. He got in, red faced and obviously shaken, and told us to be quiet, and that he would do the talking. We passed through the border post with very few questions, and no one even looked at our passports. We never found out what all the fuss was about.

Time seemed to be slipping by as we drove on, then, about ten miles from the airport, steam began to issue from under the bonnet. Stopping immediately, and obtaining water from a nearby house, we lost several minutes waiting for the radiator to stop boiling, then, after topping up the water, we were off again.

Robert dropped us off at the airport and drove off with steam again pouring from the car; I was afraid that he would not get far. Ray and I went to check in and found to our dismay that we were too late and the flight had closed. Booking a flight for the next morning, we found a taxi to take us to Antrim, which was the nearest town. We checked in at a hotel and had dinner, then Ray, whose cold was now really bad, went to bed. I thought I would check out the town, found a bar and dance hall, had a few beers and chatted with the locals. After a good night's sleep, and taxi to the airport we flew back to Birmingham and eventually home.

Three weeks later, on a Sunday night, I flew from Bristol to Dublin and checked in at a hotel where I was collected next morning and driven to John Molyhan's farm. There were about eighty heifers for me to look at, and John suggested that I take my pick, or if I agreed for him to pick them, then they would be a little less money. I was able to select sixty-one heifers that I liked and would be ready for the bull in the New Year.

All these cattle were then run through a crush where we read and recorded all their ear tag numbers. Later, in the farmhouse, all the numbers were matched with a blue card, which was the animal's passport. A ship called the Livestock Express was sailing from Dublin to Holyhead next morning, and John assured me that the cattle would be on that ship, and they were booked to travel on British Rail to Salisbury.

With business completed, we had a belated lunch of bread,

cheese and pickle, and a thick slice of boiled ham; it was delicious, perhaps because I was starving. One of his men then drove me to Dublin airport and I flew back to Bristol.

In order to arrange transport from Salisbury, I contacted British Rail to establish time of arrival of the cattle. Nobody seemed to have any information; all they could tell me was that they would phone as soon as they knew anything. As the days passed I was becoming more and more concerned at the thought of the heifers travelling all that time. It was Saturday morning when a call from British Rail at Salisbury informed me that the cattle were ready for collection. Luckily, my local haulage contractor was able to send three lorries that morning to collect them.

I went to Salisbury with one of the lorries and was surprised to find the heifers, in a lairage, lying down contentedly after being fed some hay. They were in very good condition and I could not believe they had been travelling for four days. They must have spent much of that time in comfortable lairage being well fed and watered. It came as no surprise to learn, some time later, that British Rail had given up transporting cattle, as they must have been losing money.

It was good to see my own cattle grazing on the farm. Very soon after that, Mr. Lister came to see me. He was wondering if I could take some cattle to Manor Farm, to graze the barley stubbles, and could I pay a little for the grass keep. We came to an arrangement, so I picked out twenty-five heifers that I would like to sell and moved them across. I felt that they would be in a better place for potential buyers to see them, and the remainder went to the far down. My plan was to put them to a Hereford bull for their first calving, then to a larger beef breed for their second and subsequent calvings.

The twenty-five heifers at Lister's were all sold before the end of November. Calving was planned for November and December 1969, housing them in the covered yard after they had calved. A couple of beef bulls would be hired from Ray for six weeks, from the middle of January. The calves should be well grown by the spring, and able to take full advantage of the large flush of milk

My Irish Blue-Grey cows

the heifers would provide when turned out to grass. Early grass would be available from the S24 seed crop then the heifers and their calves would spend the summer on the steep slopes.

After harvest, the calves would be sold as stores, while still with their mothers, when they look at their best, and before the store trade declined for the winter. Their mothers would then be able to calve on the new crop of S24 after the barley had been harvested.

From this time, not only did I have my own cattle on the farm, but I was looking after Ray's animals, as he was still buying the majority of the grass keep, including by now, the meadows and any grass keep available at Manor Farm. This proved to work very well and kept the farm fully stocked. Ray was building up a stock bull hiring business, and at that time there was a big demand from dairy farmers for Galloway bulls to serve their Fresian heifers.

One of my steep grazing fields was totally isolated from other cattle by arable crops. This field was put to good use by bulls, returning from their winter hires, to spend the summer and recoup their condition. This worked well so long as individual bulls were not put in with the rest, as they would pick on him with nasty results. So a number of bulls were turned out at the same time, and they all had a large scrap until they were tired, and no one bull suffered unduly from an attack, as there were always other bulls interfering. After a couple of days they settled down and enjoyed a comfortable summer on the hillside. These were the bulls that were eating the barley spilled from the overturning trailer during our first harvest of the big down.

January saw my tax bombshell arrive in the post. Despite Bernard's warning, I had not taken it very seriously as tax had not been a problem up to now. The problem arose from the two good years of 1966 and 1967 followed by the poor harvest of 1968. I had compounded the problem with the large investment in the combine, grain drier and cattle.

The demand from Inland Revenue was for several thousand pounds payable in two instalments, half in January and half in July. I consulted Bernard who was doubtful that the payment could be deferred and advised either borrowing more from the bank, or selling the cattle. There was nothing else to sell; all the grain was either sold or under contract to finance my expansion program.

First I spoke to Mr. Bell, explaining the problem, whereupon he said there was no way he could lend me any more as we were in the midst of a government credit squeeze. My immediate thought was that the credit squeeze made little difference before, why should it now? But I kept quiet. Mr. Bell told me to make the revenue whistle for their money. Not much help there then.

Next I phoned the Inland Revenue. Without revealing much about my recent expansion, I explained that I could not pay any of the tax due until after harvest, when I could sell some grain in August and pay the whole amount in September. The taxman suggested that so long as I paid interest on outstanding tax, I could pay by monthly instalments. I had great difficulty explaining that I could not pay in instalments, as I had no income, but would pay the whole amount, plus interest, in September.

The 1969 spring drilling progressed well after a period of deep snow in February, when we were able to make good use of our four-wheel drive tractor and dozer blade, for the council. The barley on the far down was under sown with S24 ryegrass, and the field at the back of the house was drilled with beans. The beans unfortunately failed to grow, apart from the odd plant here and there. It was found that the seed was at fault, and so I claimed compensation from the seed company. The field was re-drilled with barley towards the end of April.

During the drilling campaign, Mr. Lister came to see me to ask if I would like to plant barley in all of his arable fields, and how much could I pay him. We came to an agreement where by the money I paid was not 'rent', and I was to vacate the land immediately after harvest. He did not want to create a landlord and tenant situation where the tenant would have security. This was understandable, as he could want to sell one day with vacant possession. This was a large expansion of my acreage.

Mattie was confirmed pregnant in the spring and had the Shirodkar Stitch operation performed locally by her gynaecologist, who assured us that it was now a well known and proven procedure. She was advised to rest throughout the duration of the pregnancy, so we employed a live-in house maid. Jenny, who was a good worker and organiser, was also great fun, with a lovely personality and we enjoyed her company.

About the middle of May, Robin Bonifant, manager of Sykes hatchery, phoned to ask if he could see me urgently, I was concerned that there was something wrong with my management of our current multiplication flock. He came that very afternoon and, to my relief, it was nothing to do with the current flock. Robin explained that he had a flock of about 5000 hens and 450 cocks that had to be moved from their present location, as they were desperate for the hatching eggs; did I have a suitable shed?

The only shed I had was the covered yard and the manure from the cattle during the winter had not yet been cleaned out. He insisted on having a look, and soon paced it out and decided that it was big enough, but needed to be made escape proof. He suggested nylon netting tied up with string. Initially, I was very sceptical, then he explained that they would give me the birds, which were only just past their peak in their laying cycle, loan me all of the necessary equipment, nest boxes, feeders, drinkers and perching assemblies, adding that they would pay extra for the eggs. I said I would consider it.

Robin said he needed to know now because the birds had to be moved on Friday, which gave us just four days to prepare. There was no way we could clear out all the cow manure in that time, and he said we could leave it there as it was quite dry by now, and cover the whole yard with a deep layer of shavings. Robin made up my mind for me by promising to send two men to help.

We all set to work and a huge load of equipment arrived the next day We worked late into the evenings; feeders and drinkers were suspended from the roof trusses, miles of plastic pipes were connected to the water supply, nest boxes were moved in and perching areas assembled. The place was ready to receive two enormous loads of shavings on Friday morning and the birds were delivered on Friday afternoon. We left the lights on that night to avoid the birds crowding in the corners and an electrician installed a time switch and extra lighting on Saturday morning.

The birds settled in quickly and were producing at about 50%, which was very good considering their ordeal. Roger and I continued to improve the installations by replacing some of the netting with twenty feet by eight feet, ex-prefab floor panels, which I had bought at a sale some time before. We even installed a proper door for easy access for feeding and egg collecting.

It was soon apparent that, even with Jenny's help, we could not keep up with dry cleaning the eggs. Although Sykes preferred that hatching eggs were dry cleaned, they relented and suggested that we buy a couple of egg washing machines, which seemed to save our lives. Financially, the birds were a great success and they were gone by the time the covered yard was required for our cows and calves.

Harvesting went very well that year, the weather being much kinder than the previous year, Barley was again the only crop, as the beans had failed, so it was important to keep the combine going, with little regard to moisture content, and to make maximum use of the drier. The investment in the drier was paying off, and I saw little point in spending all that money and then risking the crop to dry in the sun. Immediately after harvest, some nitrogen was applied to the S24 ryegrass, to promote growth for autumn grazing. The rest of the stubbles were cultivated to germinate weed seeds and control grass weeds. The intention was to cultivate again after three weeks, to destroy any new growth and repeat the process after a further three weeks. Then the whole acreage would be ploughed during the winter. Any spare time, or periods when the land was too wet for ploughing, was spent repairing or replacing old fences.

In October Ray and I went to an annual sale of blue/grey heifers at Haltwhistle, in Northumberland. Staying at Ray's for the night, we set of early next morning in his Jaguar. The M6 motorway was now complete from Birmingham, almost as far as Kendal. There was no speed limit on motorways at that time so the journey time was reduced enormously. Ray drove until we reached the motorway then handed over to me, saying, "put her up to a hundred and stay in the fast lane". After about an hour, and just as it was beginning to get light, I saw a white van pull into the fast lane in front. I was quickly closing the distance when a large sign on the back lit up saying, POLICE STOP. I slowed the Jag to the speed of the van and followed it to the hard shoulder.

One of the police officers then explained to me that he had been asked to stop the Jaguar in the fast lane, as the police Jaguar was otherwise engaged. He reported to us that we had travelled over one hundred miles in an hour. He then went on to explain that the fast lane of the motorway was for overtaking only and not for high speed cruising. I said that it seemed the safest place to be considering the heavy traffic in the other lanes and he agreed that, at the speed we were travelling, I was probably right.

He then went through a list of reasons why our speed was excessive and unsafe; actions of other road users, the condition of the car and in particular the tyres, pointing out the horrendous scenario of a front blow out and crossing the central reservation. However, as I had not committed any offence, we were free to continue, but please, he said, a little slower. I drove to the end of the motorway when Ray took the wheel and we soon arrived in Carlisle for breakfast

The purpose of this trip to the north of England, was to buy a lorry load of the traditional blue/grey heifers, that are bred from a Galloway cow by a white Shorthorn bull. By having both types, these and my Irish heifers, on my farm, I would be able to decide which suited me best. After a cooked breakfast Ray and I drove to the sale; we were in good time so had an opportunity to look around the cattle pens, There were over eleven hundred heifers entered for sale so we had plenty to look at. These animals had a reputation for hardiness, and looked rough coated and wild, but not to be put off, we decided to try some if the price was right. We introduced ourselves to the auctioneer and the sale got under way. I found it difficult to understand what the auctioneer was saying and had to really concentrate.

After about an hour of watching the trade, I bought a bunch of eight; it was then a question of concentrating on the proceedings to buy some similar animals. During the next hour I managed to find some matching heifers, in small lots, and ended with a total of twenty. While Ray and I were arranging transport, each of the vendors made significant efforts to track me down. They were anxious to wish me luck with the heifers, and each of them gave me a pound or two pounds for each heifer that I had purchased from them. This was a custom in the north, referred to as 'Luck Penny'. Although in some cases they were difficult to understand, I got the message.

Preparations were in hand for our first calving, but in the meantime Mattie went into hospital on the advice of her gynaecologist. They discovered that the baby had not developed properly and after removing the stitch Mattie had a stillbirth. This affected her even more than the miscarriages had done, and she was a very long time convalescing, if indeed she ever recovered completely.

Jenny, who was very upset, was a great help and comfort to Mattie during this awful period. Colin, who was by now four and a half years old, was terribly disappointed, and despite hours of conversations, and as far as was possible, explanations, he became very quiet and subdued. When I returned from the hospital with the bad news, I bought him a lovely big teddy bear, which he became very fond of. I think it was, and hope it was, at least, some consolation.

Calving was a much bigger problem than I had imagined, partly because they were all first calvers, and partly my lack of experience. Even if the heifer calved successfully, the calf needed to get to its feet and suckle that all-important first milk within a couple of hours. If a cow calved near a barbed wire fence, at the bottom of a sloping field, then the calf, falling over a few times while trying to get up, would, invariably fall under the wire where it remained separated from its mother until we came on the scene. This could be several hours if the calf was born in the night.

I tried to pick out imminent cows and put them in the meadow where they were closer and easier to find. The silly cows always chose to calve close to the river, where the struggling calf would fall in and drown. If a calf was a long time being born it was often too weak to get up, then they both had to be moved to the buildings, the cow caught and tied up with a halter, milked by hand, and the important first milk fed to the calf with a bottle and teat. Not an easy task with beef cows who were not used to such close human contact.

February brought another spell of wintry weather, and Roger spent a few days snow clearing for the council. Spring drilling was rather a protracted affair due to periods of persistent rain, so the job was not completed until the middle of April. This was the month when the cows and calves were turned out into the meadow, from their winter accommodation in the covered yard, the date depending on the weather. This was great fun to watch as the calves, by now well grown, had never been outside, apart from the first few days of their lives, and they rushed across the meadow, followed by their mothers.

The calves would fail to see the river, as the banks were level, go crashing into the water, jump up on the far bank and look around in shock. Seeing their mothers on the other side, they jumped back into the water and up the bank to their mothers. Then after that initial shock, they settled down to running in a group from one end of the field to the other, and only crossing the river very carefully. I spent many happy hours watching their antics on that first day out.

There were two main projects for this summer. One was to increase the storage capacity of the old bulk grain store. This was achieved by constructing free standing "L" shaped panels from the stock of prefab floors, and some flat steel bars. These panels, when placed near the old walls, took the side pressure of the grain and enabled us to store up to eight feet deep, almost doubling the capacity.

The other project was to concrete an area through the middle of the cow yard, which would include a drive through feed passage with a removable feed fence on each side. Two drive through dung passages were constructed with concrete curbs at the edge to keep the dung off the littered area. The longer term plan was for this new concrete area to be expanded into a new lean-to extension to the covered yard, to be built when the present dilapidated sheds were demolished. This work was grant aided and as part of my application, I included a plan for using the area for drying grass seeds and also, possibly beans.

Using more of the prefab floors, Roger and I constructed a main air duct, four feet by four feet, to run the length of the new concrete. More prefab floors were used to construct a temporary bulk store. Next, galvanized, metal lateral ducts were purchased and fitted to the main duct, with hinged doors inside to control the airflow. The plan was to cover all this with grass seed or beans and to dry it with cold air supplied by a hired Lister Diesel fan. Then, as seed merchants did not take delivery of grass seed in bulk, the whole lot would have to be shovelled into hessian sacks.

CHAPTER 11

A NASTY LETTER
AND ANOTHER FARM

The 1970 harvest began in mid July when the rye grass was the first to be ready. Knowing from experience that combining would be a slow process, picking up the ripe grass which was by now lying flat on the ground, I had asked an old friend from Claverton days to bring his Class combine for a few days. Although the crop was somewhat protected from the wind by being flat on the ground, it was important to harvest it as quickly as possible to avoid the seed shedding out. A contractor baled the hay when dry, and we hauled the bales, nearly 4000 of them, back to the farm and stacked them in the hay barn for the cows in the winter. All these bales had to be handled by hand several times before they were safely in the hay barn; it was a very labour intensive operation and very hard work. This hay was not very good feed value but was better than straw. By sending some samples to NAAS for analysis, a winter-feeding program could be designed around it.

The cereal harvest was the easiest so far, and was finished by the middle of August, including the extra land at Manor Farm. I approached Mr Lister, suggesting that I might cultivate the stubbles, but no, he was concerned about the tenancy situation. I explained that the land was becoming badly infested with couch grass and would have to be cleaned at some stage. It was then that I jokingly suggested that I could relieve him of these problems by

Harvesting Barley with New Holland 1530

buying the farm from him. He laughed and jokingly said, "what a good idea". At that stage I didn't know what he was thinking, but I was glad that the seed of an idea had been sown.

My combine harvester had now completed three seasons, and as there was now a 15% grant available for investment in new plant and machinery, I decided to trade it in and buy the New Holland 1530, which was an update of my old one. This model was fitted with a dust proof cab, which was a vast improvement from that point of view, but with so much glass it was very hot inside, as the fan only delivered air of ambient temperature. The grants available for plant and machinery were primarily to encourage industry to modernise, but proved very useful in agriculture.

Our second calving was much easier than before, with everything much more organised, and with more experience on my part. We found the cattle from the north much wilder and much more difficult to handle than the Irish cattle. Another trip to Ireland was going to be necessary to expand my herd.

About this time I had a shock in the form of a letter from my new bank manager. The bank was very unhappy about my account and Mr. Dite had been appointed to the branch, specifically to sort out two accounts, one of which was mine. The letter asked me to phone as soon as possible to make an appointment to see him at the bank. When I phoned Mr. Dite, I expressed my surprise that he found it necessary to write me such a letter. He said he would explain when he saw me, and could I come down in the next few days.

I suggested that he should come up to the farm, where he could see for himself, what my business was like, and I could explain my system and plans to him, adding, when he appeared reluctant, that it would be much better than looking at figures on bits of paper in his office. He agreed to come, so I invited him to lunch and arrangements were made.

Mr. Dite arrived about eleven and immediately got down to business. He explained that the bank was very concerned about my overdraft, which had apparently turned into a permanent loan. He went on to explain that the bank was prepared to grant an overdraft for specific purposes, or for seasonal working capital. For this the bank required a planned reduction in the amount borrowed and a seasonal ebb and flow.

For my part I explained that the overdraft had always been reduced and re-borrowed for the expansion of the business. I also explained that my cash flow was managed in order to keep my overdraft close to the limit. This cash flow management gave the impression that my overdraft facility was in fact what the bank referred to as hardcore borrowing.

We filled in the usual business appraisal form, which showed a useful profit, and a high return on working capital. A look at the previous two years profit and loss accounts, together with the balance sheets, saw Mr. Dite looking much more relaxed.

At this stage I outlined my plans for the farm, which involved growing grass for seed and beans for animal feed, both to be followed by winter wheat, then barley, until grass or beans could be sown again. I emphasised that the growing of winter wheat in the rotation would not only increase my income, it would also spread some of the workload from spring to autumn, and reduce the risks. By increasing the grass seed production, more grazing would be provided for my expanding beef herd.

I impressed on Mr. Dite that the whole of the arable area would grow crops for sale, and the cattle would only get grazing and by products; this I felt would make the best use of my investment in machinery. Mr. Dite appeared to be impressed by my plans and was at last enthusiastic to have a tour of the farm. However it was almost time for lunch, and Mattie was ready to serve up.

Over lunch, which was delicious - roast beef, followed by apple pie and custard, there was a lively discussion about the national economy and the future of British agriculture. In the course of this discussion, I dropped in the idea that I would like to buy a neighbouring farm, about 200 acres, if it became available, and I said I thought it would.

Mr. Dite listened to all this in a matter of fact manner, explaining that the bank could not possibly help to purchase a farm, but would be delighted to continue to provide short term working capital in the form of an overdraft. With my figures, which included the limited production from Manor Farm so far, he thought it would be possible to arrange a loan from the Agricultural Mortgage Corporation or AMC, as it was known. Interest rates had been rising steadily over the last few years and AMC were now charging ten and a quarter per cent. I knew of farmers who were paying only three and a half on loans taken out years before.

During our tour of the farm, seeing the cattle and looking at the crops, I was able to point out the area of Manor Farm, and how well it fitted in with Whitecliff, expressing my opinion that larger farms were the farms of the future.

A few days later Mattie and I received a long letter from Mr.

Dite confirming the bank's commitment to provide working capital for the farming business in the future, and due to the uncertainties of Manor Farm, the present overdraft limit would be extended until further notice. He went on to say that, if we were successful in the purchase of Manor Farm, he would require us to borrow the purchase price, plus a further ten thousand pounds, to reduce our present overdraft.

Bernard was called in to do a cash flow and budget, on the basis that we owned and farmed Manor Farm. The calculation showed that, even with reasonably good harvests, and paying interest to AMC and the bank, forty thousand pounds was the most we could afford to borrow. This left only thirty thousand to buy Manor Farm. This was of course no use, and I expressed my disappointment to Mattie who thought I was mad to even consider buying another farm.

Some weeks passed when I again bumped into Mr. Lister, and in the course of a general conversation, he raised the subject of my buying his farm, and was I seriously interested? I said I was, but could make no progress until I had a figure to work with. He replied immediately, saying that he had consulted and given lots of thought to it, and that he wanted sixty thousand pounds.

Mr. Lister then went on to explain that the important thing, from his point of view, was to avoid his large neighbour, Col. Jack Houghton Brown, getting his hands on the place. He made it quite clear to me that he had an intense dislike for his neighbour.

Apparently, Manor Farm had once been much larger, stretching to over one thousand acres, and owned by Oxford College and rented by Mr Lister. During the Second World War, local War Agricultural Committees were formed in each county to carry forward the agricultural policies of the wartime coalition government. This War Ag., as it was known, had the power to confiscate land that was not being farmed properly, and either farm it themselves, or hand it to a neighbour to farm on their behalf.

Some eight hundred acres were taken from Manor Farm and handed to Houghton Brown's Pertwood Farm, because Mr Lister would not agree to carry out the War Ag.'s plans for increasing production. At the end of the war, for reasons I did not understand, the land was bought by Houghton Brown and was never returned to Mr. Lister. Presumably Mr. Lister bought the remaining two hundred acres, manor house, buildings and cottages.

This feud gave me a huge advantage, as Houghton Brown was the obvious buyer, if he wanted it, and this I did not know. If Mr. Lister was really serious about his neighbour, then he could not put the property on the open market and risk Houghton Brown buying it through a third party. It was time to get my valuer, Peter Hillier, to give the place the once over.

Peter arranged to look around the farm one Sunday morning. The land was sloping with some fairly steep areas, but no worse than Whitecliff, and some faced north which would make it later to grow in the spring. The buildings were well constructed from brick and slate, dating from about 1880. A single storey cow stall was built around three sides of a concrete yard, with mangers and a feed passage. Next to that was a taller building with stables and cobbled floor underneath and a substantial hayloft up above. There was also a brick and timber frame barn, providing considerable height for storage, and joined to this was a small range of two-storey general-purpose buildings. A steel framed, open hay barn with an asbestos roof situated away from the other buildings was a fairly recent addition.

A wall, separated all this from the Manor House, which was in dire condition, and Mr Lister told us that it needed six thousand spent on it just to keep it standing up. Looking up at the front, it was clear that the front wall was bulging outwards. Then, after looking at the three cottages, all of them derelict and uninhabitable, Peter was of the opinion that if we got twelve thousand for the four dwellings, we would be doing well. So that was no good. This meant that I would have to sell some of the land as well.

One Saturday afternoon in September, I was in the covered yard, bagging the grass seed which was now dry. It had been dried on the new concrete and floor drying system constructed by Roger and myself during the summer. A car arrived in the yard and a gentleman came into the shed. He introduced himself as John Cripwell, Director of the Wessex area of the National Trust. He came straight to the point and asked if I was interested in buying Manor Farm. If I was, then he was interested in buying the Manor House and the three derelict cottages, and would be prepared to pay ten thousand pounds.

I explained that we should proceed with caution, as I did not know what Mr. Lister's reaction might be to dividing the property. We decided that we might do a deal after I had secured the farm, and that I was asking twelve thousand for the part of the property that he was interested in. I promised to keep him informed. This was very reassuring as I liked the idea of selling the parts of the property that I did not require, before committing myself to the whole property. I considered that my financial situation did not justify property speculation.

All I needed now was to find someone to buy some land. Looking at a map, it was obvious that there were three fields, two arable and one water meadow, which would fit in nicely with the farm owned by my neighbours, Michael and Phillip Allard. Calling in at their place, I explained that I was trying to buy Manor Farm, and could not afford all of it, and would they like to have the opportunity to buy fifty-five acres. They were not very keen saying maybe, if they could have the buildings, or maybe, if it did not include the water meadows. Eventually, after describing it as a once in a lifetime opportunity to buy land just over the fence, and telling them that only those three fields were on offer, they began to show an interest. I promised to keep them informed and to keep it quiet, as I was unsure of Mr. Lister's reaction.

Confidence was now running high and I felt that I could risk doing a deal with Mr. Lister. I gained the impression that he had now made up his mind to sell, and I got the feeling that he meant the sooner the better, and certainly before Col. Jack heard any rumours. I offered him fifty thousand. He was obviously disappointed, and told me that he could not possibly sell for less than fifty five thousand. I asked him to give me a few days to raise some more money, then went back and said that the best I could do was fifty two thousand. He was delighted; we shook hands and he said "the farm is yours," and we agreed to hand the whole thing over to our solicitors.

The three firms of solicitors involved in the transaction agreed that the best course of action would be for me to complete my purchase of the whole property, and the very same day, complete the transfer of the two parts to the relevant purchasers. This sounded fine and I kept my fingers crossed that, if Mr.Lister were to find out, he would not withdraw from the sale. In the event, if he did know, he never mentioned it, and he moved out long before the completion took place.

Now began long and protracted negotiations between my solicitors and the National Trust solicitors. The N.T. solicitors sent us a long list of legally binding conditions that they wanted to impose on my use of the land and particularly the buildings. My solicitor, Mr. Ferris, of Farnfield and Nicholls, asked me if there was anything on the list that I could agree to. When I replied "nothing", he said, "very well, I will cross it all out and send it back"

A few days later Mr. Cripwell phoned to say that he must see me as soon as possible and could he come this evening. I agreed that he could and arranged to see him later. Mr. Cripwell was very concerned that the whole deal may collapse if I did not agree to some, at least, of the conditions set down by the N.T. I explained that the deal had been done without any conditions whatsoever, and I felt that it was an unreasonable imposition. He was very embarrassed and inclined to agree, but could not alter the fact that the N.T. needed a positive response to their proposals.

We proceeded to look through the list and, after a long discussion, I agreed not to keep pigs or make silage in the buildings. The one important condition that I would not agree to was to maintain the buildings exactly as they were, and not to alter or develop them in any way.

Another meeting with my solicitor was convened where he explained that he could agree several, unimportant items on the list. Then he would find a form of words to satisfy the N.T. on the buildings, so as not to cause me too much difficulty in future. Eventually, after a few more skirmishes, agreement was reached and the deal was all signed and settled.

Godwin Family 1971, Sue's Wedding
Brian, Ray, Mother, Sue and Myself

CHAPTER 12

A BIG BANG AND BACK
TO IRELAND

The 1971 drilling proceeded at a cracking pace, having extra help provided by my employment of Bill's son, John, who had recently been made redundant from Sykes. It was all finished by the middle of March. There appeared to be more demand for tractors and drivers for the early summer silage making campaign and now that I had three tractors, both Roger and John spent several weeks with a local contractor. Roger was making quite a reputation for himself, building the silage clamps with his four wheel drive and buckrake and he was much in demand from the local farmers.

A major project for the summer involved clearing overgrown areas at Manor Farm, removing hedges, fences and a couple of large trees. It was necessary to remove the roots, and our bulldozer blade on the four-wheel drive tractor was a huge asset. Two tree roots proved too much for the tractor so I looked up the man with the dynamite. He was still around, despite his unusual part-time activities, and agreed to come one Saturday morning. The smaller of the two tree stumps was no problem and was blasted into three manageable pieces. The larger one seemed to present more of a problem for my friend, and after drilling several holes, and packing them with dynamite, he seemed undecided about what to do next. He said that that one was going to need a lot more and started drilling and packing again. We then ran out the cable, quite a long way this time, then went back and collected our vehicles.

Taking shelter behind my Land Rover, he pressed the plunger, creating an almighty explosion; a huge chunk of the stump went straight up to an enormous height and seemed to hover over us. He said, "whatever you do, don't run, just watch it," It appeared to be coming straight down where we were! He then shouted, "RUN!" and he was gone with me hot on his heels. This huge jagged piece of wood crashed into the ground about five yards from where we had been standing, and penetrated about three feet into the hard chalk soil. We then retired to the pub for a drink and a laugh about the morning's work.

On returning home for lunch, a bit late, I found Mattie very concerned about the huge explosion she had heard, and a visit and several phone calls from irate residents in the village, complaining about broken windows. I spent the afternoon visiting the complainants, and promising to send a glazier first thing Monday to fix new glass.

Another project was to install a suitable drainage system in the water meadow, again part of Manor Farm, rotavate and level the old ridge and furrow flooding system and prepare it for planting grass seed. This involved employing a drainage contractor to plan and install the pipes, carrying out the rest of the work ourselves. Again a grant was obtained which paid for 40% of the scheme.

The harvest was finished before the end of August and yields were reasonable. The grant application to extend the covered yard was approved, so we demolished the old buildings and prepared the site for the contractors to construct the new lean-to. This would provide more space for drying the increased area of grass seed and beans, as well as accommodation for more cows and calves.

In September, I phoned John Molyhan in Ireland about more heifers and arranged a date to look at some. My brother Brian was keen to have some so we went together, flying from Bristol to Dublin, hiring a car and staying at the Four Courts Hotel in Dublin. We drove out to the farm in Co. Longford next morning where we picked out eighty-two cattle. The cattle we chose were separated from the others, then, when we were finished, they were put through the cattle crush, where we could read their ear tags - one of the men writing them down in a notebook.

John told us that the cattle would be transported to Dublin by train the next day, ready for the ship to Birkenhead in the afternoon. British Rail had ceased transporting cattle because of a serious fire on the Menai straight railway bridge, so we had to arrange road transport from Birkenhead to Wiltshire. We phoned Ray, as he knew of many haulage contractors, and asked him to arrange it.

Brian and I were invited to join John, his brother and several farm staff, for lunch in the farmhouse. We waited in line to wash our hands in a huge wooden sink, then sat around a large table laid with plates and cutlery on a thick white tablecloth. In the middle of the table was a huge joint of boiled ham, a loaf of homemade bread, a jar of pickle and some homemade butter. John's wife and daughter were busy slicing the bread and cutting the ham, passing it round the table to the hungry men.

I noticed that all the places were taken and there was nowhere for the two women to sit. It soon became clear that the women were there purely to serve the men. John would shout commands in his deep gruff voice, such as "more bread woman," and one or other would jump to it.

Two gigantic wolfhounds patrolled the territory between our backs and the walls, or cupboards, round the kitchen. If your ham included some gristle or thick rind, you simply cut it off and tossed it over your shoulder, where the dogs would noisily compete for it. For me, that was a most enjoyable meal - the food and the conversation both equally delightful.

With a barked order from John, the table was quickly cleared, the cloth shaken onto the floor and boxes of blue cards deposited in the middle. The men got up to leave, one of them throwing the notebook onto the table. John and his brother, together with Brian and I were now left at the table. I now knew the form and we set about matching the cards to the ear tag numbers in the notebook. This was made more difficult by the enormous number of cards in the boxes, John thought probably about a thousand.

While this was progressing, I took the opportunity to make some phone calls - one to Mattie, one to Ray and one to the Exported Livestock Insurance Company in Dublin. This time I knew what to expect when shown to the phone. On the previous occasion, I did not even recognise it as a telephone. It was a wooden box fixed to the wall, about twelve inches high and five by five square; a small handle was on the right side and a shaped speaking tube protruded from the front; a set of ear phones dangled on two wires from the bottom.

To make a call, you fix the headphones on your ears and wind the handle a couple of turns, which attracts the operator who asks what number you require. When I first used the phone on my previous visit, I turned the handle and expected some response, when nothing happened I turned the handle again - nothing; so I turned the handle a third time. This time I heard a very cross Irish lady say "I'll be wit'cher in a minute.". I knew from then on that you had to turn the handle and wait for the lady.

When John was satisfied that each of our animals had a blue card, he took us to see more of his cattle, then came with us to the hotel in Edgworthtown for a drink. John appeared to be on good terms with the proprietor and I expressed my opinion that he seemed a nice man. John quickly replied "Eye, he's a nice man alright, but that'll be all." Brian and I were keen to see the cattle loaded onto the train, and if possible to go on board the ship in Dublin. John told us that the train left for Dublin at nine in the morning, and that we would find the Livestock Express berthed along the north wall of the River Liffy.

After a good night's sleep we went to the station at eight in the morning. There was no sign of the cattle, only an irate steam engine driver. He was complaining about this man Molyhan, who was always late loading, and expecting him to reach the ship on time. Hot axle boxes appeared to be the main problem. Soon a line of lorries arrived and the cattle were run along the platform and directed into the open topped wagons, seventeen in each. Then with some smoke, lots of steam and noise, the train was off with time to spare.

Brian and I made our way to Dublin and found the ship along the north wall. Our cattle had been walked about half a mile from the station and were in a lairage close to the ship. Loading was proceeding at a pace, with plenty of men around to guide the cattle across the road and up the gangway; apparently the ship carried six hundred adult cattle.

As soon as the last beasts went on board we followed and introduced ourselves to the captain. He was very busy and had little time for us. I asked if we could have a quick look at the cattle on the lower decks. He said we were welcome but the ship was casting off in two minutes. We dashed down the gangway where the cattle had gone, to find a deck fitted out with small pens containing about ten beasts in each depending on their size, and all looking very comfortable on clean straw litter. No doubt there were other decks below, but we hurried back to the main deck to find the ship had cast off, the gangway was gone, and the ship was slowly moving away from the quay.

The captain shouted, "Jump, or come with us to Birkenhead." With this we jumped quickly across the widening gap, horrified to see down to the murky water as we crossed. We walked along the dock road to where we had left our hired car. It was still there and, despite John's warning, still had its wheels. It was time we made for the airport for our flight back to Bristol. At this stage I was thinking about the future of my beef herd which, if numbers were to be maintained, would involve purchasing occasional replacements. My feeling was that I had developed a good working relationship with John, and a phone call is all that would be required to buy further heifers.

CHAPTER 13

CONSOLIDATION, FIRE AND FEAR

The next three years were a period of consolidation and fine tuning, taking my story on to 1975. A new grain store was planned and built for the 1975 harvest, more about that later. In September 1975 arrangements were made with John Molyhan to send eighty heifers, big enough to go to bull in January. Nearly half of these were sold within a few weeks, with the remainder used to boost the beef suckler herd. It was important to maintain the herd size, not only to continue efficient production of beef stores, but also to keep the government suckler cow subsidy rolling in.

The cropping program was geared to increase the area of winter wheat. Grass seed production was expanded to this end, eventually growing two varieties. This was achieved by using the stable block at Manor Farm to dry one of these crops, again hiring a Lister diesel fan. This exercise was never repeated as the amount of handwork with shovels made it very difficult. Our traditional seed drying area in the covered yard still relied on men with shovels, the whole crop being turned a couple of times, then shovelled into sacks for transportation. I was determined to reduce the man-hours involved, and talked to the seed merchants about bulk transport. The above floor lateral air ducts presented us with a huge problem as any attempt to move the seed with a tractor and front-end loader resulted in their virtual destruction.

Any opportunity to carry out contract work was taken on providing that it did not conflict with productive work on the farm. A close working relationship was established with a local contractor, A. J. Legg and Son. They would send a couple of combine harvesters to help harvest the grass seed, and we would supply them with tractors and trailers for the silage making season. Col. Jack Houghton Brown grew a considerable area of grass seed and our combine was always in demand to help so long as we were not at work on our own crops. One Sunday evening there were twelve combine harvesters working in one of his large fields. A week or two was taken up by snow ploughing for the council, not every winter, but most years.

Bert Legg, of A. J. Legg and Son, became a long term friend after our working closely together on silage making and combining. Bert had set up his contracting business in 1945 after returning from his army service in the World War. He told an extraordinary story of over five years overseas without a break. He had joined the Wiltshire Yeomanry in 1939 and assembled at Wincanton where he and other farmers' sons were equipped with horses. Hundreds of men and horses now set out for the

Legg's combines on Ryegrass in "Abbysinnia"

127

Middle East going by train and ship to France and again by train to Marseille on the Mediterranean Sea. Here they boarded a ship for Palestine where they served for about a year.

It was about this time that they became mechanised, their horses being replaced by trucks and armoured cars. They were then sent to Syria to suppress the Vichy French. After that encounter they went into Iraq to quell a pro-German rebellion and to protect the friendly regime. From there they went to Persia (Iran) and met the Russians in Tehran. They had come down from the north by agreement to protect the oilfields - this was to impress upon the Russians that they were to encroach no further. The Wiltshire Yeomanry eventually arrived in Egypt in time to train with new Sherman tanks for the second battle of El Alamain. Bert was by now in command of three tanks and fortunately survived the battle, being mentioned in despatches. Many of his friends were lost, and Bert, on the 23rd October, if I happened to see him in the evening, would say how many years it was since those one thousand guns of the artillery opened up and lit up the sky.

After a long period of leave to recover after those two weeks of battle, a rumour was circulating that the ship on to which their tanks were being loaded, was to take them to Liverpool. No such luck; after being at sea for a few days they landed in Italy where they fought the Germans until the end of the war in Europe. Bert has told me that he lost a lot of friends in Italy because, unlike the desert, the vegetation gave cover to the German anti-tank guns. His tank was hit and he was lucky to survive. Bert is great company and a very good friend who lives every day as if it were a bonus.

August 1975. In the middle of harvest we had a serious fire at Manor Farm. The hay-barn nearly full of straw, a lorry loaded with straw and a bale elevator were destroyed. During the harvest period of the last three years, coinciding, as always with the school holidays, Mattie had arranged for a boy from a disadvantaged home in Swindon or Bristol to spend a few weeks on the farm. This was to provide a playmate for Colin as well as to give a country holiday to a city child.

It was probably a bit much to expect the two boys from very different backgrounds to be immediate bosom pals. However this had worked out well for a couple of years and maybe it would again. Wayne arrived about midweek and it was soon apparent that things were not working out, and the boys were not playing well together.

On Saturday, Roger had gone on a shopping trip so when the sun came out at about lunchtime, I had to drive the combine, and John drove the tractor and trailer. We were harvesting barley on the Big Down. Later on in the afternoon, we could see a large pall of black smoke rising from the trees in the village; it looked a bit bigger than a garden bonfire. John and I had stopped and were just about to go down on the tractor when I saw my Land Rover coming up the track in a cloud of dust. It was Phillippa, who had been working at the grain drier, to tell us that the barn at Manor Farm was on fire.

We returned to the farm, collected Mattie and the two boys and went to Manor Farm. The fire was by now completely out of control and the Fire Brigade were not trying to put it out, but were concentrating their efforts on protecting Roger's thatched cottage and the nearby farm buildings. I was concerned about some cars parked nearby which were already very hot. The fireman told me that if they put water on them, all the paint would come off. We watched and talked to people for a while and someone said they had seen a boy in a red jumper running away at about the time the fire started.

Discussing the fire over a cup of tea at Whitecliff, Mattie explained that as soon as she heard about the fire, she went out to the yard to find the boys. Colin was there but he did not know where Wayne was. Mattie then went out into the meadow and saw Wayne approaching from the direction of Monkton Deverill, the opposite direction to the fire; he appeared surprised by the news of the fire and seemed reluctant to go to see it.

The police arrived and began to question us to ascertain the cause of the fire. It soon became clear that the boys had been playing in some straw bales that had been tipped randomly in the cow yard at Whitecliff. Tunnels had been made and a disagreement had arisen, whereupon Wayne disappeared, wearing a red jumper.

The police then questioned Wayne, and it was clear that they suspected that he had started the fire, and constantly fired questions at him. I felt very sorry for the little boy and intervened saying that I thought they were being too hard on him. At this point one of the police officers indicated for me to go out into the hall. He then explained to me that Wayne had definitely started the fire and they just needed a few more minutes to get him to admit it, then they would be nice to him. The officer was right and a few more minutes saw Wayne admit what he had done, and only then did he start to cry. The police were then very nice to him and eventually took him away and handed him over to social services.

I felt so very sorry for that little boy, and I regret that we never found out what had happened to him. On reflection we realised that it could have been much worse. Had Wayne decided to light the straw at Whitecliff, where they were playing, and one or other of them were in the tunnels, a major tragedy could have occurred. As it was, apart from the effect on poor little Wayne, all we lost was a bit of property, and even that was covered by insurance.

Straw and stubble burning was practised widely in those days, and the smell of burning straw today, always reminds Colin of his childhood when he associated the smell of post harvest stubble burning with the approaching end to the school holidays. It was a very good and easy way of disposing of unwanted material in preparation for the next crop. This burning on a large scale required considerable planning to protect boundary hedges, trees and buildings by forming fire breaks, by ploughing and in some cases by small scale controlled burns. I must confess that I did not enjoy this part of the job as it was always a bit stressful.

After the fire-break had been prepared around the edge of a field, an old tractor tyre would be put on a pile of straw and attached to the Land Rover with a long chain. The straw was then lit and allowed to burn until the tyre was well alight. The burning tyre was then dragged around the edge of the field so that the straw and stubble burnt from all directions. This method avoided

Houghton Browm's field goes up in smoke opposite Whitecliffe

having a raging inferno near the edge of a field. Things can go wrong as experienced by our neighbours, when a huge pile of burning straw built up in front of the tyre, quickly engulfing their Land Rover; the driver making a hasty dash over the fence into the next field.

One evening three of us were preparing to burn a field near the farm and I asked one of the men to go to the house and ask Mattie for some matches. We were in the process of creating a fire-break by controlled burning, and because it was damp, a considerable amount of smoke was produced. Within about half an hour Mattie was shocked to see a fire engine come tearing up the drive and roar round the back of the house and into the field. An interesting confrontation now developed, as the firemen rolled out their hoses and my men with pitch forks protested, saying "don't put our fire out we have only just got it going."

The upshot of this was that a neighbouring farmer had called the fire service, where a stubble fire was out of control. Our thick smoke had attracted the firemen as the other fire was up over the hill. Once this was established the firemen rolled up their hoses, jumped on the engine and tore off to the next farm where the fire was soon brought under control. This stubble burning became so very unpopular with the general public that it was at first highly regulated and eventually banned; I was not sorry.

Roger and I paid a visit to Col. Jack after we heard that he had employed a contractor from Powerstock, in Dorset, to plough and reseed a very steep slope of old chalk downland. This work was grant aided and the contractors did the whole job for the same money as the grant, so the cost to the farmer was nil.

We were most impressed by the tractors; they were all County

Spreading Fertilizer on steep slopes

132

four wheel drives, equipped with twin wheels at the rear, spaced out to make an over all width of twelve feet. Talking to the drivers, we found that the extensions, rather like large flowerpots, were produced by County, and furthermore they would fit our Roadless. There were many acres of similar steep slopes at Whitecliff and Manor farms, although I was not convinced that ploughing and reseeding was the right course as I felt that the soil on the slopes would be unstable for grazing cows.

My feeling was that these slopes could be improved by the application of phosphate and potash fertiliser, and these wheel extensions may be the way to apply it. The parts and extra wheels were obtained and very soon put to the test. Roger seemed to have nerves of steel and soon became very experienced on the slopes. This type of land is common in this part of Wiltshire and very soon we had an annual contract with several farmers to spread fertiliser each spring.

The yard with the cow stalls around it at Manor Farm was converted to house some of Ray's stock bulls. I found myself more and more involved in the business of buying, selling and hiring bulls, and the premises there were ideal, and completely separate from my beef herd.

Around this time MAFF were trying to eradicate brucellosis in the national herd. This disease cost the industry millions every year. It was a serious disease, and could be contracted by humans. Many farmers and veterinary surgeons suffered its symptoms, which I am told is similar to malaria. Tests were now available to ascertain if an animal was infected, so MAFF introduced a voluntary scheme. Farmers could have their herds tested by the Ministry; if successful, or if the farmer was willing to dispose of any infected animals, they could become a Brucellosis Accredited Herd. A similar scheme had been run for several years to successfully eradicate Bovine Tuberculosis.

With the increasing number of accredited herds, the hiring of the stock bulls decreased, so Ray and I decided to ask the Ministry if we could have a licence to keep only accredited bulls at the yard, and all non-accredited bulls at Ray's farm in Worcester.

The licence was eventually granted after we had complied with a number of conditions. One condition was that the bulls must have separate transport; this was dealt with by using my Land Rover to tow a trailer. A second condition required all bulls to be tested on return by a vet appointed by the Ministry.

Another condition was for my beef herd to become accredited; this was because the same people were to be involved with the animals in both premises. Fortunately my herd was free of infection and was made accredited at the first test. Moving bulls could only be done after applying for a permit, and quarterly movement records submitted to the Ministry. After this the bull business went from strength to strength, as we could now supply both accredited and non-accredited animals.

Now that all animals on the farm were mine, apart from the stock bulls of course, I devoted some time to improving the pasture management. Previously, the scattered areas of grazing were permanently stocked with an appropriate number of cows and calves. This resulted in considerable time being spent each day visiting and checking all these cattle. Also, in the event of a herd test for TB or brucellosis, it was proving very difficult to get them back to the farm and then to their field again, complicated by the fact that the cattle were not used to being moved.

Dairy farmers at this time were using a paddock grazing system where each day the cows grazed a fresh paddock. By fencing off some short track ways along the sides of arable fields, and keeping all the cows and calves together in one herd, it was easy to move them from one field to another. The plan was for the cows to start at one end of the farm, graze each field in turn, and to reach the other end of the farm after about three weeks.

The cows had fresh grass every few days, depending on the size of the fields and with the shake of a feed bag, and a call, the animals were keen to move to the next area. Only when moving on the road to Manor Farm was it necessary to have more than one man. This system worked very well and the cows were used to being moved, which made their management much more efficient. Fertiliser was then applied, where necessary, between grazing and fences could be repaired without interference from the cattle.

The cows and calves only used the steep land, or water meadows so the rest of the land was cultivated and could not be used by the cattle, even during the winter. As it was, we always had a few cattle out wintered on one of the steep areas and it was difficult to get feed to them, especially when the weather was bad. There was a steep area at Manor Farm, suitable for out wintering at the time but was eventually ploughed when I had the hillside combine.

One very wet morning John and I set out with a Ford 4000 with a fore end loader and a flat bed trailer to feed the cows on this steep slope. I decided to go up the track to the top of the field where it was not so steep. John was putting out the hay from the trailer as I drove along close to the top fence getting more and more uneasy as the tractor and trailer kept trying to slide down the hill.

I stopped the tractor and discussed the situation with John. We decided to distribute the rest of the feed by hand then try to turn around. Returning to the tractor, I first lowered the front loader to lower the centre of gravity, and appreciated that the only way to turn round was to turn down hill, where unfortunately, the slope increased. As soon as I had turned the machine, I realized that it was not going to work; we were sliding slowly down the hill sideways, and heading for an overturn.

The Ford 4000 now became a death trap, as it was equipped with a soft, weatherproof cab, with the only door on the left, which was now the lower side. I immediately turned the tractor down the hill in an attempt to turn the machine around again and get the door to the upper side so that I could escape. This worked like a dream and I jumped out and joined John who had abandoned his trailer. The combination was now sliding toward the steepest part of the hill and we expected to see it start rolling over at any second.

But then an incredible thing happened. As I jumped from the tractor the combination had jack knifed, so that the tractor faced up the slope at about a forty-five degree angle. The trailer faced down the slope at about the same angle and was jammed tight against the tractor wheel forming a 'V' shape. The whole thing bounced and bucked down this very rough slope and came to rest close to the bottom fence. As I had left in a hurry the engine was running and it was still in gear so the wheels were slowly revolving.

Running down the hill I climbed back into the tractor and tried to turn it round to drive out of the bottom gate. It was just too wet and slippery and we were in danger of sliding through the fence, so we had to walk back to Whitecliff to fetch the four-wheel drive. We laughed about it later but realised that it could have been very nasty.

Imperial Chemical Industries, or ICI, had, at that time, a substantial commitment to the production of agricultural inputs, fertiliser, crop protection and animal health products. Consequently they were very interested in farm management and profitability in order to target their products in the most efficient way. ICI ran a scheme called the ICI Costed Farms scheme, and having developed a fairly close working relationship with ICI during the previous few years, they asked me if I would be interested in joining. It was the impression in the farming community that only the best managed farms were in the scheme, so I considered it quite an honour.

The only disadvantage of membership was a strong commitment on my part to use ICI products wherever possible. This was outweighed by the advantages of the scheme. Regular meetings were arranged with various agricultural management specialists to discuss topics such as crops, beef cattle, soil management and mechanisation. In addition an accountant from ICI made a monthly visit to collect management and financial details, in order to produce a set of accounts for the farm as a whole, and for each enterprise. A large printout was produced by an ICI computer which gave a detailed analysis of the accounts, including output per acre, output per cow, output per man, output to capital investment, output per horse power employed and many other useful figures.

Whitecliffe Farm from the top of Manor Farm

All this information was published each year and comparisons were made between farms in similar categories, in my case, arable/beef. Results were produced which placed the farm in the top 25%, the bottom 25% or in between for the various enterprises. Complete confidentiality was maintained through out by the use of a code number for each farm.

One of the conditions of the scheme was an obligation to allow ICI to arrange open days for other members, and carry out crop trials on the farm. This gave me an opportunity to visit other member's farms on their open days. I enjoyed visiting the other farms and it brought home to me what a difficult farm I had here. When holding my open days the visitors always wanted to go to the top of the hill to see the view and possibly pick out their own farms. From now on, ICI were involved in the ever more complex process of making management decisions.

These management accounts totally justified my previous policy of restricting the beef enterprise to land unsuitable for arable production, and made me appreciate the difficulties of making the beef profitable. The continued commitment to beef production could only be justified by sticking rigidly to that policy, and only if existing buildings and labour could be used.

Britain's economy was in tatters during this period, but my impression was that agriculture was performing well. The government continued to support the industry because of the balance of payments crisis, and looked to agriculture to reduce imports. Harold Wilson's Labour government had won a second term, with an increased majority, which led to a further decline in the state of the economy, and more influence being exercised by the increasingly powerful trade unions.

Eventually, the Conservatives, under Edward Heath were voted into power, but faired even worse than Labour. Industrial unrest manifested itself in strikes and walkouts culminating in a miner's strike and a three-day working week. Heath decided to call an election, having presided over the country's affairs for little more than two years. His main platform was "who do you want to run the country, the government or the unions?" The people failed to back him and Labour were again elected, settling the strike and getting Britain back to work; this proved to be only a temporary solution.

Mattie and I had found time for a seaside holiday, at least once a year, in Devon, Cornwall or Wales. It was great fun with Colin on the beach, and we even did some surfing at Woolacombe Bay one hot September; it was so hot, the sand was almost too hot for our bare feet.

October 1973 saw another frightening nuclear confrontation between America and the Soviet Union, this time because of a war in the Middle East, between Israel and her Arab neighbours, Egypt and Syria. In 1967 Israel had won what became known as the six day war and occupied the Egyptian Sinai desert and, to the north, the Syrian Golan Heights. These Arab states were determined to regain these occupied territories and, with the help of the Soviet Union, built up their armed forces, quietly and secretly, until they were ready to attack. The Israelis were about to celebrate Yom Kippur, a religious festival, when the attack came with very little warning.

My thoughts, on hearing the news, was that Israel, with her

American and French jets, would soon repulse the attacks, and destroy the pontoon bridges thrown across the Suez Canal by the Egyptians, but after the first couple of days the news was very bad and Israel was suffering a potential defeat on both fronts. We later learned what had happened.

On the northern front the Syrian tanks made good progress against the thin Israeli defences as it had taken some time for the Israeli forces to be mobilized because they were mostly civilians, called from their regular jobs. In the south the Egyptians had prepared a vast number of Soviet surface to air missiles, or SAMs, on the west bank of the canal. When the Israeli Phantoms and Mirages tried to attack the pontoon bridges, these guided weapons shot them down.

In the meantime Egyptian armoured forces poured across the canal and made a good job of repelling Israeli tanks using a new type of Soviet anti-tank missile. It soon became clear that the Egyptians were not prepared to advance more than about twenty-five miles into Sinai, which was the extent of the air cover provided by the SAMs. The Israelis decided to concentrate their forces against the Syrians in the north as they represented a greater threat to the Israeli population. In the south the enemy was hundreds of miles away across the Sinai desert.

After a few days of heavy fighting on the Golan Heights, the Israelis began to gain the upper hand and the Syrians appealed to Egypt to continue their offensive, to relieve the pressure on them. The Egyptian armour then began to charge across the desert and immediately came under attack from the Israeli air force, as they were no longer under the protection of the SAM missiles.

The Israelis now decided to go on the offensive and sent an armoured spearhead towards the canal. A 500 tonne floating bridge, which had been constructed for just such an eventuality, towed by five tanks, was pushed across the canal. Israeli armour now surged across and fanned out to the north and south, destroying all of the SAM sites. As soon as the Egyptian army lost their air cover, they faced imminent defeat and appealed to the Russians for help.

The Russians suggested that they should send troops to keep the peace and that America should do the same. The American response was a warning to the Soviets that not one Russian soldier was to set foot in the Middle East and that all their nuclear forces were being put on red alert, including the sixth fleet in the Mediterranean. The Americans also agreed to persuade Israel to accept a ceasefire, and peace was eventually restored, with much relief around the world.

CHAPTER 14

A LOOK AT EUROPEAN AGRICULTURE

Joining the Common Market was the big political debate of the early seventies and, after a referendum, we eventually joined in 1973. This decision was to effect agriculture more than any other industry, and the immediate effect was a massive increase in the price of farmland, and my becoming a millionaire, at least on paper. There was a feeling in the agricultural industry that support from Europe could only improve our situation, at least in the short term. Our local National Farmers' Union decided to organise trips to other European countries, visiting farms, markets, agricultural co-ops and associated industries, with a view to a better understanding between us and our new European colleagues.

Setting off with our preconceived ideas that Britain had one of the most efficient agricultural industries in the world, we were in for some surprises. First I joined a trip with local farmers to Germany, where the farms were small and the farmers mostly part-timers. The capital investment in machinery was extremely high by our standards, as was the investment in modern buildings. Our visit to a John Deere tractor factory was cut short one afternoon by the plant closing at 3 pm so that the workers could go home to work their farms. Maybe the few hours spent on the farm justified the high level of mechanisation.

French agriculture consisted of small inefficient farms

supported by a system of co-operation and cheap credit. This type of agriculture is widespread in France, particularly in Normandy and Brittany, but our tour took us to Reims and to farms in Champagne. There we found land, similar to our Salisbury plain, and possibly the most efficient grain producing area in the world.

Most of these huge farms had been established since the end of the Second World War, and were unaffected by the ancient traditions of French land ownership. We were impressed by the effective use of large machines and 'state of the art' use of fertiliser and chemical inputs, way ahead of our work in Wiltshire. This was where I first came across the use of 'tramlines' in the crops. The system involves blanking off certain rows on the seed drill, to create a ready made guide for spreaders and sprayers to follow with absolute accuracy. Consequently, much wider machines can be employed to greater effect, and they certainly were. As soon as I returned home I began to develop my own system, and I believe I had the first 'tramlines' in Wiltshire.

Our yields of wheat and barley were once more outstripping our storage capacity and much consideration was given to planning a new grain store. To keep the cost down, the building would need to be close to the grain drier and existing storage, so that grain could be conveyed from the drier. Lorries could use the same hardened areas for loading out; this meant demolishing some old cattle sheds. An opportunity now existed to replace the old labour intensive grass seed drying system in the covered yard - a system that had to be built up and dismantled every year. John Wallis Titt & Co produced a design for a building 90 feet in length and a 60 feet wide clear span roof. With 8 feet high, galvanised steel grain walling, the store should contain about 700 tonnes of wheat filled level to the top of the grain walls.

The first bay was a normal concrete floor and was to be used as a service area; the rest of the floor area was designed to be a drying floor. This consisted of an eight feet high, central air duct constructed from plywood, on a heavy wooden frame, designed to take the side pressure of the stored grain. A 60 hp electric fan was installed in a fan house constructed on top of the duct at the far end. The floor consisted of lateral ducts below floor level, covered by special pieces of hardwood designed to allow air to pass up through, but not allow grain or seed to fall into the duct. These hardwood ducts were also able to carry the weight of fully laden lorries so that all seed and grain can be turned, moved or loaded by tractor and loader.

The plan was to use the whole floor to dry the grass seed in a shallow layer, then when drying was completed, to store it as deeply as possible, using a minimum of precious floor area. The remaining floor area would then be used to dry and store wheat or barley, separating the grain from the grass seed with a plastic sheet or tarpaulin. Storing the grain eight feet deep could cause problems with airflow during drying if the grain came from the combine at more than 20%, so if necessary the grain was passed over the grain drier before being conveyed into the new store. In practise it rarely went on to the drying floor at more than 18%.

An added bonus of this new store was the reduction of pressure on the grain drier as several hundred tonnes could now be passed quickly through and conveyed to the new store for final drying. Now that we could handle the grass seed in bulk, it became viable to clean the crop on the farm, and avoid the excessive charges for cleaning by the merchants. So a cleaner was installed in the old barn, near the grain drier.

It was clear by now that I had developed a system of crop production that fitted the farm and suited the production of beef stores. With this realisation, a problem, which we had made some attempt to control, was that of wild oats which were increasing rapidly. The wild oat seed was very difficult to remove from cereal seed and even more difficult to remove from grass seed, so it was important that the wild oat plant was removed from the crop before it produced seeds. At this stage, this could only be done by hand, as chemical sprays were not available. This involved people, carrying sacks, walking through the crops, pulling the whole wild oat plant from the ground and putting it in the sack, then placing the sacks at the edge of the fields. These were then collected and burnt. It was fortunate that, whatever height the crop was, the wild oat was always about one foot taller, so they could be readily seen and identified.

Another problem making control difficult was the dormancy of the wild oat seed. If a plant was allowed to produce seed and it fell to the ground, it might germinate next year, or the year after, or any time up to ten years hence. Although we had made considerable efforts over the last few years using our regular farm staff, we were losing the battle against this obnoxious weed.

It had been usual to employ a couple of young people for the harvest, and Phillippa Pedley, from Monkton Deverill, manned the grain drier for several years. Phillippa took a great interest in the farm, and encouraged her school friends, and later her college friends to earn some holiday cash pulling these wild oats. The tramline system proved a great help as they divided the huge fields into strips, and the students were able to walk in the wheel tracks.

Joining the Wiltshire, Hampshire and Dorset Seed Growers Association (WHD), was a major discipline, as they inspected seed growers' farms prior to harvest, and eventually my farm became an approved wild oat free farm. Seed merchants were prepared to pay premium prices for seed produced on such farms.

1976 proved to be eventful, with the labour government in negotiations with the International Monetary Fund or IMF to stave off national bankruptcy. Local events, the Deverills Festival, the weather and a very poor harvest, all contributed to a memorable year. In February, Mattie and I had a couple of weeks in Italy, staying with friends, Roger and Angela Isiah, in Ventimelia, while Colin stayed with the parents of one of his school friends. Flying from Heathrow to Nice, in a Trident airliner, we were met at the airport by Roger who drove us on a sight seeing tour of the Riviera, on the way to his house.

After a couple of days settling in, our friends took us over the mountains and through a long tunnel called the Col de Tende, to Cunio, where we stayed on a farm with their friends. It was fascinating to see their methods of beef production, but I felt that nothing could be learned from them as the climate was much kinder and the breeds of cattle very different. An interesting day was spent at a local cattle market where I came across breeds that I had never heard of, such as the Chianina and Piedmont. Four of these giant Chianina bulls were later to come into our bull unit at Brixton Deverill, having been imported by the Ministry of Agriculture for evaluation.

On the evening we were planning to leave the farm, the farmer's wife cooked what she called a typical Italian banquet. This, we were to discover, consisted of many small courses, perhaps up to ten. We lost count as the wine flowed and the Grappa arrived on the table. All this was very enjoyable and the company delightful, but in the early hours we thanked our hosts and took our leave. The mountain pass was blocked by snow so we had to drive down the valley to Savona and then along the coast road back to Ventimelia. Thankfully it was a superb road - Autostrada nearly all the way, so we were home in about four hours.

A lovely day was spent across the border in France at the Menton festival of flowers, and on a quick visit to Monte Carlo. On another day just Mattie and I took a bus and spent a lovely seaside day at San Remo. Spending money presented quite a problem as our government had passed a law that the amount of money to be taken out of the country was restricted to twenty-five pounds per person. I remember hiding a seventy five thousand lire banknote inside my sock as we passed from Italy into France. Such was the financial state of our country at that time.

The previous summer had been drier than usual but not to the extent that the crops were effected. This was followed by a winter of below normal rainfall, and before long the dry spring quickly turned to a drought. The first major effect of all this dry weather was the lack of grass for the cows and calves, and by the middle of June they were almost back on a full winter feeding program.

Naturally, I was alarmed at the possibility of having to feed the animals right through the summer. With high temperatures and a weather forecast suggesting a continuation of the dry weather, I decided to sell the whole herd, arranging with auctioneers to have an auction on the farm. No sooner had I made an initial meeting with the auctioneer, I received a call from an old friend in Northern Ireland, Johnny Johnson, who had been talking to Ray. Johnny wanted to come over and buy the cattle to send to his farm in Scotland, where there was an abundance of grass. I immediately put the auctioneer on hold and arranged to meet Johnny at Bristol airport.

After collecting Johnny from the airport, the first stop was to see sixteen in calf heifers at Bert's farm at Winsley. I had sent them there three weeks before to help the grass situation at home. Having quickly looked at the heifers, we stopped for lunch at a pub on route to Whitecliff. At the farm, we had a quick look around the rest of the in calf heifers and the cows and calves. The calves were by now quite big having been born in November and December.

I had expected Johnny to pick out the animals that he liked, so I had Roger and John standing by to round them up for marking. Johnny appreciated that it could be difficult to pick the right calf for each cow, and to be sure in every case, so he said that he would like to take them all and particularly the in calf heifers. Having satisfied himself with the numbers of animals involved, we retired to the house where Mattie had prepared afternoon tea.

Now the haggling began and I knew I was onto a winner because he was genuinely surprised at the quality of the cattle. I knew exactly what I wanted for the cattle and had added about 10% when I had spoken to Johnny on the phone in Ireland, but had not expected to sell the whole lot. When he asked the price, I told him it was as I had mentioned on the phone. He then began to talk down the price by referring to a couple of individual cows as not quite up to the general standard, and also expressing the expense of transport to his farm in Scotland.

Johnny then made me an offer I could not refuse. He suggested that I arrange and pay for the transport, and that he would leave me a cheque for the majority of the money, for me to clear through the bank. The remaining six thousand pounds would be available in cash at his farm as soon as I could arrange to drive to Scotland, with a chance to see the cows in their new home.

This I agreed to; we shook hands and I poured two glasses of my best malt. We drank to the cows and to each other and continued our conversation, talking about the state of agriculture, the government, taxation, the weather and anything else that cropped up. It was now time to drive Johnny to Heathrow airport to catch a Tristar to Belfast. We arrived in time for me to buy him dinner in the best restaurant we could find, then afterwards we said goodbye and wished each other good luck.

Driving home alone gave me a chance to reflect on the day's events. Had I done right or wrong? I wondered if I would ever own such a super herd of cows again, and what would happen if the rain came. Oh well, I will worry about that when it happens; at least the cows contributed little to the farm income and they will not be a great loss. For now I will look forward to a trip to Scotland, and giving Mattie some extra money to spend, maybe some of it on herself for a change.

Jack Houghton Brown chaired a committee of local people to run three days of Deverill festival during June. My special responsibility was to organise an exhibition of modern farm machinery used in and around the Deverills. This involved moving lots of machinery from various farms to the chosen site, writing notes describing what the machine was for, and its cost, and mounting the notes on a post. This involved a lot of time and energy and a very impressive and informative display was there for people to see. Unfortunately, very few people were prepared to spend much time in the field as the sun was so very hot.

There were many other events, including visits to archaeological sites and experts on hand to talk about natural history. Churches were open and several special services were arranged. Exhibitions of local art and craft were laid on together with tea and cakes at the various venues. A dance with a band on a trailer was provided in our new grain store, and various fun-fair type sideshows were laid on in the meadow.

When arranging this type of event, we were all aware that it would be a disaster if it rained; we never considered the possibility of it being too hot. However, despite the heat I believe the festival was a partial success.

Because of the hot and dry weather, the harvest was to be much earlier than usual, and a barn dance by the South West Wilts Agricultural club, in my barn, had to be cancelled. In the event, our harvest was all over by the end of July, with low yields and poor quality grain. This gave us an unusual opportunity to enjoy the summer including our trip to Scotland to see the cows and collect the rest of the money.

CHAPTER 15

MILITARY JETS

A few days after harvest I received a phone call from a major in the army to say that he had been instructed to send a helicopter to my farm, pick me up and fly me around the area for about half an hour. He explained to me that he had no idea why he had to do this, but orders are orders and could we make arrangements and select a landing site.

I told him where to land and he said that tomorrow, three aircraft were flying from Odiham to Warminster and one of them could divert to my farm if it was convenient. It would be with me about three o clock. This I agreed to and began to look forward to the flight.

The reason for this flight can only be explained by going back a couple of years to a time when I began co-operating with the army on the use of some of my land for army exercises. These arrangements were made on an ad hoc basis, depending on the type of exercise and the availability of land suitable for their purposes.

On several occasions I would suggest to the major in charge that this was rather a one sided arrangement, with me providing the site for their exercises and the only thing I received was the pleasure of watching the planes. Had I been honest I would have confessed that that was a sufficient reward. However, one day, during a lull in operations, the conversation turned to the subject and the major explained that they could not make any payment for the use of the site and was there anything else they could do?

I told the major that the last thing on my mind was payment as I was very pleased to be involved, but I would like a trip in a Hunter or a Phantom. He was obviously a little surprised at my suggestion and said he did not think that that would be possible, but he was prepared to make enquiries, adding that a trip in a Hercules was much more feasible. The major went on to explain that paratroops were taken on a two hour, low level flight around Wiltshire before making a parachute jump on Salisbury Plain.

I had watched these planes on many occasions, flying very low over the farm and seeing the soldiers standing on the open ramp at the back. I said that was just the sort of thing I had in mind except the jumping out bit. We laughed and left it there, with him saying that he would see what he could do. Several months passed and I had forgotten about it when I had the phone call. I will now explain the extent of my co-operation with the army, leading to this phone call.

Of all the exercises carried out over the years, by far the most interesting and exciting was Forward Air Control or FAC. These are the soldiers who position themselves very close to or even behind enemy lines and direct aircraft to attack targets, such as buildings, vehicles and enemy troop concentrations. Cold Kitchen hill was a favourite site for the FAC as at 850 feet above sea level it gave them a commanding view of the surrounding area.

On one occasion, having agreed for three Land Rovers and about a dozen soldiers to use the hill, I waited for the low flying jets. After about an hour I decided to drive up the hill in my Land Rover to see what was going on. As I approached the top of the hill, I saw the three vehicles, two small helicopters and a camouflaged tent.

I parked my truck next to the army vehicles and walked to the tent. They were a friendly bunch, no doubt appreciative of being able to use such an ideal site. In the tent were maps of the area laid out on a table and they explained to me that they were selecting targets for attack by RAF Hawker Hunter jets.

The first target was a small white pump house on a nearby farm. It was fascinating to hear them describe the target to the pilots who were, at that time, circling around near Alfred's Tower, about ten miles away. The pilots' replies were run through a speaker for all to hear, and they wanted information about the position of hostile forces and the chances of anti-aircraft guns or missiles in the area.

After everyone was satisfied, the pilots confirmed that they were on their way, and after what seemed like a few seconds two jets were seen approaching our hill at high speed. One of the soldiers flashed a signal with an aldis lamp as they approached, they then turned sharp left, confirmed that the target had been identified and dived to attack, pulling up at the last moment and disappearing into the sky.

It was obvious to me that further targets were needed quickly, while the jets were on station. Pouring over the maps and scanning the area through binoculars, they said that the two tractors working on the hill across the valley would be ideal targets, but no way could they use them. I then explained that the tractors were mine and that the lads would love to be attacked! Roger and John were spreading manure from a store heap in the top field at Manor Farm.

The major in charge was at first reluctant and wanted to know if they were young men, and could they cope with the shock of an extremely low level attack? I assured him that they would thoroughly enjoy the experience. His mind made up, he instructed one of the soldiers to tell the pilots to attack two hostile tractors with napalm. The position of the tractors, the approach, and various landmarks to help the pilots to identify them, and the positions of hostile forces were relayed to the pilots and they were on their way. The aldis lamp was again used and the planes crossed our position at a very low level, and immediately dived into the valley in the direction of the tractors. The pilots confirmed that the targets had been identified.

We were now looking down on the planes as they crossed the valley floor and climbed the hill opposite, flying over the tractors and streaking up into the sky. All this happened so very quickly, probably as quickly as you can read about it. Fortunately, both Roger and John had seen them coming up the hill towards them, so they were not too shocked by the noise. Roger said they could see the whites of their eyes as they approached.

I well remember another occasion when I had given them permission to use the hill, saying that I would come up if an opportunity arose. It was an overcast day and there seemed to be a distinct lack of action when eventually I drove up the hill to see the cattle. Calling at the FAC base, I was informed that the RAF had sent two Hunters and they were heard flying above the cloud, but considered that it was too dangerous to descend and returned to base.

The major in charge then told me that they had sent a request to the Royal Naval Air Station at Yeovilton, and that they were prepared to send two F4 Phantoms, which were expected at any minute. Almost immediately the speaker burst into life and the navy pilots were asking for instructions, the FAC crew were elated as there was now a chance that the day would not be wasted.

After a short period of communication, I saw two Phantoms appear through the cloud base over Kingston Deverill. The planes flew around the area and then did a mock attack on a target selected by the FAC. By this time the weather was improving and a great friend of mine, Richard Phillips, appeared overhead in his Auster. On seeing the FAC base and the army helicopters, he circled round and made a landing approach, much to the consternation of the FAC. I explained that it was a friend who was probably curious to know what was going on.

Having landed, the Auster taxied up to the base and Richard switched off his engine. With much amusement, introductions and explanations all round, and two Phantoms flying slowly across the hill, the navy pilots wanted to know what was going on and who was the intruder? On being told that the Auster was flown by a friend of the farmer, they said, "if he can land then so can we," and they disappeared into the distance.

Soon they were seen coming across the far down, approaching our hill, with full flaps and wheels down in what was obviously a landing approach. They disappeared from view in a dip in the land, and arguments burst out among the FAC crew as to whether they were serious or just playing tricks. With only seconds to find out, the two Phantoms appeared, wheels just skimming the grass until they were about to pass our position, at about 50 metres away.

We then saw the wheels retract and the planes pulled up into an almost vertical climb, with the afterburners sending two long tongues of flame from their tail pipes. The noise was deafening and the ground seemed to shake as they disappeared into the clouds. There now ensued lots of chit chat and laughter between the pilots and the FAC and the Phantoms signed off and returned to Yeovilton. Another hour was spent with Richard and the FAC boys, talking about aircraft and navy pilots in particular. The crew were keen to look at Richard's plane and Richard was keen to show it off with his usual enthusiasm.

A few weeks later, Richard's enthusiasm unfortunately got the better of him. Flying his plane around the hills and diving into the valleys, he failed to pull up in time and flew through the top of some trees, ripping the wings off. Fortunately only his pride was injured, but sadly, I believe the plane was destroyed.

To go back now to my flight in the helicopter; waiting anxiously for its arrival in the meadow just south of the farmyard, it appeared, dead on three o'clock and made a perfect landing. It was a Puma; a fairly large troop and cargo carrying aircraft with two gas turbine engines. I walked across to the machine and introduced myself to the crew who were very chatty and wanted to know what this was all about. Did I know someone on high in the army?

I did my best to explain the situation and they made it clear that this was highly unusual and that I must have had quite a bit of pull, then they said where do you want to go? I said that I would like to fly over my farm and farmland and then a trip around the immediate area, and suggested that we could make it up as we go, they were happy with this.

The Puma Helicopter in the meadow

Next I was invited into the aircraft and fitted with a helmet and throat microphone. The pilot and co-pilot took their seats and I was seated between them and slightly behind in a fold away seat they called a jump seat. The crewman had by now taken up a position some ten metres in front of the aircraft and was connected by some sort of cable. The pilot then explained that first I would have a safety briefing and check that my throat mike worked. This meant that each crewman in turn said something to me, to which I had to reply, including the man outside.

At first I could not believe the sound of my own voice and repeated what I had said; this caused some laughter and I considered that the best thing was to laugh as well, which all sounded so strange on the sound system. Next, the pilot pointed to a red light in the middle of the instrument panel and explained that if that should light up at any time during the flight I was to unbuckle my harness, fold away the seat and move quickly to the rear of the aircraft; do not wait for instructions. The pilot went on to say that if I moved too slowly, it was probable that he or his co-pilot would trample me to death as they scrambled to the rear.

The crewman outside of the aircraft now assisted with starting the engines by watching for flame out, and as soon as the engines were running smoothly he climbed aboard and we took off. We went straight up to about two hundred feet then the aircraft tilted forward and we sped away towards the big down, over the trig point and on across the far down. I was shocked that we had covered the whole length of the farm in a matter of seconds and had to decide where to go?

I spotted Phillip Allard's combine and suggested that we make a low pass. With that the pilot put the machine into a dive towards the combine and circled it a couple of times at very close range. It felt like the rotor was at right angles to the ground. I could see a look of horror and bewilderment on Phillip's face and as it was a Thursday I was looking forward to seeing and hearing his reaction at the Conservative Club that evening. The pilot now wanted to know where to go again so I asked him to fly low over my local pub, 'The George' at Longbridge Deverill and then to fly around looking for more combines. We saw four more combines, but I advised the pilot not to fly so close as the drivers were not so well known to me, and might not be amused. After a very interesting flight around our local farms we came in for a smooth landing in the meadow back at Whitecliff.

The crew came into the house to meet Mattie and have a cup of tea. After a chat about army flying and farming they took their leave. I found a bottle of malt whisky and walked with them to the aircraft. I gave them the bottle and thanked them for an enjoyable trip. They said that they had enjoyed it just as much as it was something different and unusual. They then started the engines and were off to join their comrades at Warminster

One evening, I was having a drink at 'The George' I met a chap who introduced himself as Bob Morris and he told me that he flew helicopters for the army. Before long a great discussion developed about the effectiveness of helicopters in a war situation. I was saying that they must be easy to shoot down, and Bob explained how they can hide behind trees and hedgerows, and pop up to fire their missiles then drop down again behind the trees. I threw down a challenge, telling him that I would be spreading fertiliser the next day on a wheat crop, and drew a sketch map of the location of the field. If I saw his helicopter I would flash my lights, and that I would see him before he could attack.

The next morning I was spreading the fertiliser on the field at the back of the house, constantly looking around for the helicopter. Each time I turned around at the top of the field I had a good view of the surrounding area and was confident that he could not surprise me. However, on one occasion, having turned at the top, and probably about half way down the field, I heard this noise above and saw that the wheat was being blown flat all round the tractor. Looking up through the side window I saw a helicopter skid just above my cab. I opened the door and waved as the helicopter circled me once then made off up the hill. I realised that this was going to cost me a pint next time I saw Bob in the pub.

On another occasion Bob asked where I would be the next day as he could bring me some King Edward cigars. I explained that I was a committee member of our local ploughing association, and that I would be marking out the field for the ploughing match to be held at the weekend and that it was taking place on a neighbour's farm. Again I drew a map of the location and told him that it would be OK to land.

The next day was dreadfully wet and overcast and the committee members had assembled in Land Rovers, all parked in the lane adjacent to the field. I joined another farmer in his vehicle for a chat, while we waited for the rain to stop, wondering all the while whether Bob would come in this dreadful weather. Suddenly I heard the aircraft and saw Bob making a low level approach across the field, so I said "that must be my helicopter" and left the Land Rover, clambered over the fence and ran out into the field. I waved the helicopter down, bent down and approached under the disc. Unable to say anything because of the noise, Bob handed me the box of cigars and I retreated from under the disc, gave him the thumbs up and waved him away and he was gone into the murk.

On returning to the Land Rover, several of the farmers wanted to know what was going on. I showed them my box of cigars and told them that I always got them delivered like that, and inquired as to where they got theirs. Lots of laughter and expressions of incredulity ensued and it was a talking point for some time. I was to see a lot of Bob over the next few years.

The next few years I remember as being one of confidence in the agricultural industry, mainly fuelled by the European Common Agricultural Policy or CAP as it was known. The Policy had two major objectives at that time. One was to ensure that the population never again suffered rationing of food, or worse, starvation, which was the case in many areas of Europe during and immediately after the Second World War. The second was to bring the wages and standard of living of people who worked in agriculture to the same level as people who worked in industry.

During this period I gradually built up my beef herd again by buying cows or heifers locally and continuing with my arable rotation of grass seed production, wheat and barley. The ICI accounts had shown clearly that there was very little money to be made from beef production, and although I considered returning to Ireland, my early enthusiasm had been severely dented.

In July 1977 our county branch of the National Farmer's Union (NFU), organised a visit to the USA consisting of two weeks from the 27th June. About thirty farmers joined the tour and we left Heathrow on a Pan American Boeing 747 bound for Boston, where we spent our first evening. We had time to sample our first taste of American seafood and steaks, but not much time to see the city. This had to wait until the next morning when a Greyhound bus collected us from our hotel. The bus drove us through the city and then on into the countryside for the first of our farm visits.

A dairy farm in Massachusetts was our morning stop, followed by a long drive with a stop for lunch in Hartford, Connecticut, where we stayed for the night. We were up early the next morning to visit a large apple growing farm. Here, a vast area of apple trees was being farmed by a man who chewed tobacco; something I had not come across before, and won't mind if I never see again.

I was very impressed by the high level of mechanisation and small number of skilled workers. We asked how they picked all the apples? He explained that every year he chartered some jet airliners to bring pickers from Puerto Rico for the season then fly them back again. After touring the controlled environment apple stores we boarded our bus and drove on to Hartford where we stayed for another night.

The next day we boarded our coach and travelled north into New York State where we visited a dairy farm and an agricultural college before reaching our overnight stop at Syracuse. Next morning an early start took us to the famous finger lake area of the State, where we made two more farm visits. This is a very picturesque area with very long narrow lakes, some over one hundred miles in length, situated among green rolling hills.

The afternoon was taken up by our drive to Niagara Falls for the weekend. On arrival, I could not resist a quick walk to see the falls before dark and was guided by the constant roar of the water. It proved difficult to get a good view and I learnt next day that one had to cross the bridge to Canada to really appreciate the splendour of this mighty river.

Next morning our bus took us on a tour of Niagara Falls City, then crossed the bridge to Niagara Falls City in Canada where we spent the day at the falls enjoying the various tourist facilities. These included a trip on the Maid of the Mist, where the boat approaches the falls from the gorge on the lower side, and becomes completely engulfed in the spray, thankfully waterproofs were provided. We then walked along specially constructed wooden walkways that took us behind the falling wall of water, the noise was incredible.

Also, a visit was made to the bottom of the gorge via pedestrian tunnels hewn from the rock. Here, a lot of history was on display where we could read about people who had gone over the falls in barrels and various other contraptions, and people who had swum, or attempted to swim across the raging torrent in the gorge. Our visit to Niagara was completed by Saturday night at a down town night club called 'The Speak', a name derived from the old 'Speak Easy' clubs during the prohibition era.

Sunday morning was bright and sunny, just right for our flight from Buffalo to Chicago, but it was not to last. As we approached Chicago, across Lake Michigan, I could see a dense black cloudbank directly ahead. The pilot came on to say that a thunderstorm was developing over Chicago and that we might have to divert to Milwaukee to the north, but not to worry as we might just make it in. In the circumstances, I found it difficult not to worry just a tiny bit, not about diverting, but about trying to make it in! However it was OK and as the wheels touched the runway the heavens opened; it gave me the sensation of the plane speeding over the sea. By the time we had cleared the terminal building the sun returned and it felt very hot and humid.

Monday the 4th July, American Independence Day, was spent in this beautiful city of Chicago, situated on the shore of Lake Michigan. The day began with a bus tour of the city, driving along the lakeside and then down town to see the amazing modern architecture and eventually visiting the Board of Trade. Here we watched the apparent chaos of the trading floor in action, lots of people shouting to one another and waving bits of paper. Wheat, Soya, Coffee, Rice, Beef and Pork Bellies were being traded, and it was difficult to appreciate that commodity prices throughout the world were being established in this maelstrom.

We watched telex machines regurgitating reams of information from around the world. I quickly read some of the printouts coming through containing information about soil temperatures in Saskatchewan and details of frosts in Brazil. I would have liked a bit more time, but no, we were now off to the Sears Tower, the tallest office building in the world at that time. Here we took the express elevator to the sky deck where the views of the city were spectacular. Masses of skyscrapers surrounded the Sears Tower and it was strange to look down on them. The old abandoned stockyards and meat packing plants were clearly visible to the west of the city; beyond this was the endless flat expanse of the prairies. We were told that one could see 60 miles on a clear day.

We were advised that the best place to be in the evening of Independence Day was the Navy Pier where we 'pretended' to celebrate with thousands of people. About 11.30pm a most spectacular firework display began and lasted until midnight. After this the problem was to find our hotel; no one was quite sure where it was and, because of the crowds, there was no possibility of transport. Eventually, after walking for miles, we arrived exhausted and ready for our beds.

The arable farms of the mid west were next on our itinerary and proved to be the highlight of the tour from my point of view. We travelled for miles along straight, flat roads, staying one night in Rockford and two nights in Bloomington. We had an amazing night in Rockford where the local farmers had arranged a dinner and dance to welcome the Wiltshire farmers. Cowboys and cowgirls came from miles around and we danced to the music of two country bands with local singers. It was a great night.

Travelling through the state of Illinois, the land was flat and appeared to go on forever, with farms scattered around, all looking very much the same. The farms all had white clapboard farm houses, circular grain silos with elevators, and they were all growing maize and soya bean crops. It was only on visiting the farms that the difference between them became apparent. The difference was in the way they turned their maize and soya bean crops into cash.

Some were purely arable farms, marketing their crops directly, while hog farms fed their crops to pigs and other farmers fed their crops to beef cattle. It was interesting to learn that the beef farmers bought their young beef store cattle from the ranches of

Montana, Wyoming, Nebraska and the Dakotas at the sales in the fall. Rather like our cattle being purchased in the West Country for fattening on the arable farms in East Anglia.

The size of farms in this area was a surprise to us as we had expected to find very large areas being farmed on a grand scale, and to be fair there were some, but most were around 300 acres and farmed only by family labour. But this did not deter them from operating, by our standards at that time, some fairly large tractors, and often a husband and wife had one each.

It was very hot during these farm visits and we were pleased if we could find a little shade while we listened to the farmers explaining their farming systems. We endured several days in the heat of the mid west, visiting farms, feed mills and tractor dealerships. On a Friday afternoon we boarded a plane at Peoria to fly to Washington D C, checking into a hotel in Arlington. Visits were arranged to the Arlington cemetery, the Capitol, the Whitehouse and the Smithsonian Institute. In the museum I saw an example of a very early Massy Harris combine harvester. Not so very different to the 726 that I had worked on with Colin Dix.

On Sunday a bus took us to New York where we enjoyed a tour of the city, visiting Central Park, Battery Park and the Empire State building. Monday was again spent enjoying the delights and wonders of that amazing city, then catching a late night flight to London - the end of an incredible trip. I was determined that I would return to America with Mattie at some time soon.

During the last couple of days in the States, rumours were circulating about an aphid attack on our wheat crops back home. I had never heard that aphids were a problem and decided to wait until our return to find out the truth. Sure enough, there was a real problem, or at least there had been. Mattie told me how she had heard a plane spraying a neighbour's wheat very early one morning so she rang our local ADAS man, Geoff Adams, to find out why!

Geoff explained to her about the aphids and said he would look at our crops, then call in to see her. Later that morning Geoff called to say that the crops should be sprayed as soon as possible.

Mattie then set out to find the plane, which she could plainly see, but had difficulty finding the field from which it was operating.

By the time she arrived in the field, the plane and ground crew were about to pack up and move to another location. However they agreed to spray the wheat at Whitecliff before moving off, as it could be completed in four trips and Mattie agreed to pay them whatever the other farmers were paying. I was of course delighted that she had taken this action and saved our wheat from a potentially serious loss of yield.

CHAPTER 16

A FATEFUL INVITATION

On returning from the USA I was more determined than ever to move into some other business. My situation could be described as asset rich and cash poor and it was impossible to earn enough from the land to justify owning it. If I could find a suitable business to start up, then raising the money from the bank would be easy because of my assets, and I began to feel that these were being wasted, and that I was probably missing out on a huge opportunity.

Having looked at the building industry, and road transport, with little to fire my enthusiasm, the post brought an invitation to attend a seminar in Salisbury, arranged by a firm of financial advisors called Norton Warburg. They inferred in the invitation that their presentation would include something of special interest to larger farmers.

At the conference, the audience included a lot of farmers; at least they looked like farmers. The chairman introduced a number of speakers who were to speak on various subjects such as taxation, pensions and inheritance tax; the latter being of extreme importance to farmers and landowners, as the relative value of their estates compared with their earning capacity meant that their farms had to be sold. It was proving impossible for the next generation to borrow sufficient funds to pay the tax. Even if they could, they would not earn enough to pay the interest, or repay the loan.

The last speaker was from Lloyd's of London. He explained that Lloyd's was not an insurance company but an association of individuals trading and underwriting in their own right under the auspices and rules of the committee of Lloyd's, laid down by various acts of parliament over the last, almost three hundred years. Any individual could become a member, or 'Name', as they are referred to, provided that sufficient funds were lodged with Lloyd's, and that the prospective member accepted the principle of unlimited liability. This meant, he went on to explain, that in the event of a major loss, the member could lose not only the money deposited with Lloyd's but every penny he possessed. He continued by saying that this possibility could be ignored as it was most unlikely to happen, as the history of Lloyd's clearly demonstrated.

I was beginning to think that this was just a waste of a good day, as I certainly did not have a hundred thousand pounds or so to deposit with Lloyd's. The speaker then went on to tell us how farmers were in a unique situation. Instead of a deposit, a letter of credit, or a bank guarantee, could be provided by a bank or insurance company, at a low rate of interest, perhaps one per cent. On starting to underwrite, the premiums were paid into the members account and immediately began to earn interest. The money would remain on the account, earning interest, for up to three years before the inevitable claims have to be paid. Lloyd's has a three years accounting system so after three years the member is sent a cheque or asked to send a cheque to cover a loss.

Although a single cheque is received, it is made up of two parts. One is the interest earned on the premiums, which have already been taxed at source, and the other part is the profit from the actual underwriting on which the member has to pay income tax. If, as sometimes happens, a loss is incurred, a cheque is received for the interest, less any that has been used to pay the loss and this money is tax free as it has been taxed at source. Now, as a loss has been incurred on the underwriting account, a claim can be made to the Inland Revenue to refund tax paid on the farm accounts of previous years.

This was all very interesting and I felt deserved further thought. Before leaving the conference room I arranged for someone to visit my farm with a view to advising me on the problems of inheritance tax, my biggest headache at the time. One of the speakers, Nick Mercer, said he would visit the farm with a colleague, take all the financial details, such as approximate asset values, borrowings, life policies and projected earning capacity.

Nick then said that I would be presented with a written report setting out the state of my business, the potential tax take on the death of either Mattie or myself or both. The last part of the report would include their recommendations of action to be taken to enable Colin to inherit the farm in the event of our deaths. This was quite a weight off my mind as I had been worried about this for some time.

A couple of days later I phoned Nick to ask what all this was going to cost? He said that if I acted on his recommendations there would be no charge, as his firm would collect commission on any insurance policies they might recommend. I was unhappy with this, as I might not like their recommendations.

I insisted that before our meeting, I required, in writing, a charge for their work in the event that I was unable to accept their recommendations even if it was free of charge. I had gained the impression that this was no more than a sophisticated way of selling insurance. A few days later I received Nick's letter confirming our meeting, which included a quotation of his firm's charges in the event that I rejected their recommendations.

Over the next few days I was constantly chewing all this over in my mind and concluded that the meeting, with an up to date review of our financial position, would be a good exercise in itself. If it solved the problem of inheritance tax, then it would be well worthwhile. Lloyd's did not come into this thought process as I probably thought that it was a bit beyond our resources.

The appointed day arrived and I came in to wash and change and have an early lunch. Nick and his colleague arrived after lunch and we had a most interesting discussion. I furnished them with as much information as I could, and where I could not answer their questions, promised to find out over the next few days.

I thought the meeting was over and Mattie made some tea, when Nick asked if I had any thoughts about Lloyd's. I replied that I had not thought much about it as I did not know enough, and thought it was not really applicable to us as it sounded too risky. We then had a long discussion on the subject where he explained that the risks were always over-played and in any case there were many ways to minimise them. One of these ways was for just one of us to join. As Mattie and I owned half of the farm each, if only one of us was a member then we only risked half of the farm. Nick left by saying that part of the recommendations for action in his report would definitely be to apply for membership of Lloyd's. He added that the tax implications were enormous with higher rate tax at 83% and 98% on unearned income.

The report arrived in due course and, after giving it a lot of consideration, and consulting with our accountant, we decided to implement the recommendations in full, apart from the Lloyd's membership. This involved taking out various insurance policies which would pay out to Colin on our deaths; this would enable him to pay the inheritance tax and carry on farming, if that's what he wanted to do at the time. All this looked terribly expensive, but on the plus side there were considerable income tax allowances, and taxation was still at a very high level.

Mattie and I were pleased that at last we had actually done something about the inheritance tax liability problem, as it had been nagging at us for some time. Now, with that problem behind us, my mind turned to Lloyd's and it gradually occurred to me that it could be just what I was looking for. For one, underwriting would not involve me in any extra day-to-day work, as the experts in London would manage that. This would leave me free to concentrate on my farming, which, after all, was what I really wanted to do. Secondly, the fact that very little capital was required to start this business, made it attractive compared to other ideas I had considered.

After Mattie and I returned from a week on holiday in London, I decided to find out more about Lloyd's membership. Mattie was reluctant as she felt it was too risky and in any case she could not see why it was necessary; her attitude being that we were doing very nicely as we were. I remember trying to explain to her that if we were to remain in farming in the future, then we had to find ways to generate more capital to expand the size of our business, in order to maintain efficient production.

I rang Nick Mercer and he said that the best thing to do would be to visit his underwriting agency, and pay a visit to Lloyd's to find out how the whole system worked. Nick said he would go ahead and make all the arrangements if I agreed. To this I agreed, as I either had to learn more about it or forget it altogether.

My feeling was that if I could enlarge my farm business, then this is what I would prefer to do and forget Lloyd's, but land was expensive, having no relation to its earning capacity. By this time, the late seventies, borrowing was out of the question, as interest rates were through the roof, and inflation was still in double figures having hit 27% in 1975. My bank overdraft was still running at a relatively high level. The good news was that this long period of high inflation reduced the payments on my fixed interest mortgage to little more than pocket money.

I still had a substantial overdraft but was not concerned about it because, in theory at least, if you borrowed money at 18% interest and inflation was over 20% then you were better off at the end of the year. This only worked of course, if you used the money to generate cash in your business. Farming was still generating good profits and was valued by the government as having a huge contribution to the balance of payments - a constant thorn in the side of the Labour government through the seventies.

However, I had agreed to visit Lloyd's and looked forward to a day out. I met a local member of Nick Mercer's team, Keith Mollison, at Westbury train station, who was to accompany me for the day. Eventually we arrived at the offices of Kingsley Underwriting Agency where I was introduced to Robin Kingsley and Robert Hallam. After an initial chat they wanted to know how much I knew about the workings of Lloyd's. I confessed that I knew very little. They then went on to explain that the Lloyd's insurance market was made up of individuals such as myself, who joined various syndicates to carry out insurance business and that they were known as 'Names'.

At that time there were just over seven thousand 'Names', their affairs being managed by Members' Agents. These agencies, called Underwriting Agencies, also helped and advised on the selection of Syndicates. Syndicates tended to specialise in certain types of business, so there were Marine syndicates, Non-Marine syndicates, Aviation syndicates, Motor, Livestock, Life and so on. The syndicates themselves were run by Managing Agents, and in some cases they were also Members' Agents. They appointed an underwriter who would work at a desk, called a box, in the underwriting room.

Insurance brokers, licensed to work at Lloyd's, would bring business to the boxes, often visiting many boxes to complete 100% of a risk, with each underwriter taking a small share, which was called writing a line. Most of the syndicates had several hundred Names and the risk was shared equally among them proportionately to the amount of Premium Income a Name had committed himself to on that particular syndicate.

So the risk was spread among many members of many syndicates. Not only that, but if the risk was a large one then syndicates could re-insure a share of the risk with insurance companies outside the Lloyd's market and even abroad. As an individual member there was a Stop Loss Policy, whereby, in exchange for a premium, a share of the loss could be reclaimed. The business was all about spreading a risk as broadly and as thinly as possible.

Robin brought the discussion to a close, saying that a table for four had been booked in the Captain's room at Lloyd's, and that we should make a move. We all walked from the office in Fenchurch Street to Lloyd's where we were shown straight to our table. Over a delicious lunch, Robin and Robert were keen to learn all about my farming business back in Wiltshire. Robin thought it all sounded a bit risky to him. I thought that was funny and laughed, him being in the risk business.

Lunch was quickly over; there was no time to waste and we embarked on a tour of the underwriting room, stopping first at the Lutine Bell, which is rung at times of catastrophic loss. Then on to the loss book, open on the lectern. This book is constantly written up in beautiful handwriting, and contains details of shipping losses reported from across the world. It was a shock to read about so many ships in trouble at that moment.

We then began strolling around this vast underwriting room. Robin and Robert, who seemed to know lots of people, stopped and chatted at various boxes, and occasionally stopped to introduce me. At the box of an aviation syndicate, the underwriter introduced us to a broker who was there to renew the insurance of the Australian airline, Quantas. A lively discussion ensued until Robin moved us on to another box where we met a motor underwriter who explained that he re-insured motor policies written by various insurance companies. After meeting several other underwriters, it was time to hurry back to the office.

Back in the boardroom of the office and while drinking a welcome cup of tea, Robin suggested that if I wanted to begin underwriting on the first of January of the coming year, 1978, then there was not a moment to lose, for I would need to find someone to propose me, join syndicates and attend a Rota Committee interview, at Lloyd's, all in the next few weeks.

Robin was anxious to establish the level of premium income that I would like, bearing in mind that I would have to provide a deposit of £15,000 by way of a guarantee from my bank and a further bank guarantee of £60,000 to satisfy the Lloyd's means test. At that time, a maximum Premium Income limit of £250,000 for each individual Name, had been imposed by the Committee of Lloyd's, and we agreed that a £100,000 Premium Income would be a good starting figure.

At this stage I felt that I did not have sufficient understanding of the implications of Lloyd's membership, to be rushed into something that I might live to regret. I referred to the problem of finding someone to propose my application, as I did not know any Lloyd's members. Robin promised to loan me a list of members on a very confidential basis. This was ideal as I may find people that I knew, and would be able to talk to them about their experiences.

As Robin wound up the meeting he promised to send the underwriting results of Lloyd's as a whole for the last seven years, and also the results of the individual syndicates that we had met that day. He went on to explain that as Lloyd's has a three yearly accounting system, the latest profit and loss figures would be for the 1974 account year. At about four thirty, Keith Mollison arrived back at the office; he had had other business in the city, and we made our way to Paddington for the train home.

There was now a lot to think about and discuss with Mattie. I was pleased with the fact that I now had many months to consider the proposition. The bank manager, Tony Gosling, was very keen to assist as it was something new to him as well, and he said he would consult with head office. I also kept Ray informed on progress, not just because he was very interested and enthusiastic, but by the fact that we were now in daily contact, running the rapidly expanding bull hiring business.

The farm business was progressing fairly well; the ICI costings provided the information on which to base our farm policy decisions. They used the gross margin system which was far from perfect in that it did not allocate costs to particular enterprises. Fixed costs such as labour and machinery, depreciation, fuel and power etc. were divided over the whole acreage, the only concession being to the rough grazing area, where every three acres were treated as one.

These accounts consistently showed that the beef herd ran at a loss, but even so, made a substantial contribution to the overall farm gross margin and net farm income. This could be explained by the fact that labour and machinery were allocated to the beef herd, when in fact, the labour and machinery were necessary for the main arable enterprises. It proved time and time again that the beef herd was only viable on land not suitable for arable production and that any winter feed produced was to be in the form of a by product of the arable system.

An arable rotation had now been developed, growing wheat after one year of grass followed by a second crop of wheat on the lower land, and barley on the thinner soils on the hills. This was followed by more barley, some of which was under sown with grass for seed production in the following year. After harvesting the barley, the young grass was fertilised and was then used for the cows to graze; then during November and December, to have their calves. These arable fields proved much better for calving than the meadows or the steep rough grazing as they provided much better access to the cows by Land Rover.

The only real problem with this was the difficulty of magnesium deficiency and I found that the only sure way to avoid the 'staggers' was to feed a high magnesium cattle cob on the ground. This deficiency was caused by the huge increase in the production of grass and the availability of magnesium being the same as before and was therefore diluted. This area of arable land was again used for grazing in the spring, the cows and calves leaving their winter quarters, grazing the meadows then moving on to the new grass. They grazed here until the end of April, when it had to be shut up for the seed crop. By this time the rough grazing areas had begun to produce some spring grass and would support the cows and calves for the summer.

The threshed hay from the grass seed crop was baled and stored in the hay barn for feeding to the cows in the winter. The quality varied from year to year but it was never much better than straw, so had to be supplemented by purchased concentrates. However, I believed that this was preferable to using good arable land to produce hay or silage. In this way I was able to gradually increase the number of cows to about sixty, and still maintain the maximum arable area of crops.

Calving the cows on the new grass seed areas made it much easier to keep a watch on the animals with my Land Rover, but I always had to ensure that each cow had some of the high magnesium cobs every day. When a cow calved she would be away from the herd and would not leave her calf to come for her food with the rest of the herd, so I would drive around, find them and tip a few cobs (very large cow cake) on to the grass as close to them as possible.

One morning on the Big Down I was feeding the incalf cows with cobs, when an army helicopter landed nearby, it was Bob Morris. Bob told me that they were to take part in a NATO exercise during the next few days and did I have a barn for his men to use. I told him that the only barns were down at the farm and he asked me to hop in and go down to see. I explained that I had to find and feed some more cows and would see him at the farm in half an hour. He suggested that I put the bag of cobs in the helicopter and he would fly me to the cows. I thanked him but suggested that the aircraft would probably frighten the animals.

Down at the farm we soon decided that part of the new grain store would be a suitable shelter for the soldiers and that the four helicopters involved could park in the meadow. A problem arose when Bob said that a fuel tanker would need to go into the meadow to refuel the aircraft. As the meadow was very soft and wet I could not agree to that, so Bob said that they would park the tanker in the yard and the helicopters can fly in through the gate, a couple of feet off the ground and beneath the power lines, and that it would be good practise for the pilots.

The helicopters, tanker and a couple of army lorries moved into the farm during the afternoon. A number of soldiers made themselves comfortable in the barn and Bob introduced me to the major who told me that they did not want to interfere with the activities of the farm and we were to carry on as if they were not there. Sentries were stationed all around the buildings and the farm took on the appearance of an armed camp; the postman was not the only one to be surprised.

The next morning I had a chat with a couple of the soldiers and the major, before going off to feed the cows and afterwards to continue my ploughing with Roger. Returning for lunch I saw that all the soldiers were wearing gas masks and no one would speak to me until one of them pulled his mask to one side and

Helicopters moving pipes

snapped "can't you see that we are under gas attack?" and quickly reaffixed his mask; with that I left them to it.

All seemed back to normal on the following day until lunchtime when two Lockheed F104 Starfighters, with black German crosses on their wings, crossed the farm at low level. Bob explained to me that during the morning a reconnaissance plane had discovered their positions and the Luftwaff F104 fighters had been sent to take them out, so that they could not take any further part in the exercise for two days. I assume that it would take two days to move in replacements.

Bob now suggested that it would be good training for the pilots if they could do some useful work and was there anything that needed moving around the farm. The only thing that came to mind was the pile of plastic pipes near the house that could be transported up the hill, where we were installing a drainage system to stop the farm track from washing away. The major was delighted and got the helicopters on to it right away, beginning with a couple of pipes and gradually increasing the under slung loads as they gained experience.

This quickly turned into a competition to see who could carry the most and, at one stage, Bob set off up the hill with a huge bundle of these six metre pipes and seemed to be going well. The load then began to swing from side to side and, from a distance, it looked as though the pipes were swinging up very close to the rotor and I wished that he would drop them before they destroyed the aircraft. Bob brought them under control and lowered them to the ground where a soldier detached the load. Bob flew back down to the farm and the language was atrocious when I told him that I had been very worried about my pipes. All this was very interesting and the place seemed very quiet when they had all gone.

In the latter part of 1977, I received from Robin Kingsley, a full list of Names at Lloyd's. I could keep it for one week then return it by post. It was most interesting going through this booklet and I found that I knew of a considerable number of 'Names', and surprisingly some half dozen that I knew personally. These were mostly from the farming fraternity and I made an effort to talk with as many as possible. Of the five members that I discussed the merits of Lloyd's membership with, no one had a negative view and most were positive and enthusiastic. Two of them were particularly helpful and introduced me to their underwriting agents.

Mattie and I visited the two agencies during a week that we spent in London. We had a very interesting discussion about Lloyd's membership, but neither agency was looking for new members this year. Although Col. Jack Houghton Brown was not in the list of members, as I had half expected, I raised the subject with him during a lunch visit. He was the only person to be dead against the idea and explained that he could never contemplate handing over all his assets to strangers, which was what unlimited liability entailed.

Early in the New Year, I decided to join Lloyd's, and I informed Robin Kingsley of my decision on condition that I would only join syndicates of which he, or his fellow directors were members. I also explained as well as I could that I would prefer to be on steady, low risk syndicates, rather than high risk, high return syndicates. Robin agreed that this was a sensible approach, and certainly until I had built up a reserve within Lloyd's to act as a buffer. Robin also suggested that I take out an insurance policy, for a small premium, which would pay out in the event of a loss up to a certain level, after first paying the excess. These policies were called Personal Stop Loss or PSL, and the cost depended on how much cover was required and the level of excess.

George Davenport, from Codford, acted as my sponsor, writing to the committee of Lloyd's, proposing my membership. It was now up to Kingsley Underwriting Agencies to provide the necessary security documents and arrange for my attendance before the Rota committee at Lloyd's. This was subsequently arranged for some time in June. On the big day I arrived at Kingsley's office and spent a few minutes going through some of the questions that I might be asked. I was given the necessary paper work and sent on my way. Walking along those London streets towards Lloyd's on that fateful day, I found myself looking back to my childhood at Vineyards Farm. A small boy, listening to his big brother proudly explaining that Lloyd's of London was the largest insurance market in the world, where anything could be insured at a price and no risk was too great.

At Lloyd's I was shown into a waiting room with several other people whom I assumed were also candidates, as they were nervously shuffling their paper work. These people were called by name one at a time and disappeared through a door at the far end of the waiting room. After what seemed an age my name was called. I was shown into a large, imposing room, with a huge chandelier. There was a large desk with three men sitting on the far side, and a large wooden antique armchair for me.

The man in the middle introduced himself and the others, and explained that they represented the Council of Lloyd's. He went on to say that their main purpose was to make sure that I understood exactly what I was getting into. The three men asked me an easy question each in turn; then the man in the middle asked if I understood the meaning of Unlimited Liability. I replied that it was my understanding that I risked the whole of my personal fortune, not just the amount of my Premium Income Limit. There were a few more questions concerning my underwriting arrangements and agreements with my agents, and the three men got up and reached across the desk to shake my hand. They thanked me for coming and wished me well with my underwriting.

The Rota Committee recommended that my application should go forward. I arranged for my bank manager to provide the Bank Guarantee to Lloyd's, and I wrote a cheque to cover my entrance fee, annual subscription and legal fees. It was towards the end of November before I was notified that my election for membership by the Committee of Lloyd's had been successful.

My underwriting career began on the 1st January 1979, with a Premium Income Limit of £100,000(£380,000 at 2009 values). Security was provided by a guarantee from my bank for £75,000 secured by my ownership of half of Whitecliff Farm.

At about this time I kept my promise to take Mattie to the USA for a two-week holiday. This was booked through a specialist travel company, STITA, as an agricultural study tour, so part of the cost was a business expense. Colin had agreed to stay with Roger and Marilyn and we flew to Houston with Pan Am. Here we visited the Johnson Space Centre and Mission Control.

Some friends who had emigrated from Longbridge Deverill a couple of years earlier, spent a day showing us the sights of Houston. The next few days were spent on a bus tour of Texas, visiting farms and associated industries and staying in Austin, the state capital, then San Antonio, where we visited the Alamo. A visit was made to President Johnson's ranch where a runway for Air Force One, a Boeing 747, was situated at the back of the house. We then travelled to Fort Worth. At Fort Worth we had a day at the famous rodeo and spent an evening in the bar with some real cowboys and learnt the proper way to drink Tequila. The week was ended by a quick tour of Dallas before boarding a Braniff airways flight to Jamaica. Here we enjoyed the luxuries of the beautiful Club Caribbean on the north coast.

The journey home was quite traumatic, waiting all day at the airport for our Air Jamaica flight to London. The story was that our plane was stuck in the snow in Montreal. Eventually the airline decided to fly us to New York where our plane would arrive from Montreal to take us to London. This flight was most interesting as we flew up the eastern seaboard and saw the lights of several great cities, including New York. Prior to landing we were told that our plane was waiting at New York to take us to London.

On arrival it soon became clear that there was no plane and that we would be transferred to a hotel. This was very unpleasant as all the Jamaicans on the flight had their passports taken away, but not the white people. We had just got to our room when our tour manager phoned to say that he had arranged for us to take a British Airways flight, and to quietly make our way to a bus in the forecourt, doing our best not to wake the other passengers.

By the time we reached the terminal it was already light and minus 12 degrees. I was fascinated by the amount of snow clearing equipment that was available. However, by now we were very tired and quite relieved to board our plane, a VC10, which taxied out for take off. The plane just sat there for about ten minutes, then the captain told us that there was a fault with the Inertial Navigation System and the aircraft was not fit for a long oceanic crossing. He went on to explain that they might be able to fix it without returning to the terminal. In the event we spent two hours on the plane before we took off, and were by now just wishing to get some sleep.

But no, among the passengers were a number of people that I thought were probably Jews, the men had beards and wore skullcaps. These people were very noisy, calling to each other across the plane, and handing out food, as they were not going to eat airline food. We quietly complained to the stewardess, who explained that they were Miami Jews and that there was nothing she could do about the noise.

I just ignored the noise and switched off, but Mattie became more and more exasperated, and eventually she stood up and called for attention. I was shocked and pretended not to know her, wondering where this was going to end. The people were suddenly all quiet and Mattie told them that she did not know who they were or where they came from, and did not care. She went on to tell them that in her opinion they were not fit to travel on public transport, and for God's sake to be quiet. This was followed by lots of people standing up and clapping their hands, shouting "here here".

When the stewardess returned she wondered what had happened as it was all so quiet, then we all got some sleep.

As if that was not enough, the following year we took a January seaside holiday in Jamaica, taking a British Airways Boeing 747 from Heathrow. The flight was quite uneventful apart from the fact that we were sitting in the very last seats at the back, where the cabin narrows to just two seats each side, and the normal four seats in the middle. There is a very slight, almost unnoticeable wobble in the back of the early 747s, I don't know about the modern ones.

About three hours into the flight we saw the Captain approaching along the aisle, stopping to chat to people on the way. On reaching us he cheerily inquired how we were doing in this old wobble box. We told him that we were quite happy. I then went on to say that I had flown several times in the 747 but had never had the opportunity to see where he worked. "Haven't you really!" he exclaimed, just as if everyone had been to the cockpit. The Captain then suggested that when the film started I could make my way up. I thanked him very much and said that I would see him later.

It seemed to be ages before the film came on, then I gave it a few more minutes and made my way to the front of the aircraft. On reaching the spiral staircase I was stopped by the steward who said I was not allowed up the stairs. I explained that the Captain had invited me to the flight deck, so he picked up a phone, had a few words, then said he would take me up. At the top of the stairs the steward indicated for me to go forward to the flight deck whereupon the Captain, who was standing behind his seat, introduced himself with out-stretched arm and we shook hands vigorously.

My first thoughts on entering the flight deck was how small and cramped it was - an empty seat on the left, a co-pilot, Jim, sitting on the right and a flight engineer sitting at right angles facing a huge instrument panel on the right behind the co-pilot. We talked about the aircraft and I told the Captain that I was a farmer. He wanted to know all about that, and did I have a combine harvester? When I told him that I had a New Holland he said he had always wanted to drive a combine and could he drive mine if he let me have a go with his 747.

I was so surprised that I didn't know what to say. I think I said that he can drive my combine any time, but it was not necessary for me to 'have a go' with the aircraft, as he had put it. However he insisted, saying that I should take his seat at the controls and reassured me that the machine was on automatic so if I inadvertently touched anything it would be OK. It proved surprisingly difficult to step over the large instrument console between the two seats, which they told me consisted mostly of the Inertial Navigation System.

The Captain then leaned over me with a sheet of paper and showed me the flight plan, pointing out a change of course of 5 degrees and would I like to do that. I said that I didn't want to and they were all laughing. "Of course you can do it, and in any case Jim has control if you mess up," said the Captain. He then pointed out the instrument that showed the horizon and hence the attitude of the aircraft and told me to hold the control column; it seemed very sloppy in my hands. Switching off the automatic pilot he asked if that felt better. I told him that it felt as though the plane was in my hands. Now he told me to turn the control gently to the left, watching the horizon instrument all the time. It was amazing; I felt the plane bank gently to the left when the Captain said "OK bring it back level on the instrument," which I did.

The Captain said "well done" and asked Jim what he thought. Jim laughed and said "apart from the fact that we are now 10 degrees off course and have lost 2000 feet altitude, it was very good". This was followed by lots of laughter all round. I will never know whether I made that turn, but it certainly felt like it, or whether they were just having a laugh. However it was a most fantastic experience, which of course can never occur today. The Captain wrote my name and address on a piece of paper and promised to phone me to arrange a visit, but I am sorry to say he never did. I thanked them all and went down and joined Mattie in the back seat. I asked her if she had felt the plane turn and she said no, she hadn't noticed anything. We enjoyed our holiday in the Caribbean but for me the highlight was sitting in the Captain's seat on that 747.

CHAPTER 17

MAKING PROGRESS

During the last few years I had been using a New Holland combine and was still very impressed by its performance and reliability; much of this was due to Roger's operational ability and his maintenance. But as with all combines, losses over the sieves increased dramatically as the slope increased, particularly when harvesting across the slopes. For this reason we combined up and down the slopes where this was possible, but this still involved a considerable area, such as headlands, and much of the Big Down and Far Down being harvested across the slope and it was sickening to see the wheat and barley pouring from the back of the machine.

John Deere had recently introduced a medium output, self-levelling combine, the JD968H, which remained level across slopes up to 20% or 1 in 5. Up to this degree of slope, losses were reduced to the normal acceptable level, and if steeper slopes were crossed, the reduction in losses was still considerable. Having seen this machine at the Smithfield show in 1977, I arranged for one to be demonstrated in the steep field behind the house, harvesting a crop of Golden Promise, spring barley.

We were all very impressed, not only by the elimination of losses, but by the ability of the machine to cross the steepest slope without the usual crabbing, due to the weight being distributed more evenly between the two driving wheels. Admittedly, the

John Deere 968H harvesting on steep slope

machine was not so good at travelling up the slopes, but we considered that was not so important. I decided that it was an ideal machine for my particular farm and ordered one for the next harvest.

Previously, when harvesting steep slopes up and down, it was easy to run the tractors and trailers alongside the combine for transferring the grain. However, it was soon apparent that the trailers were in danger of overturning when working across a slope. Previous experience warned me as to how easily this could happen. The grain flowing from the auger on the combine always ended up on the lower side of the trailer, increasing its instability. This happened just the same, whether the trailer was on the lower side or the upper side of the combine. If the trailer was on the upper side, and an overturn occurred, then the consequences could be a smashed up combine harvester in the middle of harvest. We had to cope this year, by taking small loads and sometimes unloading the combine on the headland, but it was far from satisfactory.

Several trailer manufacturers were interested in my design for a self-levelling trailer, but only one was prepared to give me a fixed price for a prototype. The plan involved fixing the normal oscillating beam assembly, carrying the two wheels on each side, to two swinging arm type sub frames, pivoted at the front of the trailer and moved up and down by two hydraulic rams near the rear. These rams were to be operated by the tractor driver as making it work automatically like the combine was far too expensive.

We used this prototype for the 1980 harvest and ordered a second one for 1981. One of these trailers was exhibited at the Smithfield show and although considerable interest was shown, no orders were placed. It was probably too expensive and few farms would have as large a proportion of steep land as mine.

From a safety point of view these trailers were superb, and we found that we could cross our steepest slopes with a full load; the larger the load in the trailer, the more weight was imposed on the tractor's hitch. This had the effect of lowering the tractor's centre

Levelling trailer at work on a steep slope

of gravity. The trailers were also much easier to pull with equal load on the wheels and the absence of crabbing. It was soon apparent that I had the most efficient harvesting equipment in the area, for working on the hills. With grain at around £100 a tonne it was good to see the losses reduced.

British agriculture had now entered a period of uncertainty, with the spectre of over production clouding the horizon, not just in Britain but Europe as a whole. As part of the Common Agricultural Policy (CAP), a system of intervention buying had been introduced, whereby the government bought agricultural produce if the market price fell below a pre-determined level.

The government was committed to providing storage facilities for various products such as wheat, barley, beef, butter and wine. All this expense was referred to by a hostile press as, 'grain mountains, butter mountains' and 'wine lakes'. The plan was for the stored products to be returned to the market when the price increased above a certain level or in times of shortage. In practice this rarely happened, and stored products were sold on the world market, at way below the cost of production, upsetting world trade and having a detrimental effect on the agricultural economies of third world countries.

Intervention prices were decided at a conference of Agriculture Ministers of the various countries of the Common Market. The only remedy available to farmers was to continually cut their costs and increase production by the improved use of inputs, or, expanding their scale of operations. This accelerated the number of smaller farmers leaving the industry and their houses and buildings being sold for conversion to residential properties.

The fact that I had joined Lloyd's, and was able to produce two streams of income from my land, gave me an optimistic view of the future. It might be possible to earn enough money, without being taxed too heavily, eventually to purchase a larger farm and stay ahead of the game. My only concern was that, having committed myself to unlimited liability, my Lloyd's income was limited by my £100,000 limit of Premium Income earning between £7,000 and £10,000 in a good year.

I resolved to see if this could be increased for next year, on the basis that I might as well be hanged for a sheep, as a lamb. This was discussed with Robin Kingsley and the increase to the Bank Guarantee approved by Tony Gosling and my Premium Income Limit was raised to £150,000 for 1980.

Further discussions with Tony Gosling and Bernard King convinced me that there was plenty of collateral in my property to increase my underwriting for 1981.This was put into effect and my Premium Income limit was increased to £250,000 (£710,000 at 2009 values). This increase enabled me to join more syndicates, now seventeen in number, and enjoy a greater spread across the insurance market and reducing the chances of a significant overall loss.

There arose an opportunity to purchase 36 acres of land at Botany Farm, Bradley Road, Warminster - four fields of grassland divided by hedges, on the outskirts of town, and within easy working distance of Whitecliff. This could prove to be a good investment. As Tony Gosling was due for his annual visit I talked to him about finance and he suggested that I take a short-term loan, five years, and get the thing paid off and forgotten. He went on to tell me that I was now the second largest borrower at his branch and consequently, one of his best customers. I found a bottle of scotch and drank a little toast to 'The Bank, The Farm, Lloyd's of London and of course Tony and myself'.

As soon as the autumn drilling was completed at Whitecliff, we moved into the land at Warminster, removed the hedges, widened the access, ploughed the land and drilled winter wheat.

In January 1981 Mattie and I had another holiday in the States, taking a Cook's tour, flying to Atlanta where we spent a couple of days. At that time there had been a series of black child murders and the city was under curfew. If you were on the streets after nine in the evening you could be shot on sight. It was an extraordinary situation to look out of our hotel window and see this great city absolutely quiet and deserted. A bus tour took us to Vicksburg in Mississippi then down to New Orleans where we had a great time. From there we travelled along the coast to Florida staying one night at Tallahassee before travelling down to Treasure Island, in Florida, where we stayed for a week beside the sea. Then the bus took us back to Atlanta for the flight home.

The holiday was memorable because Thora Hird and her husband Sandy were on the trip and we spent several hilarious evenings at dinner enjoying her stories.

This was also the year when Colin left Warminster School and was very keen on joining us on the farm. His plan was to take a one-year course in agriculture at Lackham Agricultural College. He was very disappointed when he realized that his school results were not good enough. I went to see the Principle of the college and explained that Colin was definitely going to make a career in agriculture, unlike many of his students, and that he needed to do this course.

The Principle agreed and enrolled Colin on a day release course at Dinton for one year, while he was working on my farm. Then in 1983 Colin attended as a full time student, returning home on occasional weekends. I am unsure about his agricultural education, but he certainly had some fun! The following June, he answered an advert in the Farmer's Weekly applying for a position on an arable farm in Suffolk. Colin wondered if I would go with him to the interview. I expressed my opinion that it would be a good thing for him to do it on his own. He agreed, reluctantly. I helped plan his route and off he went in his old Fiesta.

After Colin had set off for Suffolk, I began to wonder if I should have gone with him, he had never driven so far away. I told myself that he must learn to stand on his own two feet. About one week later, he received news that he had got the job; he was delighted, and so was I.

Mr. Fison, where Colin was going to work in Suffolk, had a son who was also looking for a job, and Colin was afraid that I had done a deal to get him the job. He was relieved when I told him that I didn't even know Mr. Fison. Later I agreed to go to Suffolk with him to find some lodgings, enjoying a rare day out together. We decided to set out early on a Sunday morning and drive through central London, driving up Piccadilly and on past the Lloyd's building and generally seeing the sights.

1982 saw Britain involved in a serious conflict - this time in the South Atlantic. Ever since the Second World War, our country had been involved in fighting somewhere in the world almost the whole of the time, as the countries of our Empire moved towards independence. We were not so much resisting independence, as fighting to keep the peace between the various factions bent on seizing power. Our aim was for the establishment of democratic government, and an orderly transfer of power.

This was different. The British islands of the Falklands were invaded by Argentina, which had long claimed them as Argentinean territory, calling them the Malvinas Islands.

There was a very small garrison of British troops on the islands, and an Antarctic patrol ship. This ship was withdrawn because of the cost, and Argentina decided that their chance had come and invaded the islands. A very shocked Prime Minister, Margaret Thatcher, quickly asked the defence forces to organise a task force to retake the islands. I was very concerned at the time that this was taking on too much - the islands being over eight thousand miles away. Ascension Island in the South Atlantic was used as a staging post and the troops of the task force eventually made a successful landing in San Carlos Water, an inlet, partially protected by hills, and set up their Rapier, anti aircraft missile systems.

However, the Argentine Air Force, operating Douglas Skyhawks, English Electric Canberras and French Dassault Super Etendard fighters, put up a very strong defence. Several of our ships were lost to bombs and French Exocet, sea-skimming missiles. A huge loss to the land forces, was the sinking of a container ship, the *Atlantic Conveyor*; this was carrying all the heavy lift helicopters. This meant that the troops had to walk across the island to attack and take the capital Port Stanley. The only air cover available over the islands was a number of Sea Harriers based on our two through deck cruisers, *Hermes* and *Victorious*. This was the first time these vertical take off fighters had been used in combat, and they proved to be very effective but were few in number.

Britain had declared an exclusion zone around the islands to deter the intervention of the Argentine Navy. The enemy cruiser, *Belgrano*, was detected inside the zone and was promptly sunk by our nuclear powered submarine, *Conqueror*. After that the Argentine Navy stayed in their home waters.

In an extraordinary example of long-range bombing, a Vulcan V bomber attacked the runway at Port Stanley airport to stop the enemy from flying in reinforcements. The Vulcan was supported by several Victor refuelling tanker planes, both on the attacking flight and the return to Ascension Island. I think it was the longest bombing mission ever to be carried out in the world. Eventually the islands were re-taken and a larger defence force was established, together with a squadron of RAF Phantom fighters.

Ray's bull business was going very well, which kept us in close touch, and he was always wanting to know all about Lloyd's and was keen to join himself. I managed to talk him out of it until 1983. By then I had received cheques for my 1979 and 1980 account years.

So in 1983, despite my reservations as unlimited liability is a very personal commitment, I proposed Ray for membership and also increased my Premium Income limit to £450,000 (£1,089,000 at 2009 values), the maximum allowed by Lloyd's for an individual member. I was now a member of twenty-seven syndicates, and continued to protect my position with a Personal Stop Loss Policy.

During the last few years, crop yields had gradually increased putting pressure on my grain drying and storage facilities and big decisions had to be taken. In 1981 I had a plan to replace the old barn with a new building. This would provide a much larger bulk store, plus four, square drying bins of about 50 tonnes each. Storage would be increased from 250 tonnes in the old barn, to about 900 tonnes in the new building.

The old drier was to be reinstalled in the new system as it was considered to be good enough, as drying capacity was to be increased with the drying bins. Also, a grain drier can be operated through the night if the system should come under extreme pressure. If necessary, a larger drier could be installed at some future date.

At this stage, I asked the Ministry of Agriculture at Devizes to visit the farm, to make sure that the whole scheme would qualify for grant aid of 40% under the Farm Improvement Scheme. Mr. Cross arrived on the appointed afternoon and we had a look at the plans then went out into the yard to look at the site.

As we walked around, I outlined to Mr. Cross my intention to carry out the work during the spring next year so that the whole thing could be integrated with the storage and marketing of grain from the 1982 harvest. The new system could then be up and running in good time for the 1983 harvest, and avoid the usual last minute rush.

We returned to the house for a cup of tea and another look at the plans. Mr. Cross said he was impressed by the plans, and pointed out the advantages of replacing the existing barn. The necessary infrastructure was all in place - use of existing grain reception pit, access for lorries, electricity and drainage. In his opinion the whole scheme, including demolition and site clearance, would be eligible for grant aid.

Then came the bombshell - he did not know for sure, but this year could see the end of the Farm Improvement Scheme. He strongly advised me to make my application as soon as possible and get the scheme completed for this year's harvest. The thought of carrying out the project next year without the grant was unthinkable, as was the prospect of farming without the improvements.

I was now plunged into a rushed job, something I had been working to avoid. Firstly there were the financial implications, then the appointment of various contractors, and then the need to bring forward the selling and loading of grain. In the event, all went fairly smoothly until the last concrete floors were being laid, when a strike in the cement industry took us very close to harvest. David Barton, who had run the plant during the previous harvest, did a superb job running the new plant with temporary ladders and catwalks.

As well as increased capacity elevators and conveyors, a weighing machine was included in the system, so that the yield of each field could be ascertained. That year we achieved the magic, 3 tonnes an acre of winter wheat in Boar's Bottom. It was also possible to check the output of the John Deere combine, and we were achieving about 12 tonnes an hour on winter wheat, which was pretty good for a medium sized machine.

The following January, Mattie and I had an enjoyable holiday in the Caribbean, spending one week in Barbados and a second week in St. Lucia.

After a series of long haul winter holidays, Mattie and I decided that we would like to see something of Europe. Not being familiar with driving in Europe and looking forward to a relaxing holiday, after another year of hectic business activity, we plumped for a two-week coach tour. This proved to be very enjoyable and just what we needed, visiting Belgium, Germany, Austria, Switzerland and France. On the coach we made some new friends, Beryl and David Monk, people from Detroit, who had emigrated some years before to work for the Ford Motor Company.

We were spending a day in Lauterbrunnen when Mattie decided to take a large cable car trip up over the mountains to Murren. I have a particular fear of cable cars so she went with Beryl and David and I stayed on the ground. Looking around, I saw a mountain railway stretching up into the mountains from the village. Realising that I probably had about four hours to fill, I bought a couple of cans of beer and a sandwich and set off up the mountain, following the railway.

After about an hour of gentle climbing, I sat down to admire the fantastic view and enjoy my beer and sandwich. A few minutes later, two back packers came up and, saying hello, we were all surprised that we spoke the same language. With that they dropped their packs and sat down for a chat, introducing themselves as Richard Baruc from New York and Stephen Simmons from Colorado. They told an extraordinary story. Having finished high school, they were heading for summer camp on a bus, when they saw a poster, advertising the recently introduced airline, *People's Express* and flying to London for £99. They immediately left the bus and went to the airport, flew to London, then took a ferry to France.

The boys were concerned that they would not have enough money to fly back to the States. As harvest time was about a month away, I suggested that they might like to work on my farm. I would guarantee that they would earn enough for the flight, and we would provide food and accommodation. There was always plenty of work available at harvest - collecting bales, shovelling grain and they might even get to drive a tractor.

The American boys arrived about two weeks early and were very hungry and short of cash. One Sunday afternoon, before harvest was in full swing, I suggested that they might like to watch a game of village cricket at Kingston Deverill. I gave them directions and they walked off filled with enthusiasm. They were soon back and seemed not to have enjoyed the experience. We had a laugh as I tried to explain the intricate rules of the game and they were still not impressed. They proved to be great fun and reasonably good workers. Colin, who was now working on the farm, took them to pubs, parties and various village hall dances. There was also an occasional trip to the beach when farming allowed the time.

A small problem arose - the more money they earned, the more they spent, so I began keeping some money back to save for their flights. They were in no rush to get home as they were having such a good time. Mattie found out that their parents had no idea where they were and was horrified. Eventually, she stood over them, and made them write home. Stephen left at the end of August, and Richard stayed until almost the end of September.

They helped to make it a very memorable harvest indeed.

CHAPTER 18

AMERICAN ADVENTURES

Another parcel of land came up for sale, opposite my land in Bradley Road - only fourteen acres, but too good to miss. A long planned extension to the house was at last carried out in 1984, which involved building a new utility room, double garage and garden room or sun lounge. This was done while Colin was in Suffolk and was completed in time for a small party for my birthday. Colin returned to work on the farm for a couple of years and was joined for the 1985 harvest by Sarah Fritche, from Cornwall, introduced to us by Mattie's friend Joan Finch. Sarah looked after the grain drier and helped with the cows and calves and proved to be a fun loving member of the team, and we were all sorry when she returned to Cornwall. It was towards the end of November that I decided that I needed to get away from it all and have a little time on my own; a complete change.

Flying to Detroit, in time for Thanksgiving, I stayed with Dave and Beryl for a few days. Dave had an old pick up with a snow plough on the front; he drove it onto the ice on Lake St. Clare where we borrowed a motorised auger, drilled a large hole in the ice and did some fishing. We didn't catch any fish as probably there was too much noise from all the people and vehicles. I wondered how they knew that the ice was thick enough to carry all the vehicles.

Another treat was a visit to the stadium to watch an ice hockey match between the Detroit Red Wings and a team from New York. Dave took me to the Ford factory where he worked, showing me around the design and development department. Here cars were being designed with the aid of computers. Dave then took me to the testing department where switches were tested to destruction by switching them on and off many thousands of times.

It was soon time to move on and Dave took me across to Windsor, Ontario, where I caught a train to Toronto. I stayed in Toronto a couple of nights then took a train to Vancouver. The trip was amazing - two days and three nights, firstly through woods among frozen lakes and along the north shore of Lake Superior, to Thunder Bay. Here I saw huge grain storage elevators, holding the grain until the spring thaw would bring the grain ships in via the St. Lawrence Seaway. The train then headed for the prairies where I saw combine harvesters harvesting maize in the winter sun, but having to plough through at least a foot of snow. Other than that it was just snow, the occasional grain elevator beside the track, and more snow.

The highlight of the trip should have been the stretch through the Rocky Mountains, but this took place at night. However it was moonlight and it was like party time in the dome cars. We went over Kicking Horse Pass and the Spiral Tunnels, then Roger's Pass and down the Fraser Canyon to Vancouver. There I was met by Chris's sister and her husband and stayed with them for a few days, having a good time and seeing the city.

I took a Greyhound bus to Los Angeles - this meant crossing the border into the United States. At this point there were about a dozen passengers on the bus, some were a bit dodgy looking and roughly dressed. We all went into the customs building and were asked a few questions, passports were examined and stamped and then it was back on the bus. The bus very soon set off with only five of us on board, the others must have been denied access to the U S. Before long I decided to get off the bus at Seattle where I stayed for a few days. It was a very interesting city but I soon became bored with my own company. I spent my birthday on my own and, with Christmas coming, I was a little homesick so I flew home, having learnt to appreciate what I had.

The committee of Lloyd's had, in the meantime, increased the Premium Income Limit for an individual to £600,000 (£1,152,000 at 2009 values) for the 1985 year of account. By committing all my assets, including Manor Farm, to the bank, Tony was able to provide the necessary guarantees. The following year Lloyd's of London again increased these limits, this time to £1,000,000 (£2,079,000 at 2009 values). After discussions with Tony and Bernard, it was agreed that there was plenty of collateral to support the higher level of guarantees required from the bank as the land was continually increasing in value. So, for the 1986 year of account and thereafter, I was taking £1,000,000 of premium income and was a member of sixty two syndicates. With this level of underwriting I felt much more secure. My feeling was that if one or two syndicates suffered a major loss, then there would be plenty of profit from others to cover it. As added security, it had remained my policy, only to join syndicates that directors of my agency were members of.

At this stage it looked as though my Lloyd's income could double my income from the farm. If this happened then I could afford to pay over the odds for a larger and better farm. However I decided to wait and see; it was also important to wait and see what Colin wanted to do.

The property market was very strong in the mid eighties, and I was looking for ways to reduce my indebtedness to the bank. It was government policy to permit planning applications to develop redundant farm buildings and convert them to houses. I calculated that the buildings at Manor Farm could be worth more to me as cash than the limited income I received from Ray's bull business.

I then remembered that during the negotiations with the National Trust to sell them the Manor House, a number of restrictions were imposed on my use of the buildings. As I remembered it, there were three important ones - no keeping of pigs, no making of feeding silage and no structural alterations. At first I thought these would scupper my plans, but after consulting with my solicitor, he advised that the original agreements had been worded in such a way that they were not a problem.

An architect was engaged to survey, draw plans and obtain planning permission. Seven houses with garages were shown on the plan, with very little alteration to the outside of the brick and slate buildings. I had been assured by some of the district councillors that planning permission would be forthcoming, despite the intense opposition in the village. My architect and I addressed a meeting attended by all the villagers, where we hoped to gain some support; in fact only one person supported the scheme.

The District Council arranged a site meeting so that village people could express their views and ask questions. Several people pointed out that the buildings were in constant agricultural use until a few weeks before, so did not qualify for development as redundant farm buildings. This was of course true, but it had no effect on the District Council's decision, and planning permission was granted.

The question now arose: do I sell the site as it is, or should I develop the project myself? I was very keen to create a company to carry out the conversions and sell the individual dwellings. The argument against this course of action was the present value of the site, about £150,000 and the estimated cost of the project, about £350,000 - all extra borrowed money. This meant that the finished properties would need to sell for an average of at least £80,000 to make it worthwhile.

If the market continued to rise there was a possibility that the scheme would work, but if the market fell before the work was complete, then I would be in trouble. The risk was too much at that time and I sold the site to a builder for £160,000. The market did suffer a major reverse and it was many years before the project was completed. I lost my place as the second biggest borrower at my branch of the bank, and for the first time since I began farming, I had money in the bank.

Colin worked on the farm until July 1987, when he went to work on an arable farm in Queensland, returning to work at

Whitecliff towards the end of May 1988. On his first night at home he went to the 'Woolpack' to see if his old bike was still outside, where he had left it ten months before! What a hope? Mattie and I had a beach holiday in Yugoslavia and then I went to Texas in October with George Sheppard, leaving Roger and Colin to finish the autumn drilling. George was a drinking mate at the 'George' and the 'Woolpack' and owned the garage at Sutton Veny. I was always interested in his war stories. He had been in the RAF and flew Typhoons during the D Day landings and the battles across North West Europe.

I had watched a TV program about something called the Confederate Air Force in Texas. This consisted of World War II veterans who restored WW2 aircraft, putting on an air show every year to re-enact the important air battles of that time. George and I were having a drink one summer evening at the 'George', and I told him about the TV programme. George was very enthusiastic and said that he had a mate in the travel business, and would find out where and when the air show would be staged.

A couple of weeks later George told me it was at Harlingen, near the Mexican border in Texas, and he seemed keen to go. I said that it was a busy time for me and I would have to think about it. Colin was home working on the farm and said that he was happy for me to go; he and Roger would deal with the autumn drilling. I decided that this would be good training for Colin and made up my mind to go to Texas.

After a pleasant flight from Gatwick on a Boeing 747, George and I arrived in Houston. When asked the purpose of our visit by the immigration officer, and after telling her that we had come to see the air show, she said that it was last week! We were a little concerned that we had made a mistake and we soon discovered that there was an air show at Houston last week, but the one we had come for was at Harlingen, about 350 miles to the south. Not only that, but the officer noticed that my address was a farm so she made me report to the agricultural department. George laughed when they fumigated me and sprayed my shoes, something that I had become used to.

Next morning, we collected our hire car and set off for Harlingen, staying the night in a Sheridan Hotel. A great evening was had drinking and talking to fellow guests. As the air show was on for four days we decided to look around for a closer place to stay. We found a lovely little motel, just next to 'Ted's Diner' on South Padre Island, a long strip of land just off the coast, accessed by a long arched bridge, with signs warning of low flying pelicans. The whole population of the island had been evacuated a few weeks before, when hurricane Gilbert had struck, and several roads were still blocked by huge drifts of sand. That was the reason that all the buildings were on stilts to allow the sea to pass underneath.

The air show was fantastic, with so much to see, especially the brilliantly choreographed air battles. There were hundreds of WW2 aircraft on static display and it was possible to go on board some of the larger planes. I was lucky to have the opportunity to board a B17 Flying Fortress and try out all the gun positions, except that of the tail gunner, I was too big to squeeze in. Among the planes on display were a Spitfire and a Messerschmitt 109; these later took part in the flying display representing the Battle of Britain. George was in his element talking to his American counterparts about their flying experiences. Standing under the wing of a De Havilland Mosquito, we overheard a conversation; one of the Americans expressed the opinion that the Mosquito was not much good and was made of wood. We introduced ourselves and agreed that the aircraft was made of wood and went on to explain that it was one of the finest and the fastest aeroplanes of the World War. They were delighted to meet us and enjoyed a long chat in the shade of the planes.

This was where I met the pilot of one of the B36 Peacemakers that had flown over us at Claverton on their round the world flight all those years before. We had a long discussion about his experiences and he described how these giant planes had been rushed into service in that tense period of the Cold War. He went on to tell us how mechanically unreliable they were, and very vulnerable to attack by enemy fighters. They had been introduced

George standing in front of a Mustang

as a stopgap until the six-jet B47 Stratojet and the eight-jet B52 Stratofortress were ready. It is disappointing that not one of these extraordinary B36 planes has been preserved in flying condition, but I believe that there are a couple on static display somewhere in the States; I must find out where.

The air show was staged at a commercial airport, which caused some amusing announcements by the commentator on the public address system, such as. "I'm sure you good folks won't mind if we hold the show for a few minutes, while we launch South West Airlines to Dallas-Fort Worth." The Boeing 737 then took off through the smoke from the last battle. Then again, "Sorry folks, but we are going to hold the show while we retrieve American Airlines coming in from San Francisco, I'm sure you won't mind." The Boeing 727 then came in escorted by WW2 fighters. The passengers must have had quite a surprise.

One of the days was marred by the crash of a Martin Marauder, killing the WW2 pilot and his wife. The plane was one of three that flew in formation down the flight line in front of the crowd, flying straight and level. As the three planes turned to the left at the end of the field, the Marauder just dived into the ground, sending up a huge pall of black smoke. The commentator said a few words paying tribute to the pilot and his wife and saying that the show would go on, as that was what they would have wanted.

The re-enactment of the Battle of Pearl Harbour, which is so important in the American public mind, was the most impressive and had the most aircraft in the sky at any one time. There seemed to be an enormous number of Japanese planes, torpedo bombers coming in at low level, bombers at a few thousand feet, and dive bombers, screaming down from a great height. Add to this apparent mayhem, American fighters taking off and mixing it with the attackers, plus the smoke and noise. It was all very exciting. Then, amongst all this, some B17 bombers came in to land, one with only one wheel down, flares were fired and it climbed back into the sky.

The pyrotechnics in the battles were very impressive, and on the last day they must have piled up everything they had left, in the middle of the airfield. Then high in the clear sky, a loan B29 Super Fortress approached the field and the whole thing blew up forming a huge mushroom cloud. Rumour had it that this re-enactment of the atomic attack had prompted a letter of condemnation from the Japanese government.

After the show George and I had a couple of days on the endless, deserted beach on South Padre island before driving back to Houston. On the way, we came across a roadblock. Police cars were parked across the highway, with a small gap for traffic to pass through. Heavily armed police were leaning over them. I said to George, who was driving, "Take to the grass George". He replied "Shut up, you silly bugger, you've been watching too much television". Had anyone taken to the grass I think they would have been blown to bits.

George slowed the car and stopped next to a waiting police officer, who asked to see his driver's licence. "It's in my bag in the boot," said George. "In the boot!" repeated the officer, "I suppose you mean the trunk". He had realized that we were English and not who they were looking for and told us to get on up the road.

Back in Houston we decided to spend a day at the Johnson Space Centre before flying back to Gatwick. Here we saw the enormous Saturn 5, the rocket that made possible the Apollo moon landings and one of its five massive rocket motors. A complete lunar lander was on display, together with a command module and various Gemini and Mercury space capsules. We thoroughly enjoyed our ten days in the States, and I later heard that George had said that it was the best holiday he had ever had.

Back to reality once more - running the farm and gradually coming to the conclusion that a larger farm was necessary if we were to remain in the business. Colin was committed to a career in agriculture, but he was not content to just take over the farm from me. He was convinced that Whitecliff was too steep and awkward to be efficient enough in the future, even if this meant that he worked on or managed a farm for someone else. Mattie and I agreed that we would move if Colin could find a suitable farm and left it to him to find one while we went off to California on a yet another agricultural study tour.

We flew to Pheonix, Arizona, where we stayed the night. A

The Saturn 5 Moon Rocket

coach took us to stay the next night at Grand Canyon. The first sight of the canyon was awesome and we could not resist taking a helicopter flight to get a better view. I can't say that I enjoyed it but it was not to be missed. Our bus then took us to Las Vegas where we stayed at the Flamingo Hilton for one night. One night too many as far as I was concerned, and vowed to myself never to return. We then made a long drive to Yosemite National Park, staying for one night at the Gateway Inn, then had a few hours to gaze at the wonders of the park, snow covered mountains and sky-high waterfalls before setting off for San Francisco.

Three nights were spent in that incredible city, seeing the sights, riding the trams and giving Mattie a chance to catch up on some shopping. For me the highlight of my visit to San Francisco came after a number of us had spent the evening at Fisherman's Wharf, eating and watching hilarious street entertainers. Everyone piled into a taxi to return to our hotel, but there was no room for me, so Mattie began to get out but I said to stay where she was and that I would be back at the hotel almost as soon as they were. They set off, so I waited for another one.

Along came a big black Ford V8 with a very chatty driver. When he realised that I was leaving in the morning, he told me that there were lots of things to see and do, and he took me on a high-speed tour of the city. The driver asked if I would like to do the jumps, I was unsure as to what he meant. Then he said, "You know, the movies, Bullitt, Steve Mc Queen and all that". I can't remember what I said but I found myself at the top of the hill where the tramcars run and the driver stopped, saying that we had to wait for the lights at the bottom of the first block to turn to red.

At that instant they turned red! He slammed his foot down and we roared down the steep street, reaching the lights just as they turned green; the car bucked as we crossed the street and took off, landing some way down the next steep bit. The lights at the bottom were again red, but his foot was hard on the accelerator, and as we reached the crossing the lights turned green, and we took off, landing slightly off course and with a great screeching of tyres. With his foot hard down again the experience was repeated and we hurtled through the lights just as they turned green. We landed, nearly straight this time, and slowed down to near normal speed.

I could feel my heart pounding and my hair seemed to be standing on end. I recovered as we descended the crookedest street in the world. Then we made our way to the hotel, at high speed again, and screeched to a halt, only inches from our bus. What an experience! I thanked him and gave him a twenty-dollar tip, and he roared off in a cloud of blue smoke from his rear wheels.

It was now time to visit some farms - dairy farms close to San Francisco and fruit farms further south. There were huge fields of fruit trees of various sorts, all planted neatly in lines, often as far as the eye could see, and they were in straight lines whichever way you looked at them. More interesting to me was our visit to the Harris ranch, near Coalinga. It was a feedlot on a grand scale, where thousands of one-year-old calves were bought in, to be fattened, mostly for the Japanese market.

There were 90,000 cattle, all in outdoor pens, divided by long feeding lanes, where the feed was conveyed into mangers from large mixer lorries, continuously hauling feed from their own feed mills. It was fascinating to watch girls on horseback, moving the cattle from one pen to another and also sorting the cattle that were ready to go. I believe that the horses were a special breed called 'Cutting Horses' - either that or they were very well trained. The business also owned a hotel and service station where we stayed for one night just off the highway.

Our next stop was a large dairy farm near Los Angeles, where illegal Mexican immigrants milked 9,000 cows. The pens of cows covered a huge area, again dissected by feeding lanes. Milking parlours were provided at intervals, each serving about 500 cows. All this was made possible by the kind climate, which allowed the manure to dry quickly and provide a soft bed for the cows to lie on. We were told about a disaster that occurred when all this dry manure under the cows became very wet one hot, stormy night and produced masses of ammonia, killing many of the cows. The manure was cleared away when it had accumulated to quite a depth, and bulldozed into huge hills and abandoned.

We were told that this area where these large dairy farms were established was, once again, threatened by developers as Los Angeles continued to expand. The cows had already moved from an area that had been used to build Disneyland, and they were considering having to move even further east.

I was pleased to see that JCB had broken into the American machinery market; the farm was operating eight of the company's Loadalls, mostly in the feed preparations. The feed was bought in from all corners of the States and consisted, to a large measure, of by products from the food industry.

San Diego was our next stop, where Mattie went off to Mexico for the day and I went to the huge naval base. A day was spent at Sea World before travelling north to spend a night on the old *Queen Mary*, which is now a floating hotel at Long Beach. There were some people in our party who had crossed the Atlantic in this enormous ship many years before. Opposite the *Queen Mary* is the *Spruce Goose*, the giant wooden flying boat, built by Howard Hughes, and flown only once. I wanted to see this but the exhibition was closed during our short stay. Then we travelled north again to Los Angeles, where we saw the sights of Hollywood and Universal Studios before flying home via Denver.

Back home on the farm everything was fine and the spring work was all up to date.

CHAPTER 19

MOMENTOUS EVENTS

While we were away, Colin had obtained particulars of several large arable farms, one of which he was very keen to see. This was Bank House Farm, Pode Hole, near Spalding in the fens, so we made arrangements to visit as soon as possible. We were impressed by the quality of the land, but the several workers' houses and the main farmhouse were badly damaged by subsidence caused, we were told, by the shrinking of the fenland soil. As we knew little about that type of soil, we contacted the local ADAS office and arranged to meet their local advisor and a soil scientist at the farm for a day. They were most reassuring as to the agricultural potential of the land, tricky to work but very productive. There was a depth of soil that we, on the chalk, could only dream about. We decided to put in an offer to the agents, Bernard Thorp and Partners. I had a day out with Mattie and visited the farm once again; the wheat looked superb but Mattie was not impressed by the house or the area.

My only concern at this stage was the bad news from Lloyd's. My agents had written to say that the 1987 and 1988 accounts were likely to show a loss and would probably need some money at some stage. Discussing the situation on the telephone, I gained the impression that, although serious, it was no worse than the losses in the 1981 and 1982 years. I survived those years, paying the 1981 losses from reserves and sending a hefty cheque in the following year, claiming on my Stop Loss Policy, and claiming a substantial repayment from the Inland Revenue. This is called trading through the bad times and it gave me confidence that with my spread throughout the market, I could do so again. Knowing that I would have to provide some money to Lloyd's over the next few years was making me more cautious about buying a larger farm. Our offer of £1,700,000 for Bankhouse Farm was not acceptable and we were not prepared to increase it. We invited the agent, Mr Buteel, to Whitecliff to give us a guide as to what to expect if we sold. Now that there were no longer any buildings at Manor Farm, the land was incorporated with Whitecliff.

He advised us to sell by auction, with a guide price of £1,300,000, and sell the Warminster land separately. We were anxious to involve our local auctioneers, David Millard of Cooper and Tanner, and so they were appointed as joint agents to sell Whitecliff Farm and Cooper and Tanner were appointed to sell the Warminster land as sole agents.

Full sale particulars were produced and a date arranged for the auction of Whitecliff Farm when, one evening, I had a phone call from a Mrs. Thomas. She said that she was prepared to pay the guide price for the property, but did not want to deal with agents. I thanked her, and explained that an auction had been arranged, and looked forward to seeing her there. The next evening she again phoned and said she did not want to deal with agents, and did not want to bid at an auction, and increased her offer by £100,000. Again I explained that we would like to sell by auction, as it was all arranged, and thanked her for her offer.

At around the same time we heard that Jim White had put Keysley Farm, at Monkton Deverill, on the market. The farm had been owned by the White family since 1906. This farm was larger than Whitecliff and did not have very much steep land. It also had good access from the A303 at Willoughby Hedge, so we expected it to sell quickly at around the asking price of £2,000,000.

The solicitor for Keysley was Richard Baxter, a partner in the same office as Bill Knowles, so we quickly learned that Mrs. Thomas had been to Keysley and was obviously interested. Our solicitor assured us that there would be no conflict of interests in his office, and a Chinese wall now divided the two partners.

Later in the week Mrs. Thomas phoned again and increased her offer to £1,500,000. We had quite a long friendly conversation and I was finding it very difficult to turn down her offer. Mattie, Colin and I, after a lot of discussion, decided that if she rang again with a new offer, we would sell. In the back of our minds was the thought that if we pushed her too hard, she may buy Keysley Farm instead.

The next evening was spent in trepidation in case the phone should ring. When it did, it was Mrs. Thomas. She enquired if I had changed my mind. When I said "no", she said would another £100,000 change it? I said, "try me", and she said her new offer was £1,600,000 and that was it, no more, and she would not buy at the auction. So I said. "OK the place is yours, subject to various aspects of the transfer," and went on to explain that it was a working farm and there was much to discuss. That momentous evening was Friday the 9th of June 1989, and Mrs. Thomas promised to see me early next week.

Mrs. Thomas was quick off the mark the following week; she arrived with Mark Houghton Brown, grandson of Col. Jack. She explained that Mark would take care of everything agricultural, and that she would like to move in as soon as possible. I said that she could move in as soon as she paid the full amount and Bill Knowles was satisfied with the legalities. Mrs. Thomas said that she could pay in about one week. I replied, "OK, we will find somewhere to live".

We then began discussions with Mark about the agricultural implications. He told us that Mrs. Thomas needed the cattle sheds and grazing land for her horses, so we would need to sell the cows and calves fairly soon, and that he would buy the standing crops and deal with the harvest. However it soon became clear that Mark was not prepared to pay enough for the crops. We decided that Colin, Sarah, (who was now Colin's serious girlfriend), and myself would do the harvesting and retain possession of the grain stores until the end of December.

Mattie and I quickly found a suitable house to rent, and with Colin we moved to Packsaddle Way, Frome. This was, despite the apparent fast movement of events, almost exactly one month after selling the farm. Some good news arrived from my underwriting agents, who had now changed their name to Limestreet Underwriting Agencies. 1986 year of account had produced a profit of £102,000 and they enclosed a cheque for £50,000, the remainder being paid into my reserve account. The letter explained why so much had been retained to help fund the projected losses over the next two years.

The sad part of our move involved our black Labrador, Mutley, who got into trouble with our new neighbours, running through their gardens. When he was kept indoors he whined all day. After the freedom of the farm, we felt that it was cruel to make him stay at Frome, so we took him back to Whitecliff and gave him to Mrs. Thomas, who was delighted, and he lived happily ever after.

Sarah got a job at Whitecliff looking after the horses, and came to lodge with us in Frome. A sale of the cows and calves was arranged with Cooper and Tanner, and plans were put in hand to have a further sale on the property, after harvest, to sell all the machinery and rubbish that had collected in the previous twenty four years. An auction of the two lots of land at Warminster was held one afternoon in the 'Old Bell' and afterwards the four of us returned to Packsaddle Way to drink champagne on the balcony above the garage.

Colin and I were quite busy during this period, preparing the combine, grain drier and grain stores for the coming harvest; any spare time being spent travelling to Lincolnshire to view farms.

Mattie was on her own most of the time and she appeared to be a bit depressed. Then Sarah told me that Mattie had taken very little part in the move from Whitecliff, just sitting around instead of packing things, and she wondered if she was all right. She also told me how bad her driving was. I resolved to spend as much time with her as possible, going for long walks in the daytime, and going out at night. After harvest we joined an art class at Frome College.

Harvest time seemed to be more fun than ever, maybe because there were no crops to be planted and no cattle to look after. Colin drove the combine, Sarah drove a tractor with the levelling trailer, and I operated the grain drier and put the grain in store.

Sarah did an exceptional job and only got really scared on one occasion. That was on the steepest part of Pump House Field at Manor Farm. When following the combine, the tractor had to cross the tramlines, which were pretty deep that year, and each time the front wheels hit one, they bounced down the slope about a metre. When Colin returned across the slope he could see that something was wrong. He went to investigate and found Sarah in tears, and her little white hands were locked on solidly to the steering wheel. After that Colin drove the combine to the trailer until the steep part was finished and Sarah was able to continue.

After harvest we prepared the machinery for the sale, which was to be held in Fowl House Field, on the wheat stubble. Our Roadless Teleshift material handler could not be included in the sale because we needed it to load grain until the end of the year. The sale, generally, was a disappointment, the rubbish and small items sold well, but the good, well- maintained machines, such as the tractors, plough, and the two self levelling trailers only just made the reserve.

The combine which had now completed four harvests, failed to reach its reserve The new grain drier, having done two seasons also failed to sell, but we managed to sell it soon afterwards. We obtained permission from Mrs. Thomas to put the combine in the barn on top of the hill. Then, Mrs. Thomas, having borrowed the Teleshift on a regular basis, decided that she would like to buy it. We told her that we would sell the machine to her when we had finished with it, if she still wanted it.

Colin then went to work for Strattons at Kingston Deverill while I sold and loaded the grain at Whitecliff. Most of my time was spent at home with Mattie or travelling to Lincolnshire to look at farms. It was agreed that I would look at as many farms as I could, and if I found one that was worth another look, Colin would take a day off and come too. On one occasion I spent four or five days in Lincolnshire, staying at a hotel in Branston and meeting with land agents and farmers.

The one thing that was troubling us was the uncertainty of the proposed nitrate free zones; as yet there were no detailed proposals to consider. Most of the farms that I looked at seemed to have at least one water extraction point run by Anglian Water. If nitrogen applications were to be limited or banned in the areas where water was extracted, then agricultural production would be severely restricted.

The best farm that I found was at Maidenwell, on the Lincolnshire Wolds, but it was just too big, bearing in mind the Lloyd's situation; Colin was very keen on it and got on very well with the Farm Manager. The auctioneers were not prepared, at this early stage, to sell in lots: it eventually sold as a whole.

The Lincolnshire Wolds were similar to our chalk downs here in Wiltshire, but I suspect contained slightly better soil. I was told about another farm that was not yet on the market, at Withcall, close to Maidenwell. A council lane went right through the middle of the land, so I drove along and had a good look; it looked like just what we wanted. I asked the auctioneers to send particulars as soon as possible. They arrived in a few days and I made an appointment with the owners. Colin took a day off and off we went.

We visited the house and buildings and were not very impressed, but we had a chat with a tractor driver, who showed us around the machines - three combines and crawler tractors among others. He told us an incredible story - the crawlers were used at harvest time to push the combines up the steep slopes. We had not yet seen any slopes and until then had thought there were none.

We then went for a walk over the land, armed with the particulars and the map. As I had described the land to Colin, it was good level land as far as you could see from the road. We walked across and found that the whole length of the farm fell away very steeply after a short distance from the road. This was as steep as the worst of Whitecliff and totally unsuitable for efficient arable farming in the uncertain future. We then went across the road and found that the land, out of sight of the road, was similar but not quite so steep.

We made the long drive home talking about a wasted day.

CHAPTER 20

ANOTHER FARM

By this time there seemed to be fewer farms for sale, and, because of the nitrate situation, we lost our enthusiasm for farming in Lincolnshire and decided to wait for more information. This gave me an opportunity to manage the investment of our cash asset, which now totalled over two million pounds. Now, with the aid of my newly installed car phone, I could to keep track of interest rate changes.

The plan was to keep the money available for our own business, in case something came up, and maximise the earnings by moving the cash around, often investing it just overnight.

While all this was going on momentous events were unfolding around the world. The stranglehold over the Eastern European countries by the Soviet Union was breaking down and a score of new democratic countries were emerging as the Soviet Empire collapsed. East German citizens tore down the Berlin Wall as the Cold War came to an end; I never ever thought that this would happen in my lifetime. I even recall a discussion at Packsaddle Way about the possibility of purchasing a large tract of arable land in one of the Eastern European countries, such was the euphoria at that time.

In the meantime, the owner of our rented house in Frome came to see us, to tell us that he wanted to sell, and to offer it to us before handing the sale to an agent. We had already considered that the house was worth about £200,000 when we moved in, but the property market was now falling, and after a period of negotiation we bought the property for £145,000 and considered that we had a bargain.

Roger Singleton, from Savills, had been in contact with us regarding Keysley Farm, in case we were interested, but not having heard anything for some time, we had assumed it had been sold. Then in the middle of November I saw my old friend, Bert Legg, and he enquired how we were proceeding with finding a farm? I told him that we had given up for the winter and were awaiting developments.

Bert told me that Keysley was still for sale, and that the asking price had been reduced substantially. I discussed this with Mattie, Colin and Sarah when I arrived home, and it was agreed that I should speak to Jim White and find out if Keysley was still on the market?

Jim informed me that he had sold it to a farmer near Warminster for £1,700,000 but nothing was signed, and as the farmer could not proceed with the purchase until he had sold his own farm, Jim suggested that if I came up with the money, I could have the farm. I quickly arranged with Jim for us to look at the farm on the following day. Colin now knew the farm fairly well, as he had been crop spraying there on several occasions, whilst working for the spraying contractors.

That Saturday, we walked the length and breadth of the land and were generally impressed by the quality of the soil, in the main, much better than it had been at Whitecliff. Jim showed us the commercial grain store and explained how it worked. About 5,000 tonnes of barley was being stored for Continental Grain, from Southampton, in the converted cubicle building which Jim had built for 150 dairy cows some years before.

After chatting the whole thing through, we decided to see Jim again, and try to buy the place. Colin and I went to Keysley on the Sunday evening and the deal was done. We paid the asking price for the farm, wrote a cheque for the deposit and agreed to complete the purchase and take possession on the 1st February 1990.

We agreed that we would each ask a local machinery dealer to

Keysley Farm 1990

negotiate a price on our behalf, for all the equipment on the farm. It was the 19th November 1989, and we were now back in business with Colin taking a much more positive role in the management, and discussing the possibility of his joining the partnership, now to be called 'Keysley Farm Partners'.

We then had to consider where we were to live? The farmhouse at Keysley was in a reasonable state of repair and decoration, and it was decided that Colin and Sarah should move in as soon as possible, fixing the date for the 1st February. They were already making plans to be married in June, and we felt that it was important to have someone living at the farm.

If Mattie and I were to move into the farmhouse, we felt it would be inevitable that we would be moving out within a few years, as Colin took on an increasing share of the management. Mattie and I decided that we would stay at Frome while the cottage at Keysley was repaired.

A new roof, new kitchen, and a central heating system were necessities. The Warminster builders, Culverhouse and Co. were employed accordingly and we planned to move in some time during June. The previous owner of our house in Frome, who manufactured pine furniture, supplied our new pine kitchen.

Jim White had planned to remove all the barley from the grain store before we took over, and discussed hiring another JCB Loadall to speed up the loading. We agreed to assist by using our Teleshift, and the job was completed in a few days. A continuous procession of lorries were reversed into the store and were loaded by the two machines; one loading from one side, and one loading from the other. The lorries were weighed in and out by Peter White; the nett weights being totalled up at the end of each day, and sent by fax to Continental in Southampton.

All this proved to be very useful experience for us in handling large quantities of grain and using the weighbridge. One thing we quickly became aware of was a severe infestation of Saw Tooth Grain Beatle, which reminded me of my experience, moving into Whitecliff all those years before. It would require a thorough cleaning and spraying with insecticide before the store could be refilled with barley.

Continental were keen to continue the contract to store barley, and promised to send someone from Southampton, for the first few days of the coming harvest, to show us how the system worked and what would be required. They told us that they purchased the barley direct from the farms, and it would arrive at Keysley, dry and ready to put straight into the store.

Our job was to weigh and sample each lorry load, and to reject any loads above 15% moisture, and below 63 kilograms per hectolitre. We were also to reject loads infested with harmful insects or excessive admixture such as chaff or weed seeds. A quantity of twelve inch, perforated, black plastic land-drainage pipes, together with fans, were available for setting up a ventilation system These were important to cool the grain as quickly as possible preventing build up of damaging insects.

Consideration was given, at this stage, to handling of our first harvest at Keysley. We had taken over the growing crops of winter wheat and barley, and planned to plant the rest of the arable land with spring barley, oil seed rape and peas. There was a mobile grain drier which we decided to sell and replace with a much larger, permanent installation.

We asked T. H. White Ltd. to design a system, incorporating the existing reception-pit and grain cleaner, together with a new second-hand Lawe Denny mixed flow drier. After looking at several driers that were for sale, we eventually bought one from Trent Grain, at Burton on Trent, who were closing down. The drier was eventually delivered and installed, together with a new elevator and two screw conveyors from Whitecliff.

The existing storage for our own crops consisted of five large round silos. These we extended in height to hold about 200 tonnes each. All the barley would be sold to Continental and weighed into the large grain store.

About one week before we were due to take possession of Keysley Farm,, I was enjoying a relaxing time at our house in Packsaddle Way. Colin was at work with the spraying contractors and Sarah was at Whitecliff working for Mrs. Thomas, helping with the horses. A dreadful storm with very high winds struck the country, and I spent most of the afternoon trying to stop our neighbour's fence from crashing through our French windows.

It was the worst storm that I could remember and I was relieved when Colin and Sarah arrived home safely. They told us that there were hundreds of trees blown down and many roads were blocked. The area around Longleat had been devastated, with huge beech trees lying all over the place. Apart from the fences and a few roof tiles, our house was OK, but at Keysley, part of the grain store roof had completely disappeared.

As rumours of impending doom continued to come from Lloyd's, I joined a couple of groups to keep myself more fully and independently informed. One was the Society of Names, or SON, set up by Tom Benyon. The other was the Association of Lloyd's Members, or ALM. Both these groups produced a monthly magazine and the ALM held local meetings for members at various hotels. At these meetings the general consensus was to trade through the difficult years ahead, as in any case it was impossible to escape from syndicates with open years of account, and there were, by now, quite a number of these.

Giving up membership of Lloyd's at this stage would mean continuing to fund losses on the open years of account, without the profits of good syndicates to fund the losses. A syndicates' year of account had to be closed after three years, by an agreed figure of reinsurance, to be paid to the following year of account, in order to be fair to all the members of a particular year. This was called the Reinsurance to Close, or RITC. If the outstanding liabilities of a syndicate could not be accurately assessed, and agreement could not be reached, the account for that year remained open.

My 1987 results were notified in June 1990 and the overall loss was small and was funded from my reserves, this was encouraging, despite the bad news coming out about the 1988 and 1989 accounts.

Mattie and I, together with Mattie's disabled sister Mary, moved into the cottage at Keysley in June and renamed it 'Down in the Wood'. It had previously been known as 'The Park'. The cottage was approached down a short lane from the farm, and because of its proximity to the wood and the high hedges surrounding the garden, gave the impression of entering a wood.

June16th 1990 was the day of Colin's marriage to Sarah at a lovely church in St. Austell, and afterwards there was a reception at the Carlyon Bay Hotel. Sarah looked very beautiful in her lovely white dress and I must say Colin looked good and obviously very pleased with himself. It was a beautiful day and we enjoyed meeting our friends and relations, and Sarah's friends and relations. Bill and Frances, Sarah's parents, are very nice and we had met them several times before, so Mattie and I stayed that night at their little farm in the small village of Sticker. Colin and Sarah stayed the night at the Carlyon Bay Hotel before travelling to the British Virgin Islands for their honeymoon.

Colin & Sarah's Wedding 16th June 1990

A metal detection enthusiast, Graham Chaddock from Trowbridge, had been given permission to try his luck at Keysley. We had known him for some years as he had been to Whitecliff looking for artefacts, and he was always keen to show us what he had found. Sometimes he had interesting finds, but on the whole it was mundane items such as old nails, buttons, brooches and a few old coins. We had a verbal agreement with Graham, to share equally any money received for items of value. This only happened once at Whitecliff when Graham found a small amount of gold leaf, dating back to the early Britons.

One day during the harvest, we had decided to have an early lunch, hoping that the crop would be dry enough to combine as soon as we could get to the field. We were just about to leave the yard when Graham arrived with a little box in his hand and looking rather pleased with himself, explaining that he had something to show us.

Our hearts sank and we tried to make excuses. He insisted, so we agreed to have a quick look, but oh no, he wanted us to go to the house, explaining that we would really want to see what was in the box. We reluctantly agreed and proceeded back down to the house and seated ourselves around the kitchen table.

Graham then, slowly and deliberately, placed the box in the middle of the table and removed the lid. Inside, on a bed of cotton wool, was a most beautiful golden torc. He removed it from the box and handed it round, explaining that he had taken it home and cleaned it with soap and water. Graham told us that it was worth a lot of money, but did not mention a figure; in any case it was obvious to us that it was very valuable and we had to decide what to do? Graham was of the opinion that the article was far too important, from a historical point of view, to even consider selling it quietly, or even taking it to the States. We all agreed that it should be handed over to the authorities and we would wait and see what happened.

After handing the torc to the relevant authority, Graham told us that it had been taken to London for examination, and would be returned to Salisbury Museum to await an inquest. While the article was in London, at our request, Sotheby's, were asked to consider its value, and examined the torc. Their report stated that this torc was very difficult to value, as it was not a marketable object, but that it must be worth anything in excess of two hundred and fifty thousand pounds.

An archaeological excavation would be carried out at the site by an expert archaeologist who would give a detailed written report, with diagrams of the soil strata in the area of the find. This was carried out within a few days and the inquest was arranged for one afternoon in Salisbury where the Wiltshire Coroner would decide if the object was 'Treasure Trove'.

I visited the site while the excavation was in progress. There was quite a large hole in which the archaeologist was kneeling and scratching about with a little brush, the size of a toothbrush. When my little dog jumped in the hole, he was horrified and asked me to keep him under control, and explained that crucial evidence could be destroyed. This was not a very good introduction and I soon gained the impression that I was not really wanted at the site.

There were three members of the jury and of course the Coroner, Mattie and I and our solicitor Bill Knowles were in attendance and maybe half a dozen other people. The Coroner, after asking the names of the finders, Graham Chaddock and his friend, Reg Day, who was with him on that occasion, directed his enquiry to the circumstances leading up to the find. Graham described how he had received a signal on his metal detector, and had excavated a small hole to find an axe-head about nine inches down.

Very pleased with this find, Graham continued his search of the area, until it was almost time to go, then, as was his usual practice, he went around to fill all the holes he had made. At this particular hole, instead of replacing the soil, he put in his detector and, to his surprise, received another signal. He then dug a little deeper and found the torc lying about fifteen inches down and called out to Reg to come and have a look.

Mr. Day was next to be questioned by the Coroner and verified Graham's statement.

The Coroner then embarked on a lengthy speech on the legal position. He explained the difference in law between an object being hidden, or one that had been lost and its effect on the rules governing Treasure Trove. He outlined several points for the jury to consider and directed them to find in favour of Treasure Trove.

The jury retired for about ten minutes and on their return were asked what their verdict was?

The foreman of the jury replied that it was Treasure Trove.

The Coroner then raised the torc above his head for all to see, and claimed it as treasure on behalf of Her Majesty the Queen. .

This case had already attracted the attention of the press and as we emerged from the courtroom there were TV news cameras, and reporters asking for our reaction to the verdict surrounded us. It was strange to watch ourselves on the evening news.

By the time we had retired to a café for a cup of tea, Graham had already made up his mind to challenge the verdict, on his own if necessary. Reg Day decided there and then that he wanted nothing to do with it. Mattie and I, after discussion with Colin and Sarah, decided to back Graham and agreed to contribute fifty per cent of the huge legal costs involved.

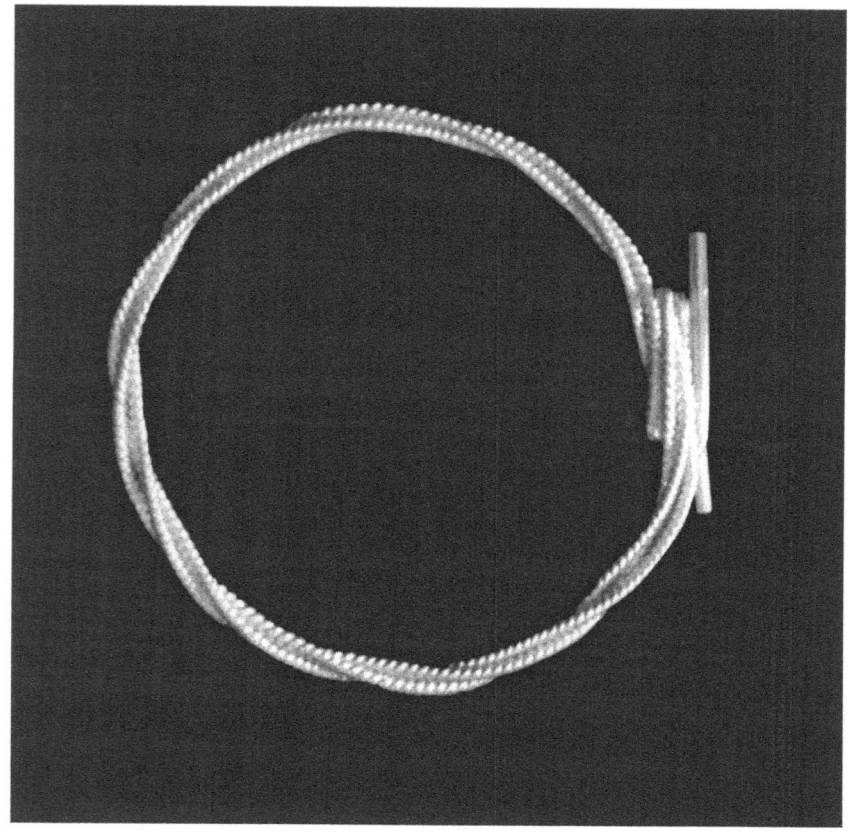

The Golden Torc

The news of the find spread quickly around the world. Newspaper cuttings were sent to us from friends in the United States, Canada and Australia. The New York Times said the treasure was worth five million dollars, while the Calgary Herald reported a value of nineteen million dollars. Where all these figures came from we will never know; all we knew was that it was a very valuable item indeed.

At about this time Mrs Thomas invited Mattie and myself to Whitecliff for a house-warming party, and an opportunity to show us the results of the small fortune she had spent altering the house. A lot of people attended, many of them were well known to us and we enjoyed it very much.

The only drink that was available was champagne, and bottle after bottle appeared as if from nowhere. Before long Mattie had had more than enough champagne, and asked for some orange juice, whereupon we were shown to the cellar to see if some could be found. There was none. The cellar was packed to the ceiling with cases of champagne. We had never seen so much.

During the course of conversation a couple of farming friends expressed the opinion that I was a lucky bugger. I said that I didn't know what they meant. "Well", they explained, "First you sold this farm for much more than it was worth; second, you bought Keysley Farm after the price had been reduced by three hundred thousand pounds; then you found some treasure worth millions".

Amid lots of laughter, I explained that it was nothing to do with luck, as I had known for years that the treasure was there, which was why I had been so determined to buy Keysley. The disbelieving lot now wondered how I had known about the treasure. I explained that, having lived at Whitecliff for so long, I had seen many rainbows all ending over Keysley!

The legal action over the treasure was to drag on for several years, with a Judicial Review in London leading, eventually, to a new hearing in Salisbury. It became necessary to engage a barrister who recommended the services of various academics and experts, to be called as witnesses. These, of course, not only had to be paid but all their expenses as well. The only lasting impression I have of the new inquest is the vast waste of time and money involved.

One point of interest remains in my memory. Our opponents in the case were 'The Crown', and they had also employed many expert witnesses. A lady 'expert' was presenting her case to the court with the aid of aerial photographs, which she had obtained at great cost, by hiring a helicopter. She made a huge mistake when saying, by way of introduction, that she was not an expert on aerial photography. This prompted our barrister to jump to his feet objecting to the evidence, and suggesting to the coroner that this evidence was inadmissible, as she was not qualified to present it. Then the unfortunate witness was asked to step down by the Coroner. This type of legal action continued all week.

In fact the only difference between this inquest and the original one was the time taken. The first lasted about half an hour, and this one lasted a whole week. The verdict was identical. If we had realised that the case would end in Salisbury before a jury we may have had second thoughts about our challenge. It is unreasonable to suppose that a jury would find in favour of a landowner, in a case involving an artefact of national importance.

Being on the losing side meant that the whole of the costs - ours and 'The Crown's - had to be borne by Graham and ourselves, and amounted to about twenty five thousand pounds each. The authorities saved up for some time and eventually awarded us an ex-gracia payment of seventy five thousand pounds, as an encouragement to other finders of treasure to hand it in. Because of the high profile of this case, there was a change in the law relating to Treasure Trove; details of the law continue to evade my understanding. The torc is now on display at Salibury Museum, in an especially constructed, secure display case.

After we had left the house in Frome, we asked a letting agent to find some short-term tenants, which they did, and the people stayed in the house until September 1991. This was an opportunity to sell with vacant possession. The property market had fallen considerably but by now we were in need of the money and decided to sell. The property eventually sold for £121,000.

So much for our bargain purchase!

CHAPTER 21

IMPENDING DOOM

Kingsley Underwriting Agencies had changed their name to Limestreet Underwriting Agencies during 1989 and many of their syndicates found themselves in trouble during 1990. Many names were joining action groups and taking legal action against their underwriting agencies, their syndicate managing agents and underwriters. Early in 1991, I paid losses amounting to about a quarter of a million by cheque and from reserves, which were by now exhausted. At this stage, with the information available, I was still hopeful that I would trade through.

The returns from arable farming continued to fall, so after our first harvest at Keysley, Colin let 100 acres of land to Clothiers, from Somerset, to fatten pigs outside. This we felt would be good for the land and save fertiliser costs for the following wheat crops.

The field was divided into one hundred pens of one acre, with electric fences, and included access tracks for the pig men's tractors. Each pen was to accommodate fifty pigs and was provided with five arcs and a double drinking trough and feeder. Two pipelines supplied each trough with water on one side, and whey from Clothiers' cheese plant to the other.

A yard was provided in a wood and Clothiers built a lairage for pigs awaiting transport and a workroom for the pig men. Electricity and water supplies were laid on, and storage tanks were installed to contain the whey, together with large silos to contain the pig food

The plan was to put weaners in the pens each week, and take about three hundred pigs to Ipswich for slaughter each week. Then, at the end of harvest, a fresh area of stubble would be fenced and the pigs gradually moved to enable us to plant wheat in October on the old pig area. There was a continuous population of five thousand pigs and we called the area 'Pig City'.

Tony Gosling, our bank manager, gave notice that he was leaving the branch and that we would have a new manager by the end of June 1991. I saw this as an opportunity to move our account to a branch in Shaftesbury, where a friend of mine, Alan Rymall, from the village was manager. I presented a business plan which he recommended to Head Office, but it was refused because of the uncertainty of the Lloyd's losses. So a meeting was arranged with the new manager, Richard Courtney, and we were able to arrange an endowment loan for Colin to buy a field of eighty acres from our neighbour, John White. I transferred a field called Loan Oak to Colin so that he had the necessary collateral.

My underwriting agents, by now were in serious trouble and their underwriting business was taken over by Bankside Underwriting Agencies. During the latter part of 1991, I made several trips to London, meeting people at Bankside, and trying to build some sort of working relationship. On one of these meetings I met Robert Hallam from the old Limestreet agency, he looked terrible and was very sorry the way things had gone. It was not long before we heard that Robert had died of a brain tumour. Ray came with me on one occasion and we found that a young man called Stephen Lumley was to deal with our accounts, at least now we had someone we could talk to. It was only a few weeks before Stephen wrote to us, asking us to meet him at Bankside Agencies to discuss the 1989 results.

At this meeting, Stephen gave us the updated situation regarding the Feltrim and Gooda Walker syndicates. The losses were horrendous. In my case over £600,000 on those syndicates alone, and many other syndicates were forecasting losses; Stephen indicated that worse was yet to come. There were sufficient cash calls to bankrupt me at this stage and my first thought was that I would lose the farm. For a couple of minutes I was shaken and in some kind of panic mode. Ray was not hit quite as badly as he was not on all the bad syndicates and also had smaller lines, meaning that he had lower Premium Income Limits, but he had gone as white as a sheet.

When I pulled myself together and explained to Stephen that we could not pay any more, he suggested that we should see a lawyer this very day, and recommended Michael Freeman of Michael Freeman and Co.

Ray and I took a taxi to Great Cumberland Place and enquired at reception if we could see Michael Freeman. The lady told us that if we were prepared to wait, then Michael Freeman would see us as soon as possible. We were shown into a waiting room where we found three men in various states of despair. One was sitting in a corner wailing quietly, 'I'm ruined, I'm ruined'.

Another man was pacing back and fore across the room, wringing his hands. The third man was sitting quietly but appeared to be in the depths of a depression. Ray and I had by now returned to our normal selves and found the situation rather amusing and we even made a few jokes, needless to say, the others were not amused.

After about an hour, the other three having been called at intervals, Ray and I were shown into a very large office, with a slightly greying Michael Freeman sitting behind an enormous desk. He explained that all he could do today was to take our names and addresses, details of our underwriting agents, and our syndicates.

When this was completed he looked very grave, and said that he would act for us and try to get an injunction stopping Lloyd's from drawing down our Lloyd's Bank Guarantees, but this would depend on the ruling of a judge in a court of law. Mr. Freeman advised us not to pay any more cash calls and to join all action groups relevant to our syndicates.

In sombre mood, Ray and I parted and went to catch our trains.

I spent the journey to Westbury in dread of reporting the day's events to Mattie, Sarah and Colin. Both Ray and I joined the 'Gooda Walker Action Group', the 'Feltrim Action Group' and the 'Limestreet Action Group' during the following week. Other groups were joined as and when they were formed.

All this was rather expensive, as you could not join an action group without paying a subscription based on the size of your line; in my case the subscriptions amounted to several thousands of pounds.

After all this I still had mixed feelings about taking legal action against Lloyd's, to avoid paying my losses. At this stage I still believed that we were happy to take the profits when they came, but were crying foul when there were losses.

All through the nineteen eighties, Lloyd's had a growing problem with their long tail syndicates. These were the syndicates that insured such things as pollution, with its increasing clean-up costs, and latent industrial diseases such as asbestosis, with no way of knowing the extent of claims over the next, perhaps forty years. The huge and increasing compensation awards by the American courts exacerbated these two problems. Ray and I were reassured by Robin Kingsley that our exposure to these risks had been kept very low and our annual syndicate reports confirmed this position.

Our problems began in the North Sea on the 6th of July 1988, when the Piper Alpha oil platform exploded in a massive fireball, and caused a huge loss of life. This single loss was a shock to Lloyd's as it became clear that some marine syndicates were badly over exposed, with inadequate reinsurance cover. It soon became evident that the reinsurance that was in place, had been taken out with other syndicates within the Lloyd's market, then a share of the risk was reinsured again within the market, then a share of reinsurance was taken by the original syndicates. This became known later as the 'spiral'.

For the last few years Lloyd's Premium Income and membership had grown dramatically. This growth had been achieved to some degree, by reinsurance being taken on by Lloyd's syndicates, instead of farming it out to some other insurance market. Brokers licensed to work within Lloyd's would cart a risk around the market, taking 15% of the Premium as commission each time they got it reinsured, and making millions in the process. It has been suggested that the names that carried 100% of the risk on Piper Alpha received only about 10% of the premium. It was obvious that there was something very wrong with the regulation of the market.

Over the following two years Lloyd's was hit by a series of disasters beginning with Hurricane Hugo, smashing into the coast of South Carolina. This enormous loss was followed by several serious disasters, including the Enchova oil platform fire, followed by Hurricane Gilbert in the Caribbean - the results of this were evident to George and I when we were in Texas, the Exxon Valdes oil tanker spillage in Alaska, the San Francisco earthquake, the Arco Baker fire, the Phillips petroleum explosion, the Australian earthquake, Typhoon Mireille in Japan and a gale which hit Britain and Northern Europe in January 1990. This was the storm that damaged the grain store at Keysley Farm.

This unprecedented series of catastrophes affected the insurance industry world wide, and as I was an underwriter my business was to pay claims. The Lloyd's motto of 'Utmost Good Faith' was very strong on my mind, and the thought of taking legal action to avoid paying made me feel very uncomfortable. This discomfort was not to last very long.

My personal disasters came from all directions in 1992. A very wet harvest resulted in the loss of a large area of peas, and the wheat that had been planted after the pigs, went down flat and rotted where it lay. Then planting the next area after the pigs was almost impossible, as it was an absolute quagmire, and we eventually spread the seed with the fertiliser spreader, and cultivated it in. The wet weather continued during the winter, resulting in the start of serious and mucky run off from the pigs and a difficult situation developing soon after Christmas. My underwriting career came to an end with overwhelming losses, marking the beginning of a long legal battle to stave off bankruptcy and save the farm. Then worst of all, Mattie became ill, more about that later.

The only bright spot that year was Manor Farm, Monkton Deverill. The tenant, Peter Dufossee, had retired and the auctioneers, R B Taylor, asked Colin to give them a price for managing the farm until it could be sold and the new owner took over. Not only did he get the contract but also he arranged a share-farming contract with the new owner, Martin Wood, which was to last for many years.

Clothiers' pigs were now in their third year and so were on their third patch of 100 acres. As I have already mentioned we encountered serious run off from the pigs' area. This started on the 18th September 1992 when we had four inches of rain during the morning and early afternoon. The resulting floodwater carved a large channel in the chalk subsoil as it made its way down the hill towards our neighbour's fields and then on to Monkton Deverill.

After leaving our property the flood entered Martin Wood's pasture land, then crossed the Hindon road into his arable field, where it flowed parallel to the road before crossing it again into a pasture field belonging to the Wiltshire County Council and farmed by Keith Burton. The flood then flowed along the valley bottom, before crossing the road once more into another of Martin Wood's arable fields. Here it spread out across a wide area as it meandered towards the river and gradually seeped into the soil and disappeared. This flow was to be repeated on many occasions during the very wet winter of 1992/93 and culminated in very heavy flows over Christmas and the New Year, the local council having to clear deep mud from the road on a number of days after heavy rain.

The original flood in September was a totally natural event caused by the exceptionally heavy rain, but the cause of the subsequent floods was undoubtedly the pigs. Due to the success of the pig fattening enterprise during the previous two years, Clothiers had increased the stocking rate from fifty pigs per acre, to sixty. The new site was situated by the farm road and sloped gently down to the bottom of the valley and up the other side to our boundary.

A total population of six thousand pigs meant that twenty four thousand little feet were constantly puddling the saturated land. This, I believe, led to the land becoming impervious to the rainwater, resulting in massive run-off every time it rained.

The run-off was doing no harm to our neighbour's arable and pasture land, as it was the middle of winter, but this did not stop Keith Burton creating a hell of a fuss and reporting us to the National River Authority. Colin and I met Keith in the valley to explain the situation and to inform him that we had already decided to bring the pig enterprise to an end.

We found Keith in a state of hysteria and screaming that the pigs must go. I expressed the opinion that there was, "not much harm done, and that in any case we would pay for any damage that subsequently emerged". This only resulted in more shouting and screaming, Keith saying that he had engaged a professional photographer to record the floods. Colin tried to explain that the position would not change until the weather changed, even if all the pigs were removed immediately. This resulted in yet more shouting and saying the pigs must go.

We left realising that we were getting nowhere and saying we would be in touch again after we had talked to the NRA. In the meantime the run off continued intermittently but by great good fortune, it never reached the river. It always spread out and soaked away in Martin's arable field.

The man from the NRA arrived at Keysley, and Colin took him to the pig field and then toured the flooded area in the valley. He was very sympathetic and helpful, saying that the type of animal husbandry we were engaged in should be encouraged, but warned us that if the run-off should reach the river, we would be fined twenty thousand pounds per day until it stopped. He agreed that there was little we could do except hope for the rain to stop. Later on, while drinking coffee in the kitchen, the NRA man suggested that we build an earth damn across the valley, just below the pig area, to intercept the flow of slurry; this we said was worth considering.

At this suggestion, Clothiers sent in two large diggers and dug some very deep holes and piled the earth into a damn across the valley; it was a very impressive operation. In the meantime Keith had complained to his landlords, Wiltshire County Council, who made an appointment for their land agent to visit the site. Colin toured the site and discussed the problem with him. The land agent was totally in agreement with us that no damage was being done to Council property, and said that he would speak to Mr. Burton. The worst thing was that after only a few days, and despite the fact that the dam was nearly forty feet high in the middle, it was already full and water was beginning to run over the top.

Another call to the NRA brought the inspector quickly to the farm. I accompanied him in his car to the pig field where we parked and he put on his rubber boots. We discussed the problem as we walked towards the valley to look at the dam. As the dam in the valley came into view, the inspector expressed his shock and alarm, and exclaimed, " If that lot goes, what happens to the village?" We watched in silence for a little while. Then he said that building the dam could have been a mistake, and we both agreed that there was little we could do about it now.

We returned to the farmhouse to discuss the situation with Colin and Sarah over a cup of coffee. The inspector looked very worried and again expressed his concern about what would happen if the dam burst. He thought that there would be considerable damage to houses in the village from the resulting flow, and that the flood would reach the river, he had no doubt. If this happened, it would be most unlikely that the NRA would bring a prosecution, as the problem had, in part at least, been caused by the NRA recommending the building of the dam.

If my memory serves me correctly, the rain stopped almost immediately. The water behind the dam gradually soaked into the ground and the problem solved itself without any further action. The pigs that were on the site were fattened in the normal way, but were not replaced by weaners, so the numbers of pigs on the field quickly fell and there was no more trouble from flooding.

CHAPTER 22

FIGHTING FOR SURVIVAL

The early part of 1992 was spent trying to decide on the best approach to save the farm for Colin and Sarah, while fighting off writs and threats from Lloyd's. Having a drink one evening at the 'Bath Arms', I overheard a conversation about the Gooda Walker and Feltrim syndicates. I apologised for interrupting and introduced myself as a member of the syndicates in question. This caused a burst of excitement around the table, and one of the gentlemen got up from his seat, shook my hand and introduced himself as Stephen Morgan.

Stephen went on to explain how he was an accountant working with Berkley Hall in Warminster and had a few Lloyd's members as his clients. We talked for some time about the problems faced by Lloyd's members and I was very impressed, not only by Stephen's knowledge of the disaster, but his enthusiasm for the action groups and the court proceedings so far. He blamed Lloyd's Regulatory Authorities for allowing the situation to develop.

Stephen said that he was a friend of my solicitor, Bill Knowles, and that he would act for me if that would help. So we arranged for him to meet me at Keysley, with Bill. When I talked to Bill on the phone, he was very enthusiastic about Stephen and recommended him to me and arranged to meet us both at Keysley. At the meeting it soon became clear that I should engage Stephen as my accountant through his firm, Berkley Hall. My accountant in London, Colin Gower, had retired from McIntyre Hudson and I had met the new man, Donald Boer, only once, so I had no feelings of loyalty in that direction.

I had great confidence in Bill, and now to have Stephen and Bill working together made me feel so much better and not so alone. They both agreed that joining all the appropriate action groups was all we could do at present, and after a long discussion about Lloyd's, the farm, and the financial situation, they went away saying that they hoped to meet me again soon, and that they would work together on a plan of action. Stephen said that he would arrange the transfer of all the files and accounts from McIntyre Hudson to Berkley Hall.

During this period I continued to attend ALM and SON meetings and action group meetings in London, and it soon became clear that there were thousands of members who were refusing to pay any more. Some of these meetings were very distressing with lots of tears being shed by rich and glamorous ladies, and hysterical verbal attacks on Lloyd's by broken and bitter gentlemen.

On several occasions I met some quite famous people who were in the depths of despair. I often managed to find some humour during the tea and biscuit interval and I found that we could even have a laugh. One very glamorous and tearful lady was the wife of an airline pilot who had used his house as security He was now at home, a broken man, unable to do anything. She said how she looked forward to seeing me. Apparently, I made her feel so much better, to the extent that on one occasion she threw her arms around me and hugged and kissed me.

The writs continued to arrive from Lloyd's so I joined a group called the 'Writs Response Group' which fought off the writs through court action. It was also very interesting to sit in on some of the action group court cases at the Royal Courts of Justice in the Strand. These cases continued for weeks and if ever I was in London with time to spare I knew just where to go. I remember one of the barristers working through a pile of files nearly four feet high; the number of documents involved in these cases was enormous, some of which were mine of course.

Mattie accompanied me on a few occasions but found the proceedings all very depressing. I was in constant contact with Ray and kept him informed of developments and made suggestions of any action that I thought he should take. It was not very long before Ray had engaged Bill and Stephen and we combined our knowledge and resources.

Spring rolled on into summer when Bill and Stephen came back with a plan, not a very nice plan, but a plan. Put very simply it involved proving that Mattie owned half of Keysley Farm, and Colin would have to borrow the money from the bank to buy my half share of the farm. I would then be declared bankrupt and Lloyd's would get a proportion of the debt and be off my back for ever after. The downside of the plan was that Colin and Sarah would be saddled with a huge debt but perhaps better than no farm at all.

This plan would only survive the bankruptcy court if my half share of the farm were sold to Colin at market value, what is referred to as an 'arm's length transaction'. This could be achieved if both Colin and I employed separate valuers, leaving them to fight over the final price. Persuading the bank to lend the money to Colin was one of the largest obstacles. This is where Stephen excelled, writing a report on Colin's farming record over the last three years, together with the farm accounts, and a detailed budget for the next three years showing how the bank was to be repaid.

With this plan in my brief case, Colin and I drove to Honiton to present it to Richard Courtney, our new bank manager. Colin had already met Richard when we were negotiating to buy the field from John White, so he was able to talk about the farm management part, and I updated Richard on the Lloyd's situation and presented our plan.

By the time we had gone through the whole thing it was time for lunch, so we walked down the street to a little restaurant, had a good lunch and a general chat and I picked up the tab. Richard told us that although he was impressed with our scheme, he would of course have to submit it to Head Office with his recommendation. We thanked him and returned to Keysley.

At our meeting in Honiton, Richard Courtney had expressed concern at the increasing level of our overdraft. We had promised Richard that there was nothing to worry about, harvest would be starting soon and there would then be plenty of produce to sell. However, on the way home from Honiton, Colin suggested that we sell the combine and offer the harvesting to contractors. This plan had two advantages, one, a hefty cheque paid into the bank at this time would impress the bank, and two, our combine was low on capacity for the number of acres to be harvested, now that we were farming Manor Farm at Monkton Deverill.

Colin quickly put the plan into effect, getting prices from various contractors, and advertising our combine in the Farmer's Weekly. Salmons, contractors near Trowbridge, owned and managed by Tony Doel, was contracted to do the work and our John Deere hillside combine was sold to a farmer in Devon who had some steep slopes to harvest.

Tony delivered a large capacity New Holland combine just prior to harvest and promised another one, should it be required. It was good to learn that we were to have an expert combine operator in the name of Alex Rawlings, who had worked for Bert at Winsley for some years, after I had left to go to Whitecliff. Alex was to prove great fun to work with, and he and Colin got on well together.

Harvest began in grand style with two New Hollands working on the winter barley at Manor Farm, Monkton Deverill, moving on to Keysley in fine weather and producing a very respectable yield. After the winter barley, there was a break, as expected, before the winter wheat and peas were ready. We had agreed with the contractors to pay at this stage for work done so far; this reminds me of a funny story.

Colin had sent the cheque, about £17,000 to Tony Dole. The same day, Saturday, Tony phoned in the evening in a bit of a state, explaining that he had talked to someone at Frome Show that day. Tony had been told that we were going bankrupt, so he would be over to collect a cheque from Colin at eight in the morning. Colin told him that the cheque had already been posted, but he was not satisfied, Colin would have to write another one!

My telephone rang quite late that evening; it was Colin to ask me to come to the farm early the next morning to explain the whole Lloyd's situation to Tony, as we were in danger of losing our contractors. With this Sarah chipped in on the conversation to ask if I could bring a drop of milk, as they had run out. I said "Yes, see you in the morning."

The following morning I walked up to the farm a little early but Tony's truck was already in the yard. I went in the back door and walked into the kitchen, knowing that Tony and Colin would be round the corner at the table out of my sight. I went across the kitchen towards Sarah, who was at the sink. Holding out a plastic bottle half full of milk, I said, "Good Morning Sarah, they let me have this little drop of milk, but they won't let us have any more," then turned towards Colin and Tony and acted surprised to see them there.

The joke almost misfired as I thought Tony was going to pass out. After he had recovered I explained all about Lloyd's and our plans for me to go bankrupt and not the partnership. The colour slowly returned to his face; we even offered to pay for the rest of the harvesting in advance but he would not hear of it. The latter part of the harvest proved very difficult as rain and wind flattened the crops, the peas were a disaster and the wheat after the pigs was a total write-off due to the increased fertility of the soil.

Harvest, during most of my working life, has been the most important part of the crop year. A farmer can work and invest inputs for almost a year, but if the harvest goes wrong it can all be wasted. For these reasons I always planned my business and private life so that I could concentrate fully on harvesting the crops; no outside commitments and no appointments were made.

So it was with some degree of reluctance that I agreed to go to Exeter to meet the South West area manager of Lloyd's Bank, Mr. Peter Lamb. I remembered meeting Peter when he was the manager of Chippenham branch, some years before, when the bank had arranged for a few local bank managers, and a selection of local farmers, to spend a few days visiting farms in France.

Being summoned to Exeter was the result of Richard Courtney

referring our bankruptcy plan to Head Office. Apparently the bank was very concerned about their own position, having granted us an overdraft, arranged a mortgage with Colin to purchase the field from John White and their provision of the guarantee to Lloyd's of London to facilitate my underwriting. This represented a total commitment by the bank of over seven hundred thousand pounds, and they were anxious to make an appointment to discuss the whole situation.

The problem with committing to a day at harvest time is the fear that it may be one of very few fine days when harvesting is possible. However, under pressure from the bank, I agreed and a meeting was arranged. Bill Knowles and Stephen Morgan agreed to attend but Colin could not be spared from the farm; this was unfortunate as he could have presented a good case for continuing the farming business in his name.

On the day, I picked up Bill and Stephen and we set off to the bank in Honiton to meet Richard Courtney who was to drive us to Exeter. We were all in good spirits and confident that the bank would cooperate as they had so much to lose themselves. Richard drove us to a modern complex on the outskirts of Exeter where we were ushered into a large room with a huge, rather grand table and chairs - a typical modern boardroom.

Bill, Stephen and I were shown to chairs on one side of the table, and Richard, after making introductions, seated himself with two bank people on the other side. We were just beginning to make a little small talk when in strode Peter Lamb. We all stood up. Richard was ready to make the introductions when Peter grasped my hand and explained that we had met before, and he was pleased to see me again. Richard completed the introductions and we all sat around, exchanging pleasantries and wondering how to start the business.

Starting the ball rolling, I said that we all know why we are here. I explained that I was a farmer in a dreadful mess financially, but the farming business was as strong as ever and in good hands, being successfully managed by my son Colin. I turned to Stephen and Bill who both backed me up. Stephen said that the profits for the last three years under Colin's management spoke for themselves, and the budgets going forward were based on realistic costs and returns from the market. Stephen handed Peter the last three years accounts of Keysley Farm Partners. Peter quickly scanned through them pausing only to look at the bottom line and made an approving comment.

We ran through the details of our plan and explained that in our opinion the only way to limit my liability to Lloyd's was for me to be declared bankrupt. I had already declared myself as no longer a partner in Keysley Farm Partners and that my wife held half of the assets.

Here I mentioned the fact that it was not just me who had a problem, but also the bank. The three men opposite nodded in agreement. I posed the question: "if you are prepared to lend the money to Colin, to buy my share of the farm from me, then he and his mother will own the farm and he will pay back every penny."

A long period of discussion ensued about how this plan could be implemented and how valuers could be involved instead of putting the farm on the open market. I said that the valuers should be instructed verbally that we wanted a low valuation. The letters of instruction should say, in my case, "Please arrange a sale to my son for the best possible price"; and in Colin's case, "Please arrange to buy my father's share of the farm at the lowest possible price".

Carefully written letters between the two valuers, giving their reasons for a higher or a lower price, whichever was the case, could be kept on file, and if necessary produced at a bankruptcy court.

Peter Lamb said that he would consider the loan to Colin when we knew what figure the valuers came up with. I replied, "We know the figure we are talking about £500,000 give or take, and that if this scheme is to succeed, then we have to employ two top national estate agents, which is going to cost, perhaps £30,000". I added, "When you decide to back Colin then we will employ the estate agents and we will get the lowest price possible in the circumstances".

I continued, "Lloyd's will eventually draw down on your Bank Guarantee of four hundred and fifty thousand pounds. I will repay you for that, and repay some of the overdraft before Lloyd's makes me bankrupt. Colin will then repay the loan over the next few years based on Stephen's projections. An alternative is for us to do nothing and the whole farm would be sold with my share and your guarantee going to Lloyd's of London".

Peter Lamb then suggested a break for coffee, as he wanted to discuss the problem with his colleagues in another room. We had coffee and the three men returned to the room looking very grave and said that there was a chance that we would be accused of planning to defraud Lloyd's of London by selling my share of the farm at an undervaluation.

I replied that that could not happen; it would not be sold at an undervaluation if two top national valuers were involved and the documentation was in order. I referred the question to my learned friend, Bill, who said very much the same but used a lot more words.

Peter then said that they would back Colin, but first they would have to check out the scheme with the bank's legal team in London, to make sure it was not fraudulent. The meeting ended with handshakes all round and we commenced our journey home, all agreed a 'job well done'.

The scheme was implemented without delay, estate agents engaged and valuations completed; all letters between agents carefully written to stand up to examination in a bankruptcy court. The agreed value of my half of the farm was surprisingly low, explained by the fact that half of a farm was not a very marketable item, and also the letters from Colin's valuer, pointing out the present slump in agricultural land values. By the time all this was ready, events at Lloyd's had moved on and we sat on these plans to await further news.

Harvest was eventually completed and the winter wheat was planted except for the wheat after the pigs, the land being an absolute quagmire. When the weather was reasonable a seven tined sub-soiler was pulled through, sometimes two tractors were required to pull it. The aim was to create drainage so the soil would dry out. The intermittent rain persisted and we eventually spread the wheat seed on the surface and then dragged the cultivator through in an attempt to cover the seed. It worked, and we produced an average yield although the land was very uneven.

By this time, the autumn of 1992, Lloyd's had second thoughts about suing members who were refusing to pay their losses, because the numbers were so overwhelming. There were now over 15,000 names and thirty action groups engaged in litigation against their members' agents, brokers, auditors and Lloyd's themselves. Lloyd's decided to have a six month long moratorium on the issue of writs, giving us names a little breathing space.

I made use of this period by carrying out some research as to what the next step should be. Despite the huge expense of the bankruptcy plan, I felt that if the bankruptcy court could be avoided then so much the better. There was the question of the field called Loan Oak, which I had gifted to Colin to provide collateral for him to buy the field from John White. There was also the money from the treasure, as I had sold the rights to it to Mattie for £100, and of course any number of transactions over the last few years might be investigated, such as the sale of our house in Frome. They might even question the ownership of Whitecliff and Manor Farms and the land near Warminster.

Tom Benyon, the founder of the Society of Names, agreed to see me over breakfast at his large home in Buckinghamshire. I arrived about half past seven and Tom was just returning from his morning run. We discussed my syndicate portfolio and potential losses and he expressed his dismay, saying there were thousands in a similar situation and it was scandalous that Lloyd's had allowed it to happen.

Tom suggested that there could be a case for an application to Lloyd's Hardship Committee, chaired by Mary Archer, but he did not feel that he could advise. He told me that the man to see was Gerald Hyam, an accountant and insolvency practitioner in London who was very much involved with Lloyd's business. We had a general discussion about Lloyd's and farming over our eggs and bacon, served by his housekeeper. I then thanked him for sparing the time to see me and headed for home.

My next step was to talk to Bill and suggest to him that we should both go to London to see this man Hyam, if I could arrange an appointment. Bill agreed so I arranged a date to meet Mr. Hyam at his office in North Audley Street. Bill and I gave Mr Hyam all the information that we could and he said that he would be happy to act for us, and for Ray as well if that was what we wanted. But first he would like to go through the information we had given him, and come back to us with a course of action.

Gerald gave us the impression that he knew what he was talking about, and he appeared to have a very close working relationship with Lloyd's. We came away from the meeting feeling that we had made some sort of breakthrough.

Gerald Hyam quickly came back to us with a letter saying that he would be pleased to act for us and stating his charges of £120 an hour plus expenses. He suggested, if we would like, to meet again at his office, together with Ray and Stephen Morgan. We discussed the situation with Ray and Stephen and a meeting was arranged.

Gerald added that as the moratorium on writs was about to expire, he suggested that it would be a good thing for him to write to the Hardship Committee expressing our intention to make an application. We agreed, as he said it could "do no harm".

At the meeting Gerald went through our syndicates and added up the losses declared so far, mine were over £1,000,000, and Ray's were about £200,000. He went on to say that this situation was going to get much worse, as there were many more bad results to come. For example, he said that he had heard a rumour that Gooda Walker Syndicate 387 was going to return a loss of 10,000%, which represented a single loss to me of £2,500,000, but this one did not affect Ray. I laughed and said that I thought it made no difference, and Gerald agreed.

Gooda Walker Syndicate 387 was a personal stop loss syndicate, so a share of the losses of hundreds of names would end up as claims on the table of 387. This was just one example of the spiral effect of names and syndicates reinsuring their risks with other syndicates within the Lloyd's market. I began to suspect that what everyone else was saying about Lloyd's was right and the regulatory authorities had been negligent in allowing this situation to develop.

Gerald then suggested that we consider a scheme put forward by a financial expert called Mr. Pilbrow. We then spent some time discussing the Pilbrow plan. I agreed to go ahead with this, which involved Sarah and Colin forming a company and trust, into which any proceeds from successful action groups could be assigned. The company, Palmfont Ltd., was formed but was never used, as there was never any money from the action groups. Although vast sums of money had been awarded in damages by the courts, there was no money to pay them. The Gooda Walker action group had been awarded damages amounting to the largest award in British Legal History.

Gerald went on to say that he would make an application to the Hardship Committee and had received the forms from Lloyd's for both Ray and me. He said that there was no hurry: delay after delay was all to the good and served to keep Lloyd's off our backs.

CHAPTER 23

A DREADFUL TIME AND
A RAY OF HOPE

As if all those setbacks of 1992 were not enough, August 1992 saw the beginnings of Mattie's mental illness, which was to cause me more heartache and despair than anything else that had happened. Since we arrived at Keysley, Mattie had worked part time, a couple of days each week, in an old people's home at Mere, Bramley House. It was the type of work that she loved, but for some reason, that summer she had lost the job but had found another position at a home in Gillingham. This did not last more than a few weeks and she was very upset when they told her that she was not up to the job.

Mattie became depressed and after the harvest admitted to me that she had been to a specialist in Salisbury, and was being treated for depression. I was most annoyed at first about not being consulted. She explained that she did not want to bother me on top of all my problems, and that she had hoped to get better, but clearly was not.

We talked all this through over the following weeks, and I went with her to Salisbury to see the specialist on a couple of occasions. We were unable to pin the problem to anything in particular, I wondered if her sister Mary was the problem, or our financial situation. As it was I never expressed any sign of despair about Lloyd's, and as far as I can remember I always had a positive and cheerful attitude, as I did for life in general.

However Mattie's condition continued to worsen, and she brought it home to me with a great shock one afternoon in September. I was ploughing in Lone Oak, a large field on the right of the drive as it approaches the A303. I saw her car parked on the drive so I stopped the tractor and walked across to see her. When I reached the car I could see that she was in a state and crying. I asked what had happened. She said that I would have to "do something, or she would drive the car straight onto the main road", meaning that she felt suicidal.

Having calmed her down a little, I persuaded her to get out of the car and I got into the driving seat, whereupon Mattie got into the passenger seat. We then drove back to our cottage, had a cup of tea and tried to talk things through. This was hopeless and I soon realised that I would have to decide on a course of action myself.

The only thing that I could think of in that short space of time was that perhaps her sister Mary was becoming too much of a burden and was causing Mattie some problems. I quickly made some phone calls and found a place for Mary at the old people's home in Sutton Veny. We packed a bag for Mary and we all piled into the car for the short journey to Sutton Veny, where we saw Mary to her new room. Mary seemed to accept that it was probably a good idea for Mattie to have a break from her for a while.

The next two weeks were like a nightmare; Mattie seemed to be going mad. I took her to the doctor and again to the specialist in Salisbury and spent much more time with her, telling Colin that he had better find someone else to drive the tractor. The situation deteriorated and she would wake me in the middle of the night and plead with me to phone the doctor. I would refuse and try to get to the bottom of what was troubling her.

Eventually I would fall asleep from sheer exhaustion, only to be reawakened by Mattie, who had phoned the doctor. She would explain that the doctor was on the telephone and wanted to speak to me. I then had a conversation with some strange doctor, who sounded a little irritated. Trying to explain the situation to the doctor, while Mattie continued to shout that she must see him now, was very difficult and the doctor eventually suggested that we meet him at some obscure village surgery to which he gave me directions. At the surgery he quickly gave her a sedative injection and suggested that I take her to our own doctor in the morning. We went home again and we both fell into a sound sleep.

Next morning, Dr. Price at Mere surgery prescribed even more tablets. A couple of nights later, Mattie awakened me in a similar state, and having failed to persuade her that the doctor could do nothing, and to wait until the morning, she was becoming aggressive and abusive. Fearing that she would call the doctor the moment that I fell asleep, I decided to phone Colin. He came down and stayed some time, talking to her and trying to persuade her to go back to sleep, all to no avail, until eventually the morning came and I was able to take her to the doctor yet again.

A few nights later a similar situation developed and Mattie was extremely abusive to me for refusing to phone the doctor there and then. I was doing everything to delay until the morning but eventually dozed off, only to be awakened by Mattie, telling me that the doctor was on the phone and wished to speak to me. This time, to my relief, it was our own doctor. We eventually agreed that I would take Mattie to his surgery early in the morning, eight o'clock if my memory serves me correctly.

Dr. Price went carefully through the notes of the last few months and then we talked about the dreadful times we had had during the last two weeks. After some consideration he suggested that Mattie should go to the Old Manor mental hospital in Salisbury. He would make the arrangements and said that I should take her there immediately.

We drove to Salisbury where she was admitted and given a room with three other patients. A nurse showed us the facilities including a day room and a smoking room where male and female patients were allowed to roam around freely. I was very unhappy with the situation and was reluctant to leave her in this place with, to say the least, some very weird people. The nurse assured me that Mattie would be quite safe as the inmates were under constant supervision. I eventually left, resolving to return that evening, and drove back to Keysley in a very depressed state.

Every evening I went to visit Mattie and found the whole place and situation most distressing. On my fourth visit, parking my car in the car park on the opposite side of the main road as usual, I walked across the road and noticed some horrendous skid marks, obviously made by a lorry.

As I entered the hospital, the nurse at reception asked me to follow her to a small room where I was introduced to the nurse in charge. The nurse explained that Mattie had somehow gone out of the main entrance and had attempted to cross the road causing a lorry driver to slam on his brakes and narrowly avoid hitting her. The nurse was very apologetic about the lapse of security and could not really explain how Mattie had been able to slip out, and assured me that they would ensure that such a thing would not happen again.

The nurse suggested that Mattie's action could have been a suicide attempt but they could not be certain. Apparently the police were involved but no charges were to be brought and the lorry driver had been in a state of shock at the scene. The police had recommended a review of security and this was to be put in hand. I thanked the nurse and then went to spend some time with Mattie, who appeared to know nothing about it.

I visited every evening, and a few nights later I was again intercepted at reception and taken to the nurse in charge. She explained that Mattie's wrists were bandaged as she had broken a picture and attempted to cut her wrists with the glass. However the damage was slight and would soon heal; apparently one of the other patients had seen what was happening and raised the alarm, Mattie refused to discuss what had happened and I did not press her.

Having made an appointment to see the doctor who was in charge of treating Mattie, I arrived early one afternoon, spent about an hour with Mattie then went to see him. The doctor explained that they were treating Mattie with drugs to stabilise her and said that it would take a long time to find the best drugs for her case as all drugs had unwelcome side effects.

However, in the meantime, they had sent Mattie to Salisbury

Hospital for a brain scan, which had shown that there was very little activity in the frontal lobes of her brain. This part of the brain was largely responsible for a person's personality. He was very sorry to have to inform me that Mattie was suffering from some form of dementia; 'Picks Disease' was suspected, but could only be confirmed at a post mortem. This would not improve and was more likely to get worse. However he was hopeful that her wellbeing could be dramatically improved by drug therapy, which would take a long time, but that she would eventually be able to return home.

I continued to visit Mattie every evening, and on one occasion the fire alarm went off. Mattie was very agitated and said that we must get out. I suggested that it was probably a false alarm; then a nurse appeared and ordered us all out as quickly as possible.

We were to assemble on a grassy area in the courtyard of the hospital where an attempt was made to count all the patients. This was proving difficult and a bit comical, as no one seemed to know how many visitors there were and many of the patients would not stay in one place.

There was a lot of smoke issuing from part of the building some distance from where we were assembled and we soon heard the approach of the fire service. They parked their fire engine in the road and raised a ladder from where they hosed water into the building and the smoke stopped quite quickly. Apparently a patient had set fire to some clothes in a cupboard. My visits to the Old Manor were not always so exciting!

Soon we were in the week leading up to Christmas and I was anxious that I could have Mattie home for the holiday. I enquired as to whether this was possible. They prevaricated and made all sorts of reasons why Mattie would be better in the hospital. I could not bear the thought of her spending Christmas in that dreadful place.

One of the problems was her medication. I said that if I was given instructions I was sure I was quite capable of dealing with tablets. Eventually they agreed that if I signed the relevant papers, which absolved the hospital of responsibility, I could take her home for a few days. Looking forward to a nice family Christmas, I collected Mattie from the Old Manor the day before Christmas Eve and we spent Christmas Day at Keysley Farm with Colin and Sarah.

This was probably the worst Christmas I have ever had. Mattie was very unwell and was unable to settle down in one place for more than a few minutes and did not join in with anything. We returned to our cottage early and I put her to bed. Thankfully she went to sleep. For the next few days I stayed with her at the cottage hoping she would improve and delay the time when she would have to return to the Old Manor.

However, about a week later, that decision was taken out of my hands when I walked up to the farm to have a coffee with Colin and Sarah. For some reason I was delayed and did not return home until about quarter to one. I found Mattie sprawled in a chair, unconscious and all her medication bottles empty on the floor. She had managed to find the medication, despite my efforts to conceal it. The ambulance arrived after what seemed to be an age and took her to Salisbury Hospital where she was treated and subsequently recovered, then after a few days she was transferred back to the Old Manor.

A few months later the hospital informed me that Mattie had improved sufficiently for her to return home, provided that she had constant care. This placed me in a difficult situation; some of our friends thought that I should give up my work and spend my whole time as her carer. Although Colin now owned and managed the farm, I enjoyed working for him and being involved in the farm's development and could not come to terms with the idea of staying at home all the time. After long discussions with Colin and Sarah, it was decided that we should advertise for a live-in carer, which we did. The advertisement in 'The Lady' attracted considerable response and I began to think that it would be an easy exercise to find someone suitable.

How wrong I was! As it transpired, the majority of applicants had even worse problems than we had! In some cases, they were even trying to escape from something, be it a husband or lover, or just trying to get away and saw this position as putting a roof over their heads. Two ladies travelled to Keysley that I considered quite unsuitable.

A third lady, who sounded very kind and caring on the telephone, explained that the position sounded ideal provided that she could bring her two dogs. We considered that this might even be an advantage. She phoned again a few days later to ask if we could meet her somewhere, as it was a long way for her to travel. She went on to explain that she was showing her dogs at a show in Gloucestershire and could Mattie and I meet her there?

She sounded so nice and genuine that we agreed, and on the day, we arrived at the show and quickly found her with her dogs. We spent a couple of hours with her and Mattie was very taken with her. She told us that she was a divorced person, living in a flat in a town, and needed to move to the countryside for the sake of her dogs, and that she would definitely take the job if it was offered. I said that we would let her know.

After talking to two local applicants we decided to offer the position to the lady with the dogs. She sounded absolutely delighted when I phoned and wanted to come as soon as possible. We arranged for her to start on the following Monday week and she said she would arrive about lunchtime. On the appointed Monday morning I received a phone call from her saying that she was sorry that she could not come, I asked why? She just said because she could not and rang off. I was devastated and didn't know what to do. I had spent hours and hours on this project and had got nowhere.

Mattie was by now living at home again so I was getting desperate for some help. I advertised again but only locally, and this time for a lady companion to come on a daily basis. A lady in her fifties came for a couple of weeks but did not wish to continue. This was when a farmer friend, Arthur Coward, from a farm near Mere, told me that his wife Christine had turned their large farmhouse into a care home. I took Mattie to see them and arranged for Mattie to go there for a trial period. This we did but Mattie wanted to come home after only three days.

Soon after this I was able to employ Kathie, a young lady who lived with her husband in Warminster. Kathie proved to be an excellent carer and Mattie liked her very much. Kathie worked from eight until five, Monday to Friday helping Mattie with her brain exercises, driving our little Fiesta on shopping trips, and taking Mattie to visit friends and relatives.

This ideal situation did not last for more than a few months. Mattie's condition began to deteriorate and she had to be admitted to the mental hospital at Devizes, where she remained for several months. Here at Devizes she was gradually stabilized and I made arrangements for her to live at Bramley House in Mere, the place where she had worked before she became ill. Mattie seemed reasonably happy there for several months, and I was able to visit her most evenings and then go to a pub for dinner and a chat. I found life was very lonely at my little house down in the wood.

I was by now a regular at my local pub, the 'Fox and Hounds' at East Knoyle, and I used to eat there quite often when I was living on my own. Ed Knight, the landlord's son, used to work behind the bar most evenings, then cut and delivered logs or worked on local farms during the day. I enjoyed talking to him

The New Holland TF44 in wheat

about his experiences on other farms and gained the impression that he was very interested in combine harvesters. Colin by this time had bought his own second hand combine for the coming harvest. I told Ed about the New Holland TF 44 and said that Colin may be looking for someone to drive it.

Before long Ed was working for Colin on an ad hoc casual basis and he operated the TF 44. At that time Colin was growing peas in the arable rotation, as they were an excellent preparation for winter wheat. Drying the peas can be difficult so Ed would cut wheat to be put through the drier during the mornings and, if the sun was hot, he moved to the peas in the afternoon. The peas were taken to Manor Farm and tipped directly into the store.

All this was really hard going as the combine had to be changed from cutting wheat to cutting peas during the hottest part of the day. The biggest part of this task was refitting the lifters to harvest the peas, which were lying flat on the ground. Because of the stony ground the damage to the cutter bar and auger was horrendous, with some fields being worse than others. This was the main reason for the eventual dropping of the peas from the rotation.

Ed proved to be an excellent operator of machinery and went on to do most of the drilling, spraying and fertilising on an increasing acreage. He was great fun to work with and he and Colin got on very well. I became quite friendly with his parents, Andrew and Doreen, and they kindly invited me to the pub for Christmas day, after they learned that I was on my own. We enjoyed a lovely late lunch with all their family. Andrew and I then went to sleep until it was time to open the pub again. It was a great Christmas day, despite my worries about poor Mattie.

During her stay at Bramley House, I used to pick up Mattie and take her to friends or relatives for Sunday lunch; sometimes embarrassing difficulties arose and I never knew what might happen. A typical example of what could occur happened on a trip to Bert and Jean's for Sunday lunch. Having enjoyed my favourite meal of roast beef and Yorkshire pudding, followed by apple pie and custard, Mattie wanted to use the toilet.

Jean showed her the way and came back into the room. I was a little concerned about what might happen and expressed my worries to Jean who suggested that we give her a few minutes and she would go and see. We continued our conversation for a few minutes when I said that I would see if Mattie was all right. In the event Jean got up to see then returned quickly to tell us that Mattie had run a bath and was lying in the water fully clothed. The need for a little chuckle was irresistible. Jean lent us some dry clothes and after a while everything was back to normal: Mattie behaved as if nothing unusual had happened.

All my worries were thrust into the background on the 26th of February 1996, when Sarah gave birth to our first grandchild, a lovely little girl. I collected Mattie from Bramley House and we drove to the hospital in Salisbury and met Evie for the first time, congratulating Sarah and Colin. Mattie did not seem to appreciate the importance of the occasion, and I wanted to celebrate in a pub on the way home but Mattie wanted to get back. Anyway I hope she enjoyed the experience.

One Saturday afternoon in April, I went off to Bath armed with a shopping list of things to buy for Mattie, provided by Bramley House. In Marks and Spencers, I struggled with the list - some of the items were underclothes. I was just considering giving it up as a bad job when I spotted a familiar face. It was Gail Gray, a lady I had met on a couple of occasions in the 'Bath Arms' at Horningsham some years before. Quickly explaining the situation with Mattie, Gail offered to help and the shopping thankfully was soon finished.

We decided to have a walk around town, looking at the shops and catching up on all the local news. I explained briefly what had happened to Mattie as we walked up and down Milsom Street and on to the Theatre Royal, where we found a restaurant nearby. We had a very good dinner and chatted about everything under the sun.

Gail enjoyed reminding me about one evening at the 'Bath Arms' when she overheard me in a conversation, when I was describing to a few friends how I had been collecting semen from bulls, and inspecting it under a microscope. She reminded me that very soon most of the people in the bar were involved in the discussion, which was punctuated by howls of laughter.

During the dinner Gail told me that she lived at Beckhampton in an annex to a large house, belonging to her brother Tim, who lived and worked in Hong Kong. She explained that she had recently completed a comprehensive renovation of the property, and now lived there in order to maintain it for her brother and family to use for their annual holiday in England.

Walking with Gail to Charlotte Street car park, she told me that she had an art studio at Beckhampton where she did interior design contracts and manufactured place mats for pubs, clubs and restaurants and that I should visit her there. She suggested the following Saturday and I agreed, saying that I would phone her during the week. I saw her off in her Fiesta XR2 and walked back to my own car, with, I must say some degree of anticipation and not feeling quite so alone.

I arrived about twelve on the following Saturday, and Gail quickly showed me around the huge house, beautifully decorated and furnished. Her studio was on the first floor of an adjacent building over a large garage for three cars. The studio was huge and very well equipped, with examples of her drawings and designs exhibited on the walls.

We then walked to her local pub, the 'Wagon and Horses', where there were several local customers and she explained that they were quite small because they worked at the nearby racing stables and were probably jockeys. Over lunch Gail told me that her brother was an accountant with KPMG in Hong Kong and had a very well paid position. When she told me that his hobby was collecting Ferraris, and he now owned five, I realised he was very well paid indeed.

I enquired where the cars were and she told me that he had one in Hong Kong and the others were stored and maintained by a specialist company in Gloucestershire. When he arrived for his annual holiday, the cars were delivered on a transporter and collected again after he had returned to Hong Kong.

As we walked back to her house, Gail told me that she had been married in Canada where she had lived for about twelve years and had a twenty-two-year-old son called Geoffrey. Geoffrey seemed to have a pretty good job in London, working in the advertising industry and living in his own flat. I remember him describing what he did at work and me not understanding a word of what he was on about. His job description was apparently a 'Media Strategist', whatever that was.

Over the next few weeks I visited Mattie most evenings and even made it to see Gail as often as I could. It was a long drive to Beckhampton so sometimes I stayed over, involving an early start to get to work at Keysley by eight in the morning. At weekends I continued to take Mattie to see friends or relatives, but she was very unwell and appeared not to be with it most of the time.

I began to think that it would be nice to get away for a while, and decided to ask Gail if she would come away with me. The last holiday I had taken was more of a nightmare than a holiday. I had decided to take Mattie on a coach tour to the Lake District, as I felt that the other passengers would be some comfort, and at least someone different to chat to. It was not a great success. We stayed for a few nights at the Windermere Hotel where they had evening entertainment. After dinner I would take Mattie to watch the shows but she would show no interest and ask to go to bed where she would sleep soundly.

I was becoming very bored with all this and talked to some of the hotel staff, enquiring where I might go for a drink and a chat. One of the waitresses told me that on Thursday evenings a crowd of the staff walked down to Ambleside to enjoy the live music and dancing; I could join them if I would like. I thanked her and agreed to meet at nine outside the hotel the next evening.

Mattie was sound asleep by eight. She still smoked a few cigarettes so I made sure that there were no matches or cigarettes in the room. left a note saying where I was and to ring reception if she wanted anything. I reported to reception that she was in her room asleep, but if there was a problem, to ring the pub at Ambleside.

When we all returned after an evening of fun, there was all hell let loose at the hotel. There was a fire engine in the forecourt so I rushed to our room to find two firemen, lots of smoke and no Mattie. I flew down the stairs to reception where they told me that Mattie had been moved to another room. They suspected that Mattie had fallen asleep while smoking and dropped the cigarette on to the carpet. The carpet had smouldered producing lots of smoke, setting off the smoke alarms.

I found Mattie fast asleep in another room, and then went to see the extent of the damage. There was just a small patch of carpet burnt very black; the smoke alarm went off before there was any smoke damage. I went back to reception in a bit of a state, apologising and promising to pay for the damage, whereupon they said that we would sort things out in the morning and not to worry. It dawned on me then how incredibly stupid I had been and I spent the rest of the night thinking about how much worse it could have been.

However, all that was in the past and I was now looking forward. So one evening I asked Gail if she would like to come with me to Scotland for a week or ten days. She said that she would be delighted and that she had some friends there and would like to see them. We decided that we would drive off on the following Monday morning, 17th June, make no arrangements and stay at bed and breakfast accommodation wherever we happened to be.

A visit was made to Gail's aunt in Glenrothies, she was a lovely old lady; she took us out and treated us to a very nice lunch. Further north we called to see some old friends of Gail's, Sue and Allan, who had moved to Scotland some years before to escape the rat race of life in Odiham. Gail had lived in Odiham for some years after returning from Canada

Sue and Allan lived in a beautiful part of Scotland, north of Alith, at the end of a long, broad valley. They told us that they could see us coming for miles. As we left them I realised that we could see their house for miles. We had a wonderful few days, visiting Loch Lomond, Ben Nevis and the Isle of Skye, my first real holiday for several years. All good things come to an end and

Gail and me in Scotland 1996

we drove home through the beautiful Yorkshire Moors, then faced the long drive back to reality.

Soon after returning from our holiday in Scotland, Bramley House informed me that they could no longer cope with Mattie as her behaviour was deteriorating. I could accept what they were telling me as on my evening visits she occasionally went to the toilet and ended up in the bath. When she washed her hair with bleach, they said that was the last straw and they were not approved to care for mental cases.

I now spent several days visiting nursing homes within easy reach and finding it very difficult to find somewhere suitable. A few days later, at the weekend, discussing the whole thing with Gail, she said that she would have a word with Aurora at 'The Close' in West Lavington, where her mother was living. Gail went on to say that when she and her brother were looking for a place for their mother, they engaged a professional person to prepare reports on various homes in the area, and 'The Close' was highly recommended.

Gail phoned about mid week to say that there was a chance of getting a place for Mattie at West Lavington and that we should visit Aurora on the following Saturday. I agreed to go to Gail's place for lunch at Beckhampton then visit the home in the afternoon.

Aurora was from the Philippines and was everything that Gail had told me about her; she seemed very kind and caring. As Aurora showed us around, Gail introduced me to her mother, who said, "Oh yes, I have known him for years!" I smiled while Gail had a good laugh.

Aurora told us that there was the possibility of a place at 'The Close' as it was called, so we made arrangements for me to take Mattie there for Aurora to assess her condition. If Mattie were to move to 'The Close', Aurora said that she would, in cooperation with Mattie's doctor and Social Worker, try gradually to reduce the medication. She went on to explain that in some care homes they found it easier to keep up the medication so that the patients were sleepy and more controllable. Medication could only be reduced, if carers were prepared to work with the consequences.

After I had taken Mattie to 'The Close' to meet Aurora and had agreed to take the room that was offered, arrangements were made to move Mattie from Bramley House. Geoffrey helped us fix up the television and reading lamps, and also put some of her pictures on the walls. I felt much happier and more relaxed and no longer felt so alone.

Mattie remembered nothing of all this and seemed to be in some sort of a trance, probably because of her medication. However, she settled in with no problems and I was able to visit most evenings, and on occasions continued on to Beckhampton to see Gail. Sometimes I stayed over but could not escape the early mornings. I hated that long drive but thankfully there were three different routes.

CHAPTER 24

SALVATION AND A HOLIDAY

By now Gerald Hyam had been representing Ray and me in negotiations with Lloyd's of London and the Hardship Committee for more than three years and it seemed at times that nothing would ever be resolved. During 1995 Llcyd's produced a settlement plan, which was put to the names for a vote.

It was quite clear that there was little to commend it and the vote to reject it was overwhelming. So long as we remained in hardship, and Gerald worked tirelessly to justify this stance to Lloyd's, they could take no action against us. The constant fear was that they would draw down our bank guarantees, which would trigger an immediate reaction from our banks to repay, in my case £450,000. This would entail an immediate sale of my share of the farm to Colin.

In July 1996, with a new Chairman, David Rowland, and a new Chief Executive Officer, Ron Sandler, Lloyd's produced another settlement offer, which would settle all 1992 and prior liabilities and provide finality to names. A very complicated document was produced called 'Reconstruction and Renewal' or 'R & R' as it was later referred to.

Each name was provided with an individual document that described how the offer affected them, after taking account of their losses, their assets and their litigation awards. This brilliant plan involved setting up a new insurance company called 'Equitas', and each name was to pay a premium to this company to reinsure all 1992 and prior years' liabilities. The form of acceptance had to be signed and in the hands of Lloyd's by 12 noon on the 28th August 1996. This would release Lloyd's Bank from their guarantee to Lloyd's of £450,000. Failure to sign and return the form would put a name once again, at the mercy of Lloyd's dreaded debt collection department.

My personal premium to Equitas was approximately £1,300,000, to be paid by Lloyd's as part of the settlement. Gerald Hyam negotiated a final settlement on my behalf, for me to pay £450,000 in three annual instalments of £150,000. I was involved in these negotiations because Lloyd's were of the opinion that the farm at Keysley should be revalued. As the valuation we had provided had been carried out in 1993, it was difficult to prove that the farm had not increased in value in the intervening period.

Gerald Hyam was in constant telephone and fax communication with Lloyd's and with me in the office at Keysley, asking questions about land values and farm profitability for at least a couple of hours before the twelve-noon deadline. As the minutes ticked by, I suddenly realised that perspiration was dripping from my forehead onto the fax machine. The deadline for me to accept the offer was very close, a few minutes in fact, when Lloyd's backed down and I was able to sign the final document and fax it to Gerald.

A condition of acceptance was for names to admit their liabilities to Lloyd's and to agree that they would never initiate any legal action against them. Also, any reinsurance recoveries accruing to names had to be paid back to Lloyd's Central Fund, and any personal earnings over £20,000 a year had to be forfeited. I believe that this settlement was better than anything I could reasonably have expected, and the amount of money that Colin and I had to pay was low because of the huge litigation awards made to members of the action groups.

It is difficult to say, with any accuracy, what my total losses were at Lloyd's, but adding my previous payments and litigation costs to the £450,000 settlement, an actual loss of about £1,250,000 sounds reasonable. I believe that this was a satisfactory result in the circumstances and enabled Colin to continue to farm at Keysley. Without this settlement and the reinsurance through Equitas, I would have had to face the uncertainty of the bankruptcy court with all its hidden dangers. Gerald had estimated that my eventual losses could have amounted to about £10,000,000 over the next few years.

My earnings from Lloyd's membership were never very great - the best result was 1986 in fact, when I received £102,000. To achieve this I was a member of sixty-two syndicates. Before that I had received an occasional cheque for about £20,000 and a couple of years, had to send a cheque to cover losses. There was a substantial saving of Income Tax of course, as rates were high at that time but this is very difficult to quantify. Looking back, and ignoring the catastrophic loss, it appears to me that accepting unlimited liability was wrong for the amount of earnings that I received. It was never going to enable me to buy a larger farm.

However, at the time of joining the risks did not appear to be very great and Income Taxes were very high. Lloyd's had a three hundred year history of successful trading and was one of Britain's great institutions, famous throughout the world. I felt proud and privileged to be a member, and felt good that I was instrumental in attracting insurance business into London. On the whole Lloyd's made my life very interesting, being personally involved in world events, and I have no real regrets.

The settlement for Ray was for about £75,000 to be paid in instalments over three years. This time limit was extended eventually for several more years, and I was pleased that Colin was able to lend some money to Ray to help him out.

However the settlement depended on the solvency of Equitas, which was always in doubt. If Equitas were to fail then policy holders could again claim from the names, so although Lloyds said that the settlement provided finality, it was in fact conditional. It was to be another ten years before Equitas was taken over by a large worldwide insurance company, Berkshire Hathaway, with a huge injection of capital, and a guarantee to relieve all reinsured names of their liabilities.

Colin and I were very fortunate that the huge debt to Lloyd's coincided with a change in agricultural policy by the EU. They had decided to pay a subsidy direct to the farmers instead of paying them indirectly through export restitutions, import tariffs and various other means of maintaining the price of home produced commodities. This meant that we were to be paid different sums for the various crops that we grew. These sums were deliberately high as the expectation was for grain prices to fall dramatically once the old system had been abandoned.

This did not happen and for three years we received the same high prices for our crops, and a substantial subsidy. This enabled Colin to pay the £150,000 each year to Lloyd's without increasing his indebtedness to the bank. I consider this to be an amazing stroke of luck as the circumstances of this were completely beyond our control.

Harvest was fast approaching and I realised that there would be difficulties as Gail lived so far away, but she was very good and came to see me quite often, coming with me in the tractor on occasions, then cooking a late dinner for us at my house and driving back to Beckhampton in the morning.

Harvesting wheat at Keysley 1995

I well remember one evening when we were combining wheat at Whitecliff for Andrew Clark. Gail and I were in the tractor following the combine, in readiness to draw alongside to take on wheat, when we noticed a thin trail of fire in the stubble behind the combine. I grabbed the CB radio and called to Alex to stop, telling him that the machine was on fire.

Stopping the tractor, we jumped down and ran to the combine. Alex was already looking for the seat of the fire with the extinguisher in his hand. I suggested that we might be able to stamp out the fire and save the extinguisher for use later if necessary. We found that burning engine oil was running down onto the ground, and that we were able to keep the fire under control, raking some burning chaff from around the straw output shaft and bearing. It was now imperative that the engine was switched off before it was damaged through lack of oil. Alex climbed up, switched off the engine, and tried to call the Fire Service on his mobile phone, but could not get a signal.

The other tractor and trailer now appeared in the field driven by Jane, which meant that we had another person to help fight the fire. Jane worked for Colin at Keysley on a casual, 'can you help out today sort of arrangement?' Jane was always cheerful and enthusiastic and lots of fun to work with.

By now the fire in the stubble was taking hold and had moved into the crop despite Gail and Jane's efforts to stamp it out. I was concentrating on keeping the fire away from the combine, which could not now be moved. Andrew now arrived on the scene in his pickup truck and we asked him to dash to the farmhouse to phone for the Fire Service.

Andrew quickly returned to say that the telephone was out of action due to an accident down the road. Thankfully, by this time, Alex had climbed on top of the combine, and had managed to make the call. Jane, Gail, Andrew and I, were able to carry on fighting the fire while Alex stood guard by the machine with the extinguisher. A fire engine arrived in the field, in what seemed like double quick time, and the firemen had put out the fire in about 15 minutes.

On later investigation, we found that the bearing on the straw output shaft had failed, got very hot and ignited some chaff nearby. Unfortunately, a rubber hose from high up on the engine, with a drain plug on the end, designed to facilitate draining the oil during servicing, had been surrounded by the burning chaff and had burnt through, draining the engine of oil. Although a small area of Andrew's wheat was destroyed, I consider that we were very lucky not to have lost the combine harvester.

After the harvest and completion of autumn drilling, Gail and I decided to celebrate her birthday, 4th November, with a few days in Paris, travelling by train through the channel tunnel. We had a lovely time visiting the Eiffel Tower, Pompidou Centre, Galleries Lafayette and then the Moulin Rouge. One evening we dined and danced on the Baton Mouche, on a very romantic cruise under the illuminated bridges over the Seine.

We spent the next few months staying at each other's houses, going to the cinema in Swindon, entertaining and visiting friends and discussing plans for the future. I was still very sad about Mattie and visited her at 'The Close' as often as I could, and feeling very unsure of myself, I was finding it difficult to commit myself totally to Gail. I made regular trips with Mattie to the Blackbury Hill hospital in Bristol, where a series of tests were carried out by various doctors, to assess her brain activity. On one of these trips I made an appointment to talk to the doctor in charge.

I explained to her my situation with Gail. A long discussion ensued. She confirmed that Mattie was suffering, in all probability, from 'Picks Disease', but it could only be positively confirmed by post mortem. She concluded by saying that Mattie's condition could appear to improve temporarily, only to get worse again, and that she would probably die within five years. She advised that if there was a chance of establishing a new long-term relationship, then I should go for it. So Gail and I discussed moving into my house and bought a new bed, and Gail had some new curtains made, and the place seemed to be coming alive again.

June has always been a good month to take a holiday from the farm. There was nothing much more to do to the crops until harvest; the grain stores were nearly empty and cleaned, and this year was no exception, so we planned a driving holiday in Western Canada. I had always wanted to go to Canada as I had studied that part of the world at school. Gail told me that she had friends near Vancouver, where she had lived for a few years, at a place called Williams Lake. Gail's 'near', meant in reality several hundred miles, but she made all of the arrangements, and contacted her friends who she wanted to visit and we flew from Heathrow to Vancouver on the 11th June 1997.

In the weeks prior to our trip to Canada, Mattie had shown a remarkable improvement in her condition, to the extent that she seemed to know who I was, and could hold a limited conversation. In fact, when I told her that I was taking a holiday in Canada, she wished to know with whom I was going. There was no way that I could tell her the truth and risk setting her back, now that she was showing the first signs of improvement since she first became ill. I told her that I was going on an organised farming tour, and she wished me a good time and seemed quite happy with that.

Our Canadian trip, to which we had both so looked forward, was dampened, to a certain extent, by my worries about Mattie. However we had a wonderful time. From Vancouver we boarded a ferry to Salt Spring Island where we stayed with Ron and Margareta Nordine. Margareta met us at the ferry port in her '56 Cadillac convertible', then we went on to meet Ron who was working on his fishing boat.

After a couple of nights we took the ferry back to Vancouver and our hired car. We headed south into the United States to visit Sue and Stan Birkland in Birch Bay, WA. Crossing the border involved stopping at a barrier and being asked questions such as 'are you carrying any spirits?' I said 'yes' just as Gail said 'no', and we laughed. This of course aroused suspicion and we were directed to the customs shed for full interview and to pay some duty. With Gail as navigator, it was easy to find Stan's place - they were living on the very edge of a golf course; Stan just lived for his golf. We spent a couple of hours with them with Gail talking about old times with Sue. Travelling further south we spent the night with Lesley and Allan Rankin. Seeing the sights of Bellingham took up most of the morning before it was time to hit the road to Seattle.

Unknown to her brother, Tim, Gail had booked us a room in the same hotel that he was staying at for a conference, and he was flying in from Hong Kong that very day. Having found the hotel and checked in, we were sitting in the lobby for a few minutes, when in came Tim who went straight to the desk. As he was checking in we crept up and stood beside him; he was so shocked and pleased to see us as he had no idea we were in Seattle.

The three of us spent the next day together seeing the sights of the city - much more fun than my previous visit when I was on my own. We then drove north into Canada and up the Fraser Canyon on our way to Williams Lake. Don Docherty had built his own log cabin on the edge of an Indian reservation in the foothills of the Rockies, living there with his wife Sylvia. It was a super place to live among the mountains, lakes and all the wildlife of the area.

Don took us for a look around Williams Lake where we did some shopping, had a bite to eat, then went on to a construction yard. Here log cabins or houses were being built from huge logs. Every piece of timber was then marked and the whole house was dismantled, packed into a container and shipped off to Japan.

Three very pleasant days were spent at Don's, then we got into the car, travelling north to Prince George where the weather turned very cold and snow was falling - the town looked very bleak. We continued north, then turned east through Pine Pass in the Rockies and headed towards Peace River. I had learned about this area in my geography class at school; it was the most northerly wheat growing area in the world.

Progress was slow through the pass owing to the damage to the road by the severe frost, signs continually warning us of frost heave. I was doing my best at picking a way between the cracks and the raised slabs of the road; some slabs were up to six inches above the others. Just as I thought we were doing well, the offside front wheel crashed into one of these jagged steps and burst the tyre. By the time I had changed the wheel and got moving again, I began to think that we were going to be late finding a place to stay, but it transpired that we were by now over the worst and soon arrived in Grand Prairie.

Having found a place to stay in Grand Prairie, we discovered that the lady of the house was interested in interior design, so she and Gail had lots to talk about. After a while we enquired if there was any possibility of visiting a farm in the locality. She made a few phone calls and arranged for us to pick up a friend of hers that evening, and he would take us to a relative with a large arable farm. Driving a few miles north towards Sexsmith, we picked him up and then drove for about fifteen miles over gravel tracks. It was now past eight o'clock and we were concerned that we would be too late to see anything, but we had not taken into account the fact that we were in the far north and it was light until about eleven thirty.

Arriving at last at the farm, we met Ray Seers and his wife Pat in their beautiful home. He showed us around the barns and his equipment, including two John Deere combines, a Caterpillar tractor with rubber tracks and an air seeder. The sprayer was a small, unimpressive machine and it occurred to me that very little spraying was necessary to produce the crops. It transpired that the crops grown were all genetically modified to be resistant to Roundup.

So the crops were sown with the air seeder, then, when it had grown to a certain stage, together with all the weeds, it was sprayed with Roundup, a safe, non-toxic and biodegradable weed killer. As the growing season was very short, fungal diseases were not such a problem as they are at home in the UK. This was the first time that I had seen GM crops grown commercially as this technology is not allowed in the UK or Europe.

Before we went back to the house, Ray was keen to show us inside a relatively new barn. It proved to be a well- insulated building and was equipped with a variety of wood working machines, including power saws, planer, lathe, sanders and drills. Ray explained that the winters were pretty grim, and with no farming to do, he spent his time making furniture. He showed us a few examples of his work - some items were very beautiful and well made.

Ray and Pat then took us to see an elk farm where elk were kept for their antlers, producing velvet. We saw large freezers full of antlers. Then back to the farmhouse where we were told about the history of the Peace River district. The Canadian Government of the time promised to build a railway through the region, and an ancestor of Ray's set out from Edmonton, three hundred miles away, with a horse and cart, to claim some land and build a farm. A year later he returned to Edmonton to collect his wife and family.

During the course of conversation there arose a little difficulty. Ray told us that he and his wife were planning to visit relatives in the west of England soon after our return, and that they would like to visit my farm and Gail's studio. This was likely to prove embarrassing as Gail's studio and my farm were forty miles apart and worst of all we had pretended to be a married couple.

After spending the night in Grand Prairie we visited a huge lumber mill and had a conducted tour. We found it most interesting to see how the trees went in at one end of the mill and came out at the other end as four by two's, shrink wrapped in polythene packs, and loaded on a train for the first part of their journey to Japan.

The forklift truck that was used to unload the lorry loads of trees coming in from the forests was immense. It would pick up the whole load and deposit it onto the base of an elevator where the trees were propelled into the mill. As the trees ascended they were cut to length and selected to go in different directions. All this appeared to be controlled by girls in glass cabins suspended over the machines.

We then decided to take what was called a forestry road towards Jasper, saving many hours of driving. Local people were of mixed opinion as to whether we could get through that way, but the consensus was that we would definitely get as far as the coal mine, whatever that meant. We decided to give it a go, and set out early next morning, enjoying a lovely drive through some really wild country, keeping a constant lookout for bears, which they say that Canada is supposed to have. However we did see a wolf on the road travelling in our direction, he looked lost and hungry.

The road was in good condition for the first hundred miles or so then we came up to a road block and the Indian lady with the stop sign explained that we were to await an escort, when there were enough vehicles. As we had seen only one other car the whole way we wondered how long this would be. We waited and waited, but only for about an hour; at least we could see the 'coal mine'.

Eventually a four-wheel drive escort vehicle arrived, and by now there were six vehicles waiting and we were instructed to follow in convoy. This was easier said than done. The road surface had disappeared and we were soon travelling through a sea of deep mud. Keeping the car moving and in the right direction took all of my concentration. After about eight miles we were through, the car absolutely covered in mud, and soon arrived in the town of Grand Cache. Finding what appeared to be the only motel in town, with a car park covered in heaps of mud that had fallen from cars, we went into a muddy reception office and checked in. The next thing was to find a car wash. I eventually found a place where I could hire a pressure washer and the car was soon spic and span.

Continuing towards Jasper in the morning, we arrived about mid afternoon in lovely clear sunshine; the mountains looked spectacular. I was most interested in the railways so we drove up to the yellow head pass through the Rockies. Here we saw freight trains of enormous length with containers stacked two high on the flatbed trucks. We went back to town to find a place to stay and watched a large herd of elk wander through the town, grazing where and when they could. We wanted to photograph the mountains but were tired and decided to leave it until the morning. Alas, in the morning the mountains had completely disappeared in the murk. We wandered around town in the rain then motored along the ice field parkway towards Banff.

The rest of our holiday was very interesting and enjoyable - staying a few nights in the delightful town of Canmore, visiting the Kicking Horse pass, and waiting with hoards of Japanese tourists to see a long freight train pass through the spiral tunnels, where the front of the train comes out of the mountain and passes under its own tail still heading in. There are two of these tunnels, constructed to double the distance travelled and halve the gradient, to replace the original 'big hill,' notorious for runaway trains.

We went on a 'Snow Bus' trip on to the Athabaska Glacier with, once again, hundreds of Japanese. The snow buses were designed for travelling over the ice on the glacier and had massive tyres and a huge ground clearance. It was possible to walk under them by just bending your back. We then drove for several days back to Vancouver, taking a route to the south, closer to the US border, enjoying the mountains, lakes and most of all the cherries. We went to see Don's sister in Burnaby before setting off to the airport for the flight home, wondering all the while about Mattie and what to expect when we eventually arrived.

CHAPTER 25

DESPAIR, AND A
SECOND CHANCE

After getting some sleep, I returned to my house. I saw Mattie in the evening; she seemed surprisingly well and wanted to know about my holiday, and I began to feel pretty bad about the whole situation. This was to be the beginning of the worst week of my life, as the next morning, Mattie's social worker phoned me at the farm, sounding very cross, and telling me to make up my mind as to what I wanted to do, and to stop two-timing Mattie as she could now come home.

I was distraught; this was the very situation that I had sought to avoid, having taken advice from her doctors in Bristol and having discussed the position with Aurora. The advice was that any improvement in Mattie's well being could only be temporary, as she was suffering from the brain disease diagnosed by the brain scans when she first went to the Old Manor.

Gail was in a dreadful state and was convinced that I no longer loved her. I spent the weekend in turmoil; eventually deciding to leave Mattie, as there was no way that I could cope with her again. I was dreadfully worried about the effect this would have on her illness, but decided that it was now or never. Monday was the worst day of my life.

I went to work as usual and discussed the situation with Colin who was also very concerned about the effect on his mother's

269

illness, but agreed that the current situation should not continue. To complicate the situation still further, Ray and Pat Seers from Canada were due at the farm after lunch. They arrived with one of their English relatives and looked around the farm with Colin explaining what we grew and how we do it, all very technical. A very successful visit, Ray said he would have talked to Colin for hours if he could. Pat was very keen to see Gail's studio, so I was involved in embarrassing explanations as to why it was forty miles away and that we were not yet married.

I drove to Beckhampton with Ray, Pat followed with their relative in his car, dropping them off with Gail and dashing back to ' The Close' to tell Mattie that I was leaving her. Taking her out in the car, we went to a nearby pub where I explained what had happened and what I wanted to do. She was shocked and extremely cross, especially when I explained who Gail was, as she had met her on occasions when Gail was visiting her mother. During the course of this conversation I realised how poorly Mattie had been, as she had no idea that it was 1997 and could not recall the last three years at all, which of course helped me explain why this situation had arisen, and as always she seemed very understanding.

I took Mattie back to 'The Close' where I had arranged to meet Colin. He had a long talk with Mattie and tried to reassure her that he would make sure that she was looked after, and that everything that had happened with me was probably for the best. The next few days were hell, with Mattie saying awful things about Gail, and threatening to sell the farm if we moved into my house at Keysley. This was a worrying prospect, as the whole farm would have to be sold, ending Colin's career, totally undermining all I had achieved in my negotiations with Lloyd's, and destroying my lifelong ambition.

When I told Gail that we were no longer able to stay at my house she was very upset, and thought that the farm was more important than she was. We then spent a weekend at a very expensive country hotel where I hoped we might re-establish our relationship. It was a lovely place but we were not very happy as

I was racked with guilt at having deserted Mattie in her hour of need.

My relationship with Colin and Sarah deteriorated for a couple of years, mostly because they did not see eye to eye with Gail, and I even stayed away from the farm for about three months and considered doing something else.

To my great delight, Jack, my second grandchild, was born on the 25th October 1997. It was wonderful to see Colin and Sarah looking so happy and the little one in perfect health. My mind was cast back to the days when Mattie and I were trying to have a family, and suffering such ill luck. Even now Mattie is being deprived of the joys of her grandchildren growing up.

In September 1998 Gail was diagnosed as having breast cancer and had to have a mastectomy. I could scarcely believe our bad luck and felt as if I had been hit with a hammer. I was amazed by how well she faced up to it; she just dealt with it in her stride. I was very proud of her and felt much better myself. In the back of my mind was this awful fear of the 'big C' coming back to strike at our happiness.

Eventually I went back to work at the farm, but the forty miles drive there, and forty miles back was a real drag, and I was not very happy. Gail and I spent a great deal of time looking for a house within easy reach of Keysley and eventually found one at Wanstrow, near Frome. When we first saw it in November 1999 it was just a shell and the builders were busy finishing the house next door.

The builders, Innovations Ltd., were a pair of unlikely developers, Steve Key and Geoff Evans, who got together and bought a plot of land to build five houses. Contractors were engaged to carry out the heavy work such as concreting, block work, plastering and roofing. The rest of the work was divided between them. They considered that the project would see them through to their retirement. Three of the houses were sold and occupied, but the builders had permission to show us around one of them, to give us an indication of the standard of finish we could expect.

Steve and Geoff expected us to be interested in number four, the one nearing completion, but number five had a separate old building, probably an old farm barn. This building was to be a garage with a studio up above, accessed by an external staircase. This had obvious attractions for Gail and would provide facilities for her to continue her artwork.

After a period of negotiation, changing the planned layout of the first floor from four bedrooms to three, and planning the addition of a conservatory, we purchased the property to be completed as soon as possible in the New Year. I was able to buy a half share of the house by using the proceeds of some long forgotten insurance policies that matured when I was sixty. Gail's brother Tim kindly purchased the other half.

The builders immediately stopped work on number four and concentrated all efforts onto our house. We left them to get on with it while we flew to Santo Domingo and embarked on a Caribbean Cruise for Christmas. It was a lovely ship and it visited Cartagena in Columbia, the San Blas Islands off Panama and Limon in Costa Rica. I was interested in the activities in the port of Limon, where our ship was docked, as it seemed to be very busy. Cranes were lifting containers from ships and other cranes were loading and unloading containers to and from lorries. I learned that most of the lorries were engaged in transporting containers to and from the Pacific coast, this was to avoid the shipping costs of the Panama Canal. Truckers were able to earn very big money compared to other jobs. With poor roads, ropey old lorries and very little regulation, accidents and death were common.

We then sailed on to Cozumel, an island off Mexico. Next we docked for a couple of days in Havana, Cuba. This was a fascinating visit where we came across two separate economies, the Cuban and the U S Dollar economy. U S Dollar shops were well stocked but the Cuban shops were nearly empty. The only people to have cars were party officials or people who had kept their nineteen fifties American cars in running order. We saw very large old cars powered by very small engines, probably Trabants from Eastern Europe.

Before we left the safety of our ship we were warned that we should not board the Camel Buses. These proved to be very large Russian articulated buses, carrying up to three hundred people, and we were told that every aspect of human life from conception to death was experienced on board. The world has moved on since those dramatic days in October1962, but sadly the Cuban people still yearn for freedom.

Montego Bay, Jamaica, was our next stop before returning to Santo Domingo and our flight back to Birmingham. There were three flights for this cruise, ours to Birmingham, a second one to Manchester and a third plane to Gatwick. It was very amusing waiting for our luggage, as we continued to see bags with Manchester or Gatwick on their labels, and very few for Birmingham. We were about to give up when our bags suddenly appeared on the carousel; thankfully picking them up we made our way back to Beckhampton.

We now set about fitting out our new house. Everything had to be chosen; this was of course just up Gail's street and the list was endless - a kitchen, bathroom, tiles, taps, colours, light fittings and curtains. The farm was quiet at that time of the year so I spent a few weeks driving from Beckhampton to Wanstrow every day. I spent my time making shelves, fixing curtain rails and poles, making a padded headboard for our bed and fitting out the study for Gail's computer.

Steve was a great help with suggestions as to which fixings to use on the various walls, as my experience with domestic DIY was very limited. After we moved in, the builders still had work to complete outside, and in the garage and studio. When all this was done we had a second move and transferred all Gail's studio paraphernalia. I constructed a large plan chest for Gail and then made a workbench for myself in the garage.

When all the work was complete, the caravan that had been used as the site office and mess room had to be lifted onto a trailer by a mobile crane. Also in our back garden was the builder's toilet, which had to be lifted right over the house. We very often used that toilet ourselves, and when it was suspended over the house, I ran to Steve and asked if he had seen Gail. He said "no" and I said that I was pretty sure she had gone to the toilet. He looked up at the little object in the sky and laughed heartily.

My mother died on the 22nd April 2000, at the grand age of 97. She was active and lived alone, right up to the last few days, close to Sue at Bradford on Avon. Mother was very independent and it was fortunate that Sue could visit two or three times a day to enable her to stay in her own home. It really struck me at this time the huge advantage a woman has if she has a daughter. Sue would get the shopping, take mother to various appointments, and take her to visit friends, as well as carrying out the hundred and one things that need to be done.

For the last several years of her life, her birthday, 15th September, was celebrated with a lunch and family get together with about fifty friends and relatives. This has continued every year since her death and has been called the 'Godwin Gathering'. This takes place at the Great Cumberwell golf club, which is owned and run by my niece Marion and her husband Adrian. It is an enjoyable way to remember her and meet up with members of the family at least once a year.

I have tremendous admiration for my mother who must have been very tough. Just feeding her family under the conditions that existed at Claverton must have been hard going enough; then to keep the farm and family together for ten years after my father died was amazing. Today, it is very difficult to imagine running a household with one coldwater tap over the sink, no hot water, no inside toilet or bath and no electricity. How did she manage without a fridge? I remember the sink and cold water tap being installed, so before that the only water was in the dairy.

Religion was very strong in my mother's life, and I believe that during her last days she was convinced that she was going to join 'Daddy' in heaven. In her younger days she insisted that her family were brought up in the traditions of the church and I am sure this was partly the cause of her hostility to Chris all those years before. I have been told that before I was born, my father employed a young couple, the man was to help on the farm and the girl was to help Mother in the house. They lived in the attic

My Wedding to Gail 2001

and somehow my mother found out that they were not married and promptly threw them out.

Settling into our new house was no problem; a small garden to look after and a pub just across the road seemed good to me. However, I began to realise that our relationship would probably be improved if I divorced Mattie. This was quickly and quietly carried out without, I hope, any serious detrimental effects on poor Mattie. On the 7th July 2001, a very hot day, Gail and I were married at Shepton Mallet Registry Office, and stopped for a drink at Cranmore on the way home. Gradually our lives and happiness continued to improve and I began to feel that I had been granted a second chance in life. Our house is within easy reach of Keysley Farm and my relationship with Colin and Sarah gradually improved over time.

As soon as the Lloyd's debt had been paid off in 1999, with wheat at £120 tonne, the price of wheat fell to around £65 or £75 for the next few years. Once again the EU changed the subsidy system in 2000 and farmers were to be paid what was called a 'Single Farm Payment'. This subsidy was paid on every acre of the farm irrespective of whether anything was produced or not. This put farming firmly in the market place - no longer would a farmer have to grow a crop in order to receive a subsidy.

Mother's death was obviously not unexpected as she approached the magic 100 years of age and anyway she was of a previous generation. Much harder to bear was the sudden and unexpected death of my brother Ray. I knew nothing until the Wednesday evening of 10th March 2004, when I had a phone call from Chris to say that Ray was dead. I was so shocked that I didn't know what to say. A few minutes later I phoned back to find out what had happened. Apparently Ray had been suffering some pain in his leg and the doctor had been prescribing painkillers. Over time there appeared to be no improvement so Ray was sent to hospital on the previous Friday for observation. More painkillers were administered over the weekend, and certain tests were carried out at the beginning of the week.

On the Wednesday morning it was discovered that the painkillers had caused internal bleeding, and despite the efforts of the hospital, Ray's life could not be saved. Ray's death was a great loss to all of us; me in particular as he was always a kind of father figure, and we had worked together for many years. I was very fortunate to be asked by his family to make an address at his funeral in the little church at Mamble near his home in Worcestershire.

People from all corners of the country, farmers, cattlemen, horsemen, huntsmen and men from the racing fraternity, together with friends and relations, attended Ray's funeral. Over 500 people - the church and the village pub were totally overwhelmed, the service being relayed outside by a speaker system. The headstone on his grave in the little churchyard at Mamble has a carving of a bull, and the words, 'The Bull Man'.

Ray could be described as a great character, being a man of his time, very little education, but an absolute wizard at mental arithmetic, gradually stifled in his last few years by modern regulations. Above all, he was utterly fearless, never afraid of man or beast. Ray was not a big man but when he was handling the bulls, even the large continental breeds, he was always the master, totally in charge, talking and reassuring the animals the whole time. This was the result of experience and technique developed over the years, which I always tried to emulate.

Colin continued to farm efficiently during this period, concentrating on his most profitable crop - first year winter wheat, leaving land fallow if he saw no chance of growing a profitable crop. He managed to increase his acres by contract farming for other farmers. Colin was still farming at Manor Farm, Monkton Deverill, and had been farming Whitecliff Farm for several years. Then, after sharing the cost of a combine with Robert Brown at Hindon for one season, Colin was able to farm the one thousand acre farm for himself.

Farming some two thousand acres gave Colin huge economies of scale and bargaining power when buying inputs. This proved to be very profitable despite the low prices for wheat and oil seeds. During this period Colin had been storing wheat and oil seed rape for Centaur Grain and had increased his storage capacity by building more grain stores and utilising the stores at Whitecliff and Hindon.

In 2006 Colin lost the contract on the one thousand acre farm that he had been farming for three years, because Robert Brown decided that he would like to farm it himself. This meant that the economies of scale that had been enjoyed, and on which profits depended, would disappear, and I believe Colin became disillusioned with farming in this country. He took his family to Australia for a Christmas holiday, and to take a second look at Australian agriculture. A serious drought and the potential effects of global warming on an already very dry continent gave him second thoughts.

Colin then decided to give up the farming on the other two farms, sell most of his machinery, dispense with Ed Knight as his tractor/ combine driver and concentrate on his storage business. He continued to farm the 800 acres at Keysley, employing a contractor to do the drilling and combining. Helping him with this decision was the EU policy of paying farmers for various environmental and wildlife projects. These continually reduced the area that he could farm at Manor Farm and Whitecliff Farm, as did the increasing importance of shooting, and the growing of crops for pheasant cover.

Ed left at this time and concentrated on building up his firewood business, investing in a log processor and renting one of Robert Brown's yards including a large shed. Before very long he was processing hundreds of tons of timber into logs and delivering to households. Ed's father, who had retired from the 'Fox and Hounds', was very much involved with the log business.

Colin is now planning to increase his grain storage capacity to about 28,000 tonnes at Keysley, and is in the process of designing a scheme which will satisfy the planning authorities - not so easy in an area of 'Outstanding Natural Beauty', or AONB. If this all happens then perhaps Ed may come back and work for Colin at harvest time when the log business is quiet.

CHAPTER 26

AND FINALLY

It is now January 2009 and I am coming to the end of my story, although I hope I will have a few more years to live and reflect on a most interesting life. Mattie and I spent thirty one years of happy married life. apart from her occasional bouts of depression, caused, I believe, by her miscarriages and her perceived failure to produce the family that she dreamed of. Mattie has spent the last fifteen years in homes or mental institutions and it makes me so sad to think she has missed out on all those years. I have not seen her for many years but Colin, Sarah and the children visit her regularly and report to me. They tell me that she seems to be happy in her own little world. I would love to visit her but Colin thinks that it may destabilise her and make things worse. As things are, I can at least remember her as she was.

Looking back over my life I realise how lucky I have been, living my life as I would have wished, and enjoying fitness and good health. My work place has been the beautiful living countryside, my short experience of great cities of the world has only reminded me of my extreme good fortune. There have been a few 'downs' in my life, as in most lives, but the 'ups' have more than made up for them. And I have lived through a period of relative peace with none of my nearest and dearest having to endure the horrors of war.

My business life has brought me into close contact with so

many different and interesting people - Farm Workers, Mechanics, Engineers, Veterinary Surgeons, Scientists, Solicitors, Bankers, Underwriters and Insolvency Practitioners to mention just a few.

I have witnessed the huge changes that have taken place in my lifetime, from early telephone and radio systems to the Internet and mobile telephones. I cannot imagine life without a telephone or electricity as was the case at Vineyards Farm. Air travel is no longer only for the very rich, now there is regular, safe and reliable air travel for everyone. When I was in my teens it was only possible to fly to somewhere like America if you saved up for many months; at the time I thought that I would never be able to fly to places like that. Now it is normal to fly to New York and back for the price of a weekly wage, and friends of ours have flown to New York to do their Christmas shopping.

The changes in agriculture in my lifetime have been amazing. When I was born on my father's farm the main motive power was provided by horses and I remember the first tractor arriving at the farm. It was a Fordson. It ran on paraffin, after being started on petrol by cranking the engine with the starting handle. This machine produced about twenty-five brake horsepower, had a clutch cum brake, three gears and a pulley wheel for driving stationary machinery by means of a flat canvas belt. Gradually various implements were modified to be used behind the tractor, having their shafts replaced by a drawbar. On most machines a man was still required to work the controls on mowers, binders and seed drills etc, as if the machine was pulled by horses.

This reminds me of a sad event when I was very young. It was haymaking time and my father was mowing in the front paddock with two of his horses, Captain and Toby. A rabbit hole caused Toby to break his leg and he had to be destroyed. Father was very fond of his horses and I remember that it was like losing one of the family. However, the very next morning two men arrived at the farm to convert the mowing machine, so that it could be pulled by the tractor.

Over the years a steady development introduced diesel engines, crawler tractors and eventually four-wheel drive. Electrical systems were introduced and included electric starting and lights. Hydraulic systems became common and were continuously improved to operate implements attached to the three-point linkage, including automatic depth control of ploughs and cultivators. Operation of remote hydraulic rams on implements became possible. Mechanical power could be transmitted to implements on the move by a power take-off shaft located at the rear of the tractor. The number of gears available to the tractor driver has increased, as has his comfort, with power steering and push button controls.

Early efforts to provide the driver with protection against the weather proved disastrous in the unlikely event of an overturn and many people lost their lives. Legislation saw the introduction of crush proof safety cabs. These were so noisy that drivers damaged their hearing, leading to more legislation to produce quiet cabs with heaters and air conditioning. The latter was common for tractors many years before it became available for cars. With the

The driver was unhurt, thanks to crush-proof cab, 1979

introduction of quiet cabs came radios and cassette players, no longer are tractor drivers cut off from world events.

Today a large range of tractors are available, from quite small garden tractors to enormous machines of several hundred horsepower. The larger tractors are now equipped with an automatic satellite steering system which maps the field and can steer to within two centimetres of the last run across the field. Implements can be put in and out of work in exactly the right place without the driver having to watch for the marks on the ground, making the whole operation very efficient. The application of seed, fertiliser and sprays can be done in the dark if necessary, without missing strips or overlapping.

Harvesting machinery has developed from the horse drawn binder producing sheaves of corn, which had to be stooked to finish ripening; then, with a massive amount of labour, carted to a rick, thatched and eventually threshed when the threshing machine trundled onto the farm. Soon after the Second World War came the combine harvester, producing grain in sacks, like the Massey Harris 726 I worked on with Colin Dix. This development saw the introduction of 'in sack' grain driers. Tanker combines saw the gradual change to bulk handling of grain from the field to drying and storage, then loading onto bulk transporters by bucket loaders or elevators and augers.

Output from combine harvesters has increased from two tonnes an hour to sixty plus and cutting width from eight feet to thirty-five feet. These wide machines are difficult for the driver to control accurately for hours on end, so first a laser steering system was introduced and now of course the satellite system is used.

A print out of the yield in the form of a contour map can be produced at the end of each day to enable the farmer to investigate the reasons for any low yielding areas of the field. If applicable, this contour map can be used to control the application rates of fertiliser spreaders and sprayers as they move across the field. This is an increasingly important facility as costs of inputs continue to rise. The operator sits in a pressurised, dust free, cool environment with all power operated controls. In the early days of combine harvesters the driver was exposed to long hot days sitting in dust and noise. All this technology can only be applied efficiently on the larger farms.

I have failed in my long-term ambition to hand over a viable farming business to Colin, but with the high price of land and its limited earning capacity, I do not feel so bad about that. I have great confidence in Colin, and I am sure he will continue to farm successfully at Keysley, and develop his grain storage company. His planning application has at long last been approved so I am looking forward to seeing the new grain stores being built.

As has been the case over the last few years, I foresee more farms being farmed by large companies, farming thousands of acres, the land being owned still, by the farmers. Increases in regulations, Heath and Safety, Employment Regulations, Environmental Concerns all make life more difficult for the individual family farmer, and the numbers are falling rapidly.

The number of dairy farmers continues to fall, but perhaps not the number of cows. When I was a boy every farm had a few cows and if they were in a village, they also had a milk round. When I went on holiday as a boy to Marshfield, I used to help deliver the milk in large churns, measuring out the required amount with a long handled dipper at each house. The cows appear to be concentrated into larger and larger dairy units milking hundreds of cows and enabling the dairymen to have time off like the rest of society. There are plans to build a dairy with 8000 cows in Lincolnshire and I am sure that there will be more. In these modern dairy units the cows are well looked after and want for nothing. Being professionally operated, they are clean, tidy and hygienic producers of food, and the vast quantities of waste can be used to produce electricity before being returned to the land to grow the crops for the cows.

Most of the wheat stored at Keysley is milled at West Country mills and made into chicken feed. The lorry drivers who collect the wheat, also deliver the chicken feed to the poultry farms. They tell us about these farms having hundreds of thousands of chickens producing millions of eggs. Every farm used to have a few hens, as we called them in those days. The surplus eggs were purchased by the Egg Marketing Board and were collected by local packing stations. This has long gone the same way as the Milk Marketing Board. Big business is the name of the game and accountants control big business.

Commodity markets are likely to become much more volatile as globalisation continues apace, and I foresee sudden shortfalls in world food supplies, leading to rising prices and riots around the world. This will be followed by large surpluses a year or two later leading to sharp falls in returns to the farmer. The gradual, long term increase in the cost of oil for fuel, and manufacture of fertiliser and chemicals must mean a continual increase in the cost of inputs.

In many areas of the world, water will be a limiting factor in the production of food. Bearing in mind the, as yet, unclear effects of climate change and the desertification of large areas of the world's farmland, the long-term prospects for agricultural profitability are good, provided that your farm is in the right place. The challenge to produce enough food for the world's growing population, at prices that they can afford to pay, is massive. The present ban on the growing of Genetically Modified Crops in Europe and elsewhere will end quite soon, leading to a reduction in the use of pesticides and opening up a new era of crop production - maybe even a second agricultural revolution. The dangers are that farmers could be exploited by the great multi-national biotech companies - this must not be allowed to happen.

I have farmed through a period when farmers were considered to be important members of the community, and the supply of food was high in people's minds. Since the great production surpluses of the 1980s, nobody seems to care anymore and farmers are just people who get in the way on the roads at holiday time. When moving large machines on the roads farmers and their workers are subject to verbal abuse from other road users. People just assume that their food will come from somewhere. Supermarkets have contributed to this malaise by providing produce from all over the world, at reasonable prices, and people are no longer committed to eating local seasonal food.

Global warming has manifested itself in recent years with our long run of mild winters and lack of snowfall. In my early days two or three periods of snow fell during most winters, and about every five years or so we experienced a severe blizzard or ice storm. The rapidity of the changes makes me fear for the future of the human race, and talk of saving the planet is misguided, the planet will survive quite happily without us.

These few words in this book cannot possibly be enough to convey to the reader, the wonderful and interesting life I have had. In my now seventieth year it works out at just over thirteen hundred words per year, just over one hundred words per month. I have just picked out some of the highlights as I remember them - some sad moments and some very funny moments but of course there were many, many more.

It was a great surprise when Evie came home from school with a poem to study for her homework. She had assumed that it was just a poem, not realizing that it was based on an actual event in our family history.

INCENDIARY
That one small boy with a face like pallid cheese
And burnt-out eyes could make a blaze
As brazen, fierce and huge, as red and gold
And zany yellow as the one that spoiled
Three thousand guineas' worth of property
And crops at Godwin's Farm on Saturday
Is frightening.
An ordinary match intended for
The lighting of a pipe or kitchen fire
Misused may set a whole menagerie
Of flame fanged tigers roaring hungrily.
And frightening, too, that one small boy should set
The sky on fire and choke the stars to heat
Such skinny limbs and such a little heart
Which would have been content with one warm kiss
Had there been anyone to offer this.

Vernon Scannell.

Lightning Source UK Ltd.
Milton Keynes UK
UKHW020839191019
351913UK00009B/169/P

9 780755 213405